T0137743

Strategic Urban Health Communication

Charles C. Okigbo
Editor

Strategic Urban Health Communication

 Springer

Editor
Charles C. Okigbo
Department of Communication
North Dakota State University
Fargo, North Dakota
USA

ISBN 978-1-4939-4473-6   ISBN 978-1-4614-9335-8 (eBook)
DOI 10.1007/978-1-4614-9335-8
Springer New York Heidelberg Dordrecht London

Springer is part of Springer Science+Business Media (www.springer.com)

Foreword

This new book *Strategic Urban Health Communication* has come at a most auspicious time for the involvement of communication professionals in promoting good health practices at local, regional, national, and global levels. As the world becomes increasingly more urban and our health challenges continue to require more than the usual bureaucratic approaches to manage, there is an urgent need to adopt integrated and strategic communication methods that take advantage of proven techniques of advocacy, behavior change, persuasion, promotion, public enlightenment, publicity, and customer relationship management. This is the message of this new book.

The global health situation has improved dramatically in all world regions, both developed and developing—the world has recorded an impressive decline in child mortality and maternal mortality rates. Some diseases have been eradicated completely and the incidence of epidemics and pandemics has reduced in the last two decades. Prevalence of HIV/AIDS, Tuberculosis, Malaria, and Measles has dropped drastically. Fewer people are contracting HIV.

Average life expectancy has increased worldwide, even in developing countries from 45.4 to 68.2 years in the last 60 years. Higher standards of living, improvements in hygiene, and medical progress are some of the factors that have made key contributions to this trend. (Source: World Health Statistics 2012). Such dramatic achievements or developments mask many areas of underperformance, especially in developing countries where health challenges have persistently been pervasive. HIV/AIDS, Tuberculosis, Malaria, Measles, Pneumonia, Diarrhea, etc. continue to challenge improvements in life expectancy in developing countries. Rapid urbanization which is a worldwide phenomenon but more serious in developing regions complicates the global health situation and calls for more urgent use of strategic communication methods which are known to have been successful in other spheres of human communication.

There are three elements required in sustained improvements in global well-being. These are sustained leadership, effective communication, and participatory engagement. The least common factor among these is strategic planning, which is illustrated in many of the 17 chapters of this book. From the world of professional advertising we know the value of strategic planning because all our communication activities begin with a sound knowledge of consumers and how they can best be engaged. Effective gathering and qualifying of consumer data enable accurate identification of the audience that then informs what messages are articulated, how they are packaged, and the most effective and efficient vehicles for their delivery.

The Saatchi model of strategic communication adopts the use of the OIIC tool (Objectives, Issues, Insights, Challenge) which enables the communicator to focus on the key objectives of the communications, identity issues that could be obstacles to the solution, and using the Xploring tool, mine insights that would provide windows of opportunity to unlock the challenge. Contemporary health communication already employs such analytical tools but needs more of these in more disciplined and focused approaches, with clearly identified audiences, benchmarks, and milestones for measuring success.

It has been proven that behavioral changes are key assets in proactively managing health care, especially in developing countries. Inculcating healthy habits and influencing the adoption of positive attitudes toward health and environmental issues will lead to more sustainable improvements in public health. Global health promotion today requires multidisciplinary and multimedia approaches that embrace the proven technologies of human communication in all its ramifications from advertising to personal selling. Our health is much too important for us to manage while leaving out some professional communicators who are well versed in strategic uses of communication for education and behavior change. The book illustrates the value of planning and integrated marketing communication approaches that ensure effective engagement of key stakeholders in a holistic manner that delivers the necessary enlightenment, behavioral change, and improved well-being. Indeed, there is no better option in health communication to adopting strategic methods that begin with planning and end with assessment and evaluation.

Udeme Ufot
MD/CEO
SO&U/Saatchi, Lagos, Nigeria

Contents

Contributors

Susan Adamchak   FHI 360, Durham, North Carolina, USA

Vinita Agarwal   Salisbury University, Salisbury, Maryland, USA

Momtaz Uddin Ahmed   Department of Economics, Dhaka University, Dhaka, Bangladesh

Rukhsana Ahmed   Department of Communication, University of Ottawa, Ontario, Canada

Francisco Armada   World Health Organization, Kobe, Japan

Kriss Barker   Population Media Center (PMC), Shelburne, Vermont, USA

Kristine Berzins   Ecologic Institute, Berlin, Germany

Khongorzul Byambajav   Information, Monitoring and Evaluation Division, Ministry of Health, Ulaanbaatar, Mongolia

Angela Chang   Communication Department, University of Macau, Taipa, Macau, China

Arul Chib   Nanyang Technological University, Nanyang, Singapore

Elizabeth Crisp Crawford   North Dakota State University, Fargo, USA

Christine A. Eith   Johns Hopkins University, Baltimore, Maryland, USA

Jennifer J. Edwards   Howard University, Washington, DC, USA

Holly Greb   Programs for Assessment of Technology in Health (PATH) Research Institute, Hamilton, Ontario, Canada

Karen Hardee   Hardee Associates LLC, Arlington, Virginia, USA

Yumi Kimura   Center for Southeast Asian Studies, Kyoto University, Kyoto, Japan

Zahirul Hasan Khan   Natural Resources, Canada

Kenneth A. Lachlan   University of Massachusetts, Boston, USA

Jennifer Liku   FHI 360, Durham, North Carolina, USA

Patchanee Malikhao   Fecund Com Consultancy, Bangkok, Thailand

Charles C. Okigbo   North Dakota State University, Fargo, USA

Chuka Onwumechili   School of Communications, Howard University, Washington, DC, USA

Amit Prasad   World Health Organization, Kobe, Japan

Cornelius B. Pratt   Temple University, Philadelphia, Pennsylvania, USA

Kiran Prasad   Department of Communication and Journalism, Sri Padmavati Mahila University, Tirupati, Andhra Pradesh, India

Yagaantsetseg Radnaabazar   Social Development Department, City Governor's Office, Ulaanbaatar, Mongolia

Jennifer Reierson   University of Minnesota, Duluth, USA

Jan Servaes   Department of Media & Communication, City University of Hong Kong, Kowloon, Hong Kong

Renata Schiavo   Mailman School of Public Health, Columbia University, New York

Patric R. Spence   University of Kentucky, Lexington, USA

Carol A. Stroman   Howard University, Washington, DC, USA

Margaret U. D'Silva   University of Louisville, Kentucky, USA

Steve Sohn   University of Louisville, Kentucky, USA

Vijay Sharma   New Delhi, India

Thanomwong Poorisat   Nanyang Technological University, Nanyang, Singapore

Priscilla Wamucii   University Canada West, Calgary, Canada

Malea Hoepf Young   Catholic Charities, Alexandria, VA, USA

About the Authors

Susan Adamchak, Ph.D. is a Scientist with FHI 360, a major international development organization. She has 30 years of international experience in more than 30 countries, including residence in Namibia and Zimbabwe. An expert in monitoring and evaluation, Dr. Adamchak has focused most recently on the integration of family planning and HIV services, and on measuring service integration and data quality concerns. She also has extensive experience in research, evaluation and education on adolescent reproductive health and HIV/AIDS programs. She is the lead author of the *Monitoring and Evaluation Resource Guide for Young Adult Projects*. She has also worked in the areas of population policy development, private sector family planning programs, and quality of care. Prior to joining FHI, she served as team leader for nearly a dozen process evaluations of USAID-supported programs. Dr. Adamchak holds a Ph.D. in Sociology from Brown University. She is an adjunct professor at Kansas State University.

Momtaz Uddin Ahmed Ph.D. is a Professor of Economics at the University of Dhaka with forty years of teaching and research experience in Development and Economics. He has published widely in national and international journals. He is the author of *Essays on Contemporary Development Issues in Bangladesh*; the editor of *Current Status and Future Perspectives of Rural Development in the CIRDAP Member Countries*; and the co-author of *Small and Medium-Scale Enterprises in Industrial Development: The Bangladesh Experience* and *Rural Development Outlook—A Review of IRD Programmes*.

Rukhsana Ahmed Ph.D. is an Associate Professor in the Department of Communication, University of Ottawa. Her primary research area is health communication with an emphasis on interpersonal communication across cultures and within organizations. Her research also focuses on communication for development and issues related to multicultural media, religious diversity, and gender. She has published in communication journals, health studies outlets, nursing journals and in journals at the intersection of health, communication, and culture. She is currently co-editing books on health communication and mass media and on medical communication and co-authoring a book on health literacy in Canada.

Francisco Armada, Ph.D. is a Technical Officer for The World Health Organization located in Kobe Centre, Japan. He is a specialist in urban health. He was a health officer in the Ministry of Health, Venezuela, for more than a decade, and held several leading positions between 2002 and 2006. During that time he was involved in the implementation of universal health care through Barrio Adentro. He obtained a Ph.D. in the Department of Health Policy and Management at the Johns Hopkins University School of Public Health, where he also received an M.P.H. His academic research focuses on the political determinants of health.

Kristine Berzins is a Transatlantic Fellow at the Ecologic Institute in Berlin. Her research focuses primarily on European energy and climate change policy. Previously, Kristine Berzins worked in foreign affairs and international development in Washington, DC. This publication was drafted when Ms. Berzins was a research analyst at Population Action International, where she helped evaluate how demographic factors affect climate change mitigation and adaptation in developing countries. Kristine Berzins has an MPhil in International Relations from the University of Cambridge in the United Kingdom and a BA in Political Science and History from Yale University in the United States.

Khongorzul Byambajav is the Deputy Director of the Department of Information, Monitoring and Evaluation of the Ministry of Health, Mongolia. She received a master's degree in public health from the University of Leeds, UK. She leads assessment initiatives in the health sector, including performance appraisal of health institutions, monitoring and evaluation of health programs and policies

Angela Chang, Ph.D. is assistant professor in the Department of Communication at the University of Macau. She holds a Ph.D. in Communications and Advertising from the Union Institute & University, USA. Chang has conducted research on advertising strategies, audience preferences, media uses, consumer behavior, and eye-tracking protocols. Her publications include a book, many book chapters, and journal articles, academic and technical reports. Her articles have appeared in the *Chinese Journal of Communication Research, the Journal of Advertising,* and *Modern Advertising.*

Arul Chib, Ph.D. is a faculty member at the Wee Kim Wee School of Communication and Information and Assistant Director of the Singapore Internet Research Center, Nanyang Technological University, coordinating the Strengthening Information Society Research Capacity Alliance (SIRCA). Dr. Chib studies mobile phone healthcare systems, particularly in the resource-constrained environments of developing countries. He pursues action-oriented research with marginalized communities, in varied cross-cultural and socio-economic contexts and actively conducts research fieldwork in communities in Indonesia, the Indian and Nepalese Himalayan region, Peru, Singapore, Thailand, Uganda, and China. Dr. Chib has published in *the Journal of Health Communication, International Journal of Communication, the Asian Journal of Communication, the Journal of Computer-Mediated Communication, and New Media & Society,* amongst others.

Elizabeth Crisp Crawford, Ph.D. is an assistant professor of communication and advertising at North Dakota State University. She received her B.A. from St. Norbert College, her M.A. from Marquette University, and her Ph.D. from the University of Tennessee. She manages the National Student Advertising Competition (NSAC) case study, advises NDSU AdClub, and publishes in the areas of mass communication strategy, message design, and mass communication education. Dr. Crawford has published in a variety of academic journals including *Social Marketing Quarterly*, *Journalism and Mass Communication Educator*, *The International Journal of Selection and Assessment*, and the *Journal of Health and Mass Communication*.

Jennifer J. Edwards, Ph.D. specializes in community health training, curriculum development, and health program assessments and she is passionate about promoting health equity, access to services, and community sustainability. She has been a management consultant for national health organizations including the American College of Physicians, the National Osteoporosis Foundation, and the Federation of State Boards of Physical Therapy. She conducts health research in cancer among vulnerable groups.

Christine A. Eith, Ph.D. is Assistant Professor in the Division of Public Safety Leadership at Johns Hopkins University. She is the author of *Delinquency, Schools, and the Social Bond.*

Holly Greb is Program Associate for the HIV/AIDS and Tuberculosis Global Program at PATH in Washington, DC. At the time this publication was being developed, Ms. Greb was Program Coordinator at Population Action International where she initiated and managed the organization's Youth Program which provided grants and training to local, youth led reproductive health projects based in multiple countries. She has worked in many countries, and has a particular interest in the intersections of global health, diplomacy and security. She is currently completing her MPH in Global Health at the George Washington University and holds a BA in International Relations from the American University in Washington, DC.

Karen Hardee, Ph.D. has been a social demographer for 25 years, a senior fellow and deputy director of population and reproductive health for the Health Policy Project at the Futures Group in Washington, DC., and has been visiting senior fellow at Population Reference Bureau. She is also president of Hardee Associates LLC. Dr. Hardee has extensive global experience in population and development, family planning and reproductive health, HIV/AIDS, gender integration, climate change, evidence-based policy, and monitoring and evaluation. Dr. Hardee has also worked at John Snow, Inc., Family Health International (now FHI360), USAID and the U.S. Bureau of the Census. She holds a Ph.D. from Cornell University's Population and Development Program.

Zahirul Hasan Khan, Ph.D. is Research Scientist at CanmetENERGY-Ottawa, Natural Resources Canada. His research focuses on developing innovative technologies especially relating to environmental management. He is an expert in emission and air pollution control sciences and passionate about issues of global sustainable development. He has presented at many professional, national and international conferences.

Yumi Kimura Ph.D.   is a researcher at the Center for Southeast Asian Studies in Kyoto University, Japan. She worked as a consultant for projects on urban health metrics at the WHO Kobe Centre. Her current research is based on health and nutritional assessment in the community, especially for the elderly population. She received her Ph.D in Public Health from Kyoto University.

Kenneth A. Lachlan, Ph.D.   is Associate Professor and Founding Chair of the Communication Department at the University of Massachusetts, Boston. He has published his research in journals such as *Journal of Broadcasting and Electronic Media, Journal of Applied Communication Research,* and *Communication Studies.* His research interests include the psychological effects of mass media, crisis and emergency communication, and quantitative research methods.

Jennifer Liku, MA   is a social science researcher with a background in social work and sociology and a keen interest in youth issues. She has conducted research in many health areas that include national demographic and reproductive health surveys, and has managed projects on female genital mutilation, youth reproductive health, sexually transmitted infections, condoms and integration of reproductive health and HIV counselling and testing services. Her research engagements extend to Uganda and Zimbabwe. She has presented extensively at national and international meetings. Jennifer is currently working on youth and adolescent sexuality.

Patchanee Malikhao, Ph.D.   received a Ph.D. in Sociology from the University of Queensland in Australia, a Master of Arts degree in Mass Communication from Thammasat University in Thailand, and a Master of Science degree in Printing Technology from Rochester Institute of Technology (RIT), Rochester, New York. She has extensive experience in Communication for Social Change, Social Science Research Methods and Data Analyses in Belgium, Australia and the US. She has been a researcher and lecturer in the School of Public Health at the University of Massachusetts, Amherst, and is currently a consultant in Bangkok, Thailand.

Charles Okigbo, Ph.D.   is Professor of Communication at North Dakota State University, and was formerly Head of Policy Engagement and Communication at the African Population and Health Research Center, Nairobi, Kenya. He had been senior lecturer in mass communication at the University of Nigeria, Nsukka and Executive Coordinator at the African Council for Communication Education. He engages in action research in health and development communication, and has consulted for many UN agencies including UNAIDS, UNICEF, UNFPA, UNESCO, and WHO.

Chuka Onwumechili, Ph.D.   is Professor of Communications and Culture at Howard University where he serves as the interim Dean for the School of Communications. His research interest is in the intersection of culture, development and communication. He has published books and peer-reviewed articles in many areas of communication and was formerly Vice President at the Digital Bridge Institute (DBI) in Nigeria.

Thanomwong Poorisat received her bachelor's and master's degrees in Communication Research from the Wee Kim Wee School of Communication and Information, Nanyang Technological University (NTU), Singapore and is currently a PhD student at NTU, majoring in communication research. Her research interests are in cognitive processing and health communication, specifically among less-educated non-Western audiences. She has presented in many conferences of international associations such as the International Communication Association, the Association for Education in Journalism and Mass Communication, and the Association of Internet Researchers.

Amit Prasad, is Technical Officer and Health Economist, Health Division WHO, Kobe Japan. He has coordinated the development of WHO's Urban Health Equity Assessment and Response Tool (Urban HEART), which is increasingly being used by cities, globally, for planning and monitoring action. Currently, he leads WHO's initiatives on urban health metrics and works closely with country officials on capacity building and developing global standards on metrics. Previously, he has worked for several years in WHO (Geneva), and at the Harvard School of Public Health. Mr. Prasad received his education in economics and international development from Harvard University.

Kiran Prasad, Ph.D. is Professor in Communication and Journalism at Sri Padmavati Mahila University, Tirupati, India. She was also Associate Professor in Communication Studies, College of Applied Sciences, Ministry of Higher Education, Oman, Commonwealth Visiting Research Fellow at the Centre for International Communication Research, University of Leeds, UK, and Canadian Studies Research Fellow at the School of Journalism and Communication, Carleton University, Ottawa, Canada. She has researched and published extensively in communication, health, and development, she is series editor of *Empowering Women Worldwide*, a book series published by the Women Press, New Delhi.

Cornelius B. Pratt, Ph.D. is a professor in the Department of Strategic Communication at Temple University, United States. He also teaches at Temple University Japan. He is a consultant to the African Public Relations Association. Pratt is also an honorary visiting professor of mass communication at Bingham University, New Karu, Nasarawa State, Nigeria. He served for nearly six years in the communication program of the U.S. Department of Agriculture, Washington, D.C., and for 11 years on the faculty of the College of Communication Arts and Sciences at Michigan State University, the last eight years as full professor. He serves on the editorial-review boards of six academic journals, including *The South East Asian Journal of Management, Public Relations Review*, and the *Journal of Pubic Relations Research*. He is coeditor of *Case studies in crisis communication: International perspectives on hits and misses* (New York: Routledge, 2012). His research interests include communication for national and regional development, particularly in emerging economies; international and strategic communication; and health communication. His health work focuses on the challenges of health-care delivery in high-risk populations.

Yagaantsetseg Radnaabazar, MD, Master of Medical Sciences, is an official of the Social Development Department, City Governor's Office, Ulaanbaatar, Mongolia. She is in charge of overseeing the implementation of health related objectives set out in the plan of action and socio-economic development direction for the Ulaanbaatar city and administering the coordination of activities of implementing agencies, NGOs and professional associations, with regard to improving health services quality and accessibility and ensuring healthy environment for city residents.

Jennifer Reierson, Ph.D. is an Assistant Professor of Public Relations in the Communication Department at the University of Minnesota in Duluth, MN. Prior to her graduate studies, she worked at an advertising, marketing, and public relations agency group, Flint Group. She has been involved in risk and crisis communication, and has also taught communication at the College of St. Scholastica, Minnesota. Her research is varied, covering interests in risk and crisis communication, public relations, and work-life tensions. Her recent research has focused on marginalized or non-dominant populations with a focus on policy and systemic change opportunities.

Renata Schiavo, Ph.D. is a public health and global health specialist with significant experience in developed and developing country settings, including the U.S. and several countries in Europe, Latin America and Africa. She has wide experience on strategy design, program development, direction and evaluation, and research design, implementation and analysis. She focuses primarily on strategic health communication for behavioral, social and organizational change, non-profit strategic planning and management, and strategic partnerships in public health and for non-profit ventures. Dr. Schiavo is currently working with leading public health/ global health organizations as the *Founder and Principal of Strategic Communication Resources.* Her recent experience includes the National Association of Pediatric Nurse Practitioners (NAPNAP), Solving Kids' Cancer, World Bank, World Health Organization (WHO), UNICEF, and the US Office of Minority Health Resource Center (OMHRC). She was Adjunct Assistant Professor of Public Health at New York University, and she is now at the Mailman School of Public Health, Columbia University, New York. Renata is the author of a book on *Health Communication: From Theory to Practice* (San Francisco: Jossey-Bass, 2007 and 2013) and many other publications on public health topics. She has recognized expertise on a variety of public health/global health topics and has participated in scientific panels, expert consultations, and advisory boards for leading organizations such as the American Public Health Association (APHA) and the World Health Organization (WHO).

Jan Servaes Ph.D. is Head and Professor, Department of Media and Communication at City University of Hong Kong. He has been UNESCO Chair in Communication for Sustainable Social Change at the University of Massachusetts, Amherst (USA), Honorary Guest Professor at the Huazhong University of Technology and Science (HUST), Wuhan, China; Researcher at the 'Brussels Center for Journalism Studies' (BCJS), Belgium; Editor-in-Chief of '*Telematics* *and Informatics'* (Elsevier), and Editor of Book Series on 'Communication for Development and Social Change', and 'Communication, Globalization and Cultural Identity'. Servaes has undertaken research, development, and advisory work around the world and has published extensively in development communication, health, intercultural communication and social change. His latest book is *Sustainability, Participation and Culture in Communication: Theory and Praxis*, Bristol/Chicago: Intellect/University of Chicago Press, 2012.

Patric R. Spence Ph.D. is Associate Professor of Communication at the University of Kentucky. His recent research has been published in *Sociological Spectrum*, the *Journal of Modern Applied Statistical Methods*, *Communication Research Reports*, and the book *Real Data Analysis*. His research interests include crisis communication, applied research methods, and organizational communication.

Carolyn A. Stroman, Ph.D. is Professor of Communication in the Department of Communication and Culture and a Research Associate in the NOAA Center for Atmospheric Sciences (NCAS), Howard University. Her research interests are in health communication and behaviors, cultural diversity and risk communication. Dr. Stroman is the Editor of *The Howard Journal of Communications*.

Malea Hoepf Young, M.P.H. works on health education and healthcare access for refugees resettled in Kentucky. She formerly worked as a research associate at Population Action International, focusing on issues related to urbanization, population and the environment, and HIV/AIDS. Ms. Hoepf Young is a graduate of Kenyon College, holds a Masters degree in Public Health from the University of North Carolina at Chapel Hill, and has ten years of professional experience in the field of global health. She has worked for numerous global health organizations in Washington DC, the International HIV Alliance in Hyderabad, India, and in Rwanda through the United States Peace Corps.

Chapter 1
Strategy: What It Is

Charles C. Okigbo

Strategy is one of those common everyday words and concepts that we understand so well and use even appropriately, but still find difficult to define and explain in precise terms. However, once we define and explain them, they become permanently embedded in our minds and we see their applications all around us. Strategy has been used implicitly in different ways, but formally seen as the art of planning and implementing with considerate care to achieve predetermined objectives. Strategy derives from the Greek where it has clearly military references as "office of general, commander, leader and to lead." In this military sense, strategy refers to a *broad* plan of action designed to achieve a predetermined objective. In this sense, strategy or grand strategy refers to high levels of engagement distinct from operations and tactics, which are concerned with the *specific* conduct of an engagement. Having a good strategy which leads to effective operations and tactics is a sine qua non for successful engagements in many spheres of life, especially in business, communication, corporate affairs, health management, and politics, among other areas.

Sun Tzu's classic book, *The Art of War,* first published around 400 B.C. is one of the many resources in trying to understand strategy (Wing 1999). According to Tzu, strategy makes all the difference between success and failure, and it is the essence of living, which makes it worth studying for individual, organizational, and societal success. Tzu positions strategy as the great work of the organization, which marks the difference between life or death, and survival or extinction. Therefore, its study cannot be neglected (Wing 1999). Strategizing is necessary to triumph over the inevitable conflicts and challenges of warfare in particular, and life in general.

Being strategic can make all the difference between success and failure. It is a deliberate, systematic, well thought-out plan and engagement, and not a serendipitous or trial-and-error approach to problem solving. For instance, in the area of health management, the eradication of diseases in communities and individuals staying healthy do not come about accidentally; they require careful planning, implementation, evaluation, and continual attention to know when it becomes necessary to stay the course or change tactics. Different countries today are challenged by

C. C. Okigbo (✉)
North Dakota State University, Fargo, USA
e-mail: Charles.Okigbo@ndsu.edu

C. C. Okigbo (ed.), *Strategic Urban Health Communication,*
DOI 10.1007/978-1-4614-9335-8_1, © Springer Science+Business Media New York 2014

different health problems that manifest in the global burden of diseases, which are being addressed through different health intervention strategies with varying levels of success. As the largest ever systematic research to chart the global distribution and causes of all major diseases, injuries, and health risk factors shows (Murray et al. 2012) widespread progress in global health is still accompanied by persistent problems that require extensive strategizing, consistent policies, and continuing attention from global actors and national leaders.

Strategy is so essential for success it is the essence of being and acting. Not to be strategic is to leave oneself or one's organization at the mercy of the vicissitudes and vagaries of life, without plans or preparation. The unexamined life is not worth living, according to Socrates, and similarly, the unstrategic entity, be it an institution, organization, or country, does not stand a chance in today's highly structured world. Although strategy is not a strange word, there is hardly any consensus on its precise meaning, nor is there a paucity of views on how it is applied practically.

There is no end to new ways of expressing strategy. For instance, the US Military has embraced Marine General Charles Krulak's proposition on "The Strategic Corporal," a term that invokes the empowerment of low-level unit leaders to take independent actions and make major decisions in the face of hostile, neutral, and friendly forces. This has now been widely adopted by Australian and Canadian military formations. But what does strategy really mean? Mintzberg (1987) provided five definitions, and later in association with two others (Mintzberg et al. 1998) identified 10 schools of strategic management. It is convenient to explain strategy through seven windows or frames of meaning all of which are heuristic tools for understanding strategic health communication as applied in urban settings.

Seven Windows on Strategy

In common parlance, strategy means a plan, and being strategic implies thinking ahead for the best ways to meet a challenge. There are many ways of conceiving and understanding strategy, with almost all of them showing it to be a deliberate plan, ploy, pattern, position, perspective, thinking, and competition. In ordinary everyday situations as well as in high-level organizational and corporate contexts, we must engage in some level and kind of strategic thinking, which is the art of staying on top of our situations to achieve our personal or corporate goals. As Dixit and Nalebuff (1991) expressed it, we must practice strategic thinking at work as well as at home; whereas businesses must use good competitive strategies to survive, politicians have to devise campaign strategies to get elected. Sports coaches must plan strategies to win. Managing communication programs in urban health care requires strategic planning and implementation, which can take different approaches and ways of redressing the situations. Mintzberg (1987) provides five definitions of strategy as plan, ploy, pattern, position, and perspective. All of these point to the direction of forethought and careful consideration.

Strategy as a Plan As a plan, strategy is "some sort of consciously intended course of action, a guideline (or set of guidelines) to deal with a situation" (Mintzberg 1987, p. 11). By this definition, it is implied that strategies are developed deliberately and ahead of the actions that are adopted to achieve the particular objectives. In the area of health care, it is expected that different levels of care will demand different approaches to strategy. A strategic approach to health care planning can involve adoption of three levels of prevention: primary, secondary, and tertiary, each requiring different plans for meeting specific objectives. Whereas primary prevention focuses at prepathogenesis of a disease and is often synonymous with health improvement, promotion, and protection, secondary prevention focuses on minimizing damage by early engagement in pathogenesis and reduction of disease severity. The third level, tertiary prevention, will seek to alter postpathogenesis or recovery phase by reducing the impact of damage and providing optimal treatment.

Although strategies are plans, not all plans are strategic. This is the sense in which some argue that the term plan is much too static and unless it is properly qualified, it may lack the necessary connotations of scheming and calibrating carefully and in an anxiously anticipatory manner to achieve a predetermined position. Many routine health care practices reflect more of bureaucratic and routine actions than people's deft moves and strategies for better health. Some childhood immunizations and winter flu shots originally started as parts of grand plans (strategies) but have since then lost their edges due to routine applications without much thought to mechanisms for achieving more effective or efficient results thereby becoming a-strategic. The apparent intractability of polio in Nigeria shows why strategies must attend even the most basic routines such as childhood immunizations, which are nearly effortless. Strategies are usually broad general plans; when they are specific, they are best seen as tactics.

Strategy as a Ploy A ploy is another way of describing strategy, especially in those contexts where reference is made to specific actions or maneuvers which are intended to present an illusion or deception. Mintzberg (1987, p. 12) explained it as "really just a specific maneuver intended to outwit an opponent or competitor" and thus it is different from a grand plan or design. Examples can include parents who use song and play to get their children to eat their vegetables and spouses who use various guises to get their partners on board strategic and thought-out family planning methods. The ploy is similar to the idea of creating illusions to obscure reality, which Wing (1999, p. 78) refers to as "a specific tactical maneuver designed to keep the opponent at a constant disadvantage."

Sun Tzu emphasized the use of illusions or ploys and believed that strategists who understood and employed this technique were invincible. Sun Tzu exclaimed in awe of such strategists: "Subtle! Intangible! Seemingly without shape. Mysterious! Miraculous! Seemingly without sound. They master the destiny of their opponents" (Wing 1999, p. 78). Illusions or ploys may be effective strategies but they present ethical dilemmas that must be resolved by asking serious questions about the value of truth and honesty and whether the end justifies the means. The line between strategies (as grand plans) and tactics (as specific maneuvers or ploys) can be so thin to be indistinguishable sometimes. However, strategy as a pattern of occurrences is not controversial.

Strategy as a Pattern Another sense in which strategy is more than just a plan is the scenario of looking at resulting behaviors in a post hoc (after the fact) manner. When the behaviors accumulate in a systematic way, we have a pattern that reflects a string of actions or results that could arise from well laid out plans but could as well have come from no such plans. Strategies as patterns can be realized without preconceived plans, just as some plans can lead to unrealized objectives. Trying to find the strategies in the string of actions or patterns of behavior is analogous to a situation of *grounded theory,* where the explanatory paradigm evolves (post hoc) from obtained results. Whereas deliberate strategies (like nongrounded theories) show planned approaches, observed patterns as strategies (or emergent strategies) show that "patterns developed in the absence of intentions, or despite them…" (Mintzberg 1987, p. 13).

Like grounded theory which suggests that our theory emerges inductively from the data (that is from the ground up), thereby contrasting with the traditional deductive approach, strategy as a pattern is also inductive and unfolds, cascades, rolls, and emerges from the extant situations and conditions. The results can be unanticipated or unplanned, but not any less interesting and significant. Not being based on preconceived plans, the situation is similar to that in which the investigator does not know what would result from the investigation ahead of time. New trajectories of disease infections in urban areas sometimes present emergent patterns that are apparent "after the fact" and must be interpreted contextually and inductively.

Strategy as a Position One of the results of successful strategizing (whether as deliberate planning or emergent patterning) is the close association that people make between an achieved or realized *position* and the activities that lead to it. In this sense, strategy becomes a mediating or intervening force and a reflecting mirror that shows how well an implementing agency such as a health care organization has positioned itself or its programs. This view of strategy as position leads us to expect different health communication programs to be seen differently depending on how the managers employ relevant communication design elements to achieve predetermined objectives of public perceptions by their relevant stakeholders. For example, many population communication programs today are being implemented by various organizations whose cognate strategies position them appropriately to rent specific spaces in the minds of their publics. Such positions are the results of strategic planning as well as emergent activities that may not have arisen from deliberate planning.

In one of his various interpretations of strategy, Michael Porter (1998, p. 55) asserted that "strategy is the creation of a unique and valuable position involving a different set of activities." Flavored by his characteristic admiration for competition, he adds that "the essence of strategic positioning is to choose activities that are different from rivals" (p. 55). When many organizations fail to have clear strategies, the blame should be on leadership and general management. As Porter (1998, p. 70) saw it, "general management is more than the stewardship of individual functions. Its core is strategy: defining and communicating the company's unique position, making trade-offs, and forging among activities."

Our view of health communication as practiced by such organization as The Population Council, UNAIDS, UNESCO, UNICEF, WHO, and The World Bank, among others, derives largely from the strategies of the respective organizations in positioning themselves through their programs in the global, national, or local health communication environment. In branding promotion terms, strategy helps them to establish a "niche"—but not in a thoroughly competitive mode as is often the case in product or service branding where the market is populated by competitors. Instead of competitive strategies, many global health organizations are disposed to promoting cooperative or collaborative strategies because they often have a common enemy in the diseases or health conditions they are created to fight. Thus, niche is not necessarily the position occupied by one particular health organization but the totality of the branded environment that results from the strategic activities of the relevant organizations that operate individually and/or collectively in the domain.

Strategy as a Perspective A macro view of strategy shows it to be a *perspective,* a worldview, or a philosophy of being (metaphysics) that is more than planning, plotting, patterning, or positioning, but it can indeed incorporate all four and much more that reflect our essence of being. It is indeed our collective response to our world and in that sense our understanding and response to how the world works as well as how and why our environment is to be controlled. Strategy as philosophy must emphasize the social and shared aspects of our beliefs more than our individual idiosyncrasies. Even though an individual actor can be guided by a personal strategy, strategy as a perspective and philosophy is best expressed as collective intuition. As Mintzberg (1987, p. 17) explained it "strategy is a perspective shared by the members of an organization, through their intentions and/or by their actions." A major challenge of designing successful health communication strategies is finding correct ways to read the collective minds of program designers, implementers, and beneficiaries in a congruent manner that builds synergy, collaboration, and cooperation instead of antagonism and disagreement. The notion of strategy as a perspective buttresses the view that it is a concept and an abstraction which exists only in the minds of the interested parties. Every strategy is an invention of one or more minds designed to achieve clear objectives that lead to establishing a position and ultimately underlining and clarifying a worldview or perspective. Yet another window on strategy shows it to be a thinking and implementation process.

Strategy as Thinking Thinking and strategizing are often associated and sometimes used interchangeably. Strategic thinking is the art of weighing options and taking steps to get ahead. Although Dixit and Nalebuff (p. ix) explain it as "the art of outdoing an adversary, knowing that the adversary is trying to do the same to you" there are many nonadversarial situations where we engage in strategic thinking. They are correct, however, in arguing that strategic thinking is pervasive in our everyday lives, as we have to engage perpetually in weighing competing options and choosing the best approaches. But all the thinking and patterning will amount to very little without successful implementation. So strategy is also implementing or execution, as it is sometimes referred to.

Stressing the overarching importance of correct strategy implementation, Nielson et al. (2008, p. 61) explain that "a brilliant strategy, blockbuster product, or breakthrough technology can put you on the competitive map, but only solid execution can keep you there." There are many plans or strategies which are just that: plans or strategies. Some good plans may go unimplemented while others may be poorly executed. A wrong approach can be taken in strategy execution, thereby making it difficult to achieve desired organizational results. In the long run, the best strategies will prove so in their execution, which are also reflective of strategic approaches. Yet another window on strategies is the competitive approach, which is the characteristic view in many military and business operations.

Strategy as Competition Many explanations of strategy are based on the view that the human environment is largely competitive and our opponent's gain must be our loss. In an update on his numerous explications of the place of competition in effective and efficient organizational performance, Michael Porter (2008, p. 79) concluded that "in essence, the job of the strategist is to understand and cope with competition." This is an elaboration of his earlier view in *Competitive Strategy* (Porter 1998) where he had argued that "every firm competing in an industry has a competitive strategy, whether explicit or implicit. This strategy may have been developed explicitly through a planning process or it may have evolved implicitly through the activities of the various functional departments of the firm." By extension, organizations and indeed nations engaged in urban health programming are in implicit or explicit competition with themselves, while at the same time cooperating or collaborating with each other as the case may be.

It is the realization of the new, constructive, and actionable roles for governments and business organizations in the pursuit of strategic competitiveness and global prosperity that have fuelled the new world standards that were set in Alma-Ata and as the Millennium Development Goals (MDGs). The historic 1978 Alma-Ata international conference on primary health care articulated a set of guiding values for health development, health services, health needs, and the fundamental determinants of health, culminating in the launching of the very ambitious "Health for All" movement. The MDGs have set new standards, which even if they are missed, underline the need for strategic planning and keeping a focus on a few priority areas of global health challenges. The difficulty in closing gaps in health outcomes between communities and nations is not a matter of fate but reflects differences in policies and strategies. Individual health organizations, communities, nation states, and the entire world community need well-articulated strategies. Not surprisingly, much emphasis is being placed on strategic planning today because of the significant benefits that can accrue from explicit strategy formulation.

Of the various ways of seeing strategy, planning and perspective are the most applicable in health communication contexts because they are most useful at this time of convergence of media, messages, and people to achieve the desirable objectives of better health for all humanity. The view that the job of the strategist is to understand and cope with competition is a valid one because of the limitations that finite resources place on interventions and implementation programs. The world's resources are sufficient to meet the health needs of the world's peoples but only if there are appropriate strategies in terms of plans and perspectives to address the perennial problems that appear to be intractable in the face of competing priorities. The science of health care must interface with the art of human culture to address the world's problems of health communication in both urban and rural contexts. The solutions are sometimes easier on paper than in the field because some strategy problems are "wicked" in the sense that traditional processes cannot resolve them; they can only be tamed. John Camillus (2008, p. 102) explained that "it's impossible to find solutions to wicked strategy problems, but companies can learn to cope with them" through organizing brainstorming sessions to identify the various aspects of the problem, holding retreats to share perspectives, running focus groups to understand various viewpoints, and involving stakeholders in developing future scenarios in order "to create a shared understanding of the problem and foster a joint commitment to possible ways of resolving it."

Strategy as an Art and a Science Is strategy art or science or both? Strategy as a carefully thought out plan or perspective is both an art and a science. If it was an art only, it would mean that only highly creative people would be successful strategists, for an art is largely based on creativity, intuition, and innate qualities of individual artists. And if it was solely a science, it would mean that only systematic applications of standard rules and procedures (essential scientific methods) could be applied. But as it is, strategy is both a science and an art. Strategic planning requires some amount of artistic creativity and a modicum of cognitive knowledge commonly associated with the scientific process. As an art, strategy has an intuitive, creative, and qualitative aspect to it, especially at the level of considering and choosing between alternative approaches and scenarios. But it is certainly also a science because it often involves sophisticated statistical forecasts, collecting and analyzing vast amounts of data, using scientific modeling techniques, real options, and operations research analyses. The debate about whether strategy is an art or a science is akin to the argument on the merits and demerits of qualitative versus quantitative research methods. The truth is that both methods are valuable, although not necessarily equally, depending on the prevailing situations. They both have important roles to play in strategic planning processes.

To say that strategy is an art is not to equate it with capriciousness, arbitrariness, and unreasoned decision making. Rather it is to recognize that as important as measurements and matrices may be, there is still room for creativity, intuition, and artful maneuvering. Strategic planning that does not combine artistic and scientific perspectives is likely to fall victim to political machinations and environmental endangerment.

Conclusion

Strategy has never been out of fashion because limited resources and ever changing terrains require planners and implementers to be on their toes as they aspire for
maximal benefits that come from judicious deployment of resources. In the realm
of health communication in urban contexts, the challenges are evident in the ever
changing landscape for media, messages, publics, health problems, and public policies. Yesterday's strategies are not likely to remain as effective today and tomorrow,
nor are the effective strategies in Asia likely to play with equal efficacy in Africa
or Latin America. So the work of the health communication professional is to be a
perpetual student of strategic communication always on the lookout for opportunities to plan better, employ ploys where appropriate, shift positions where necessary,
and keep the perspectives of the organization in view at all times. Strategy is the
creation of an effective communication approach to address health problems and
situations with purposive plans aimed at improving the chances for better health
for all, in line with the defined goals, targets, and standards. Strategy requires organizational leadership not only in the business sector where it is more obvious but
also in social services areas, including health care and management. Strong leaders
who are willing to exercise professional judgment and work collaboratively as team
members are essential. The need for strategic thinking in tackling urban and global
health problems is greater today than at any other time in our history.

Although infectious diseases, maternal and child illnesses, and malnutrition now
cause fewer deaths and less illness than previously, still noncommunicable diseases
such as cancer and heart disease have become dominant causes of death and disability. Although life expectancies for men and women are improving, and the scourge
of HIV and malaria is declining, yet on balance, more people will be spending more
years of their lives afflicted by more illnesses. We may live longer, but for many,
in both rich and poor countries, it will be years of disability. We need better health
communication strategies to put these new developments in context for better attention from health planners and policy makers. Not only are there new global threats
but there are still big gaps in progress for some regions of the world. There are also
disturbing gaps within countries with many in the urban areas experiencing the
worst consequences of different kinds of diseases and afflictions. Poor sanitation,
maternal, newborn, child mortality, and communicable diseases are prevalent and
persistent serious concerns in many urban areas in many industrializing countries.
In many industrialized countries, there are some enormous health challenges relating to environmental degradation, cancers, and life-style diseases all of which require more strategic interventions and better uses of strategic communication. The
appalling global and regional situations are avoidable and these problems do not
stem from ignorance of biomedical science but rather from lack of adequate strategies. Not to strategize effectively is to leave oneself and one's institution to the vagaries and ravages of nature, which is not always kind to the indolent non-planner.

References

Camillus, J. C. (2008, May). Strategy as a wicked problem. *Harvard Business Review, 86*(5), 98–106.

Dixit, A., & Nalebuff, B. (1991). *Thinking strategically: The competitive edge in business, politics, and everyday life*. New York: Norton.

Mintzberg, H. (1987). *The strategy concept 1: Five Ps for strategy* (Fall, Vol. 30 of California Management Review, pp. 11–24). University of California

Mintzberg, H., Ahlstrand, B., & Lampel, J. (1998). *Strategy safari: A guided tour through the wilds of strategic management*. New York: Free Press.

Murray, C. J. L., Ezzati, M., Flaxman, A. D., et al (2012). GBD 2010: A multi-investigator collaboration for global competitive descriptive epidemiology. *Lancet, 380*, 2055–2058.

Neilson, G. L., Martin, K. L., & Powers, E. (2008). The secrets of successful strategy execution. *Harvard Business Review, 6*, 61–70.

Porter, M. E. (1998). *Competitive strategy: Techniques for analyzing industries and competitors*. New York: Free Press.

Porter, M. E. (2008). The five competitive forces that shape strategy. *Harvard Business Review, 1*, 78–93.

Wing, R. L. (1999). *The art of strategy.* Translation of Sun Tzu's The art of war. London: Thorsons/HarperCollins.

Chapter 2
Strategic Communication Campaigns

Elizabeth Crisp Crawford and Charles C. Okigbo

Introduction

One of the best ways to promote good health in society is through the use of communication campaigns to inform and educate the public about healthy habits and good health care. Although the importance of mass communication in promoting health is widely acknowledged, creating effective communication campaigns can be a complex process. Health messages have a variety of characteristics that differentiate them from other types of mediated messages. Among these are the sensitivity of health issues, the fear that some health messages evoke, the attendant feelings of resistance to some health messages, and the complex nature of many health problems. Many health messages focus on sensitive and personal issues such as sexually transmitted diseases, substance abuse and addiction, abortion, and mental illness. Because these subjects are difficult and emotional for many audience members, they can be especially challenging to develop effective communication campaigns to check.

Many communication campaigns fail on account of audience members resisting the messages because they contradict adopted habits and ingrained behaviors. Successful health campaigns have to address these behaviors directly or indirectly in an accepting or nonthreatening manner, using appropriate emotional and/or logical persuasive appeals, designed to elicit desirable attitudes and behaviors. Some health campaigns that evoke fear may seem to work but only for a limited time only because audience members eventually overcome such fears or learn to avoid the messages that evoke fear. This was the case with some of the early HIV/AIDS campaigns, which became less impactful with time. Many people go back to their old habits after the campaigns conclude. Old habits die hard, even when we know they are unhealthy and need to change. Attitude and behavior change as a result of health communication is a complex process. We cannot expect desired outcomes to be realized all the time from programmed interventions.

E. C. Crawford (✉) · C. C. Okigbo
North Dakota State University, Fargo, USA
e-mail: Elizabeth.c.crawford@ndsu.edu

C. C. Okigbo (ed.), *Strategic Urban Health Communication,*
DOI 10.1007/978-1-4614-9335-8_2, © Springer Science+Business Media New York 2014

Health communication campaigns are a subset of general communication campaigns. Interventions to change health-related practices take a variety of forms involving both interpersonal communication and the mass media. Therefore, creating effective health communication campaigns requires a thorough understanding of the various media channels available, as well as the issues and appropriate strategies for delivering the messages to achieve the best results possible.

Communication Campaigns

Communication campaigns are all around us and it is impossible to avoid them in our contemporary environment of traditional communication and the new social media. A communication campaign is a series of coordinated messages or other promotional efforts that are purposively designed to achieve predetermined goals or objectives. According to Paisley (1989, p. 16), communication campaigns are defined with reference to their objectives and methods, with the former focusing on "one group's intention to influence other groups' beliefs or behavior, using communicated appeals." Atkin's (1981, p. 265) definition of communication campaigns as "promotional messages in the public interest disseminated through mass media channels to target audiences" illustrates a methods approach. The methods for communication campaigns today encompass more than the mass media to include special events, interpersonal communication, and personal influence.

Communication campaigns are presented in different forms and they serve different purposes, with the most popular ones being for promoting political causes and candidates. Others are for public health and wellness, public welfare and safety, and promoting charitable causes. Most communication campaigns are sponsored by entities such as governments, private companies, nonprofit organizations, communities, and social change advocates. Successful public communication programs today require mass communication campaign strategies, as evident in the investments of time, money, and other resources in many of today's political campaigns. Success or failure in elections is largely determined by campaign managers' skills in staging effective communication (including new social media) campaigns. The strategies may include opposition research, specific audience targeting, constant adjustment of the messages, and minute-by-minute tracking of issues. In the age of digital communication and 24/7 news cycles, constant attention must be paid to message delivery, audience reaction, and unintended results. In recent years, the US presidential campaign has provided the arena for testing the most competitive communication campaign strategies that underline the supreme importance of timing, packaging, monitoring, and image management. One single incident, no matter how seemingly innocuous, can spell doom if allowed to snowball into a crisis.

Next to political campaign managers, the other proficient users of communication campaigns are product and brand marketers who are willing to pay any price to deliver their messages to the right audience through the right channels at the right time. Some communication campaigns are more effective than others. In 1984,

Apple aired only one short commercial during the Super Bowl telecast and created a buzz that is still talked about today because of its uniqueness and fascinating creativity. And, the US Advertising Council has affected generations of Americans with the indelible messages of such public service announcements as the historic American Red Cross campaign (1945–1996), polio eradication (1958–1961), AIDS prevention (1988–1990), and domestic violence prevention (1994 to present). However, there is no silver bullet or magic formula in producing effective communication campaigns.

Health Communication Campaigns

Communication is a critical tool in health care awareness and education, and the campaign approach is a necessity in health communication. If health communication is understood to mean the use of communication strategies to inform choices that influence health (CDC 2011), health communication campaigns must imply the strategic devices for influencing target audiences with messages designed to promote positive health-related knowledge and decisions.

To resolve the many health-related problems of our contemporary society through personal conviction or public enlightenment, it is important to create consistent messages that the audience can understand and embrace. A campaign approach to health communication can help the health communicator design and disseminate effective messages consistently and strategically. Health communication campaigns can take many forms, address different objectives, and use a variety of media. They are usually designed:

1. To influence people's beliefs and actions toward their health or the health of others.
2. For specific target audiences or groups, and hardly for the entire population.
3. For implementation within a particular span of time.
4. To be integrated with various media and other communication efforts to educate an audience about a health-related topic (Rogers and Storey 1987).

Both the mass media and personal influence are useful channels for health communication campaigns. Ideally, they should complement each other instead of being used in isolation. It is foolhardy to organize health communication campaigns that disregard personal influence through face-to-face communication although the power of the mass media in reaching mass audiences is unquestionable. Mass media campaigns are ideal for creating awareness, especially in emergency and crisis situations, while personal channels are more effective in situations requiring persuasion, attitude change, and behavior modification. The mass media tend to have an upper hand in health communication campaigns that require mass audience exposure, reliance on public discussion as a means of public education, and needing the support of media authorities or agenda setters to support the message (NHS Health Development Agency 2004).

Although many health problems such as outbreak of disease epidemics and the gradual pervasiveness of cardiovascular disorders deserve and demand the use of campaign approaches, in some situations, this may be an overkill, as a set of mediated simple messages may suffice. The fight against polio in Nigeria has been waged through a variety of health campaign approaches, with less sterling results to show for the huge efforts that have often involved local and international partners working in concert in comprehensive campaign modes. More encouraging results have been achieved by the President of Nigeria leading the Minister of Health and the Commissioners of Health in polio-affected states in noncampaign but impactful efforts to wipe out polio from the country (Eze 2013).

The chances for success in health campaigns increase with the use of multiple strategies and paying attention to the circumstances of the target audience, relating interventions to theoretical and tested models, providing appropriate and clear information, and ensuring there are resonant choices and options available for audience members' consideration (NHS 2004). It helps a great deal to have a well-structured and comprehensive campaign plan that is built on a solid structure with the standard steps associated with communication campaigns. Designing a health communication campaign usually involves planning for a nine-step process that begins with a situation analysis and ends with an evaluation exercise.

Designing a Health Communication Campaign

An effective communication campaign requires a definite structure, usually expressed in these nine elements: (1) situation analysis, (2) goal/objectives, (3) target audience, (4) strategy, (5) tactics, (6) media of choice, (7) calendar/timeline, (8) budget, and (9) evaluation. Research plays a vital role within each of the nine elements. This generic template for communication campaigns is adaptable to specific scenarios in such areas as advertising, fundraising, health, and public relations among others. Underlining the structure is the strategy, which provides direction for all efforts and flavor for all messages. Strategy is the key to a successful campaign. With reference to advertising campaigns whose methods are also applicable in health campaigns, Shultz and Barnes (1995) aver that without strategy there is no campaign, only a series of ads or commercials or communication elements that may thrill the audience without any lasting impressions.

A health communication campaign plan identifies what is to be done, why, by whom, for whom, through what media, within what time frame, and with what results. Such a plan can be as short as two pages or as long as 100 pages. Regardless of the length, it shows that considerable thought has been exercised in designing the plan and that the key people involved in the implementation or supervision understand the purpose and the courses of action. Although research is critical at every phase of the planning and at each stage of implementation, it is the foundation on which all other activities are built. At the precampaign phase, formative research is essential to guide the initial campaign design. Starting with research helps campaign designers to determine what approach, media, and message are the best fit for the audience. In addition, formative research can help to determine if any messages or media would not enhance the campaign (Atkin and Freimuth 2013).

Qualitative research is especially beneficial during the formative phase of pre-production. The qualitative approach focuses on understanding concepts, meanings, definitions, characteristics, metaphors, symbols, and descriptions that research participants from a targeted group can provide to help the researcher obtain relevant insights from the audience's perspective (Berg 1989; Morrison 2002). During this phase, focus groups, observations, and in-depth interviews can help the researchers understand the health issue from the audience's perspective.

Situation Analysis

The first step in health communication campaign planning is to analyze the prevailing situation or health problem by dissecting the whole into pieces to separate causes from symptoms and try to locate the true sources of the malignancy. Fortunately, there are usually basic office records such as annual and project reports, periodic assessments, and the views of people in the trenches who are familiar with the situation and can be engaged in focus group discussions or be required to produce their analyses of the situation. Part of analyzing the situation is describing the history of the problem and previous communication efforts that have related to the health issue at hand. Assessing previous failures and successes can help inform a future campaign. At this point, practitioners might want to evaluate the opportunities and problems that their client or employer might face during the course of a new health campaign. Sometimes, paying attention to the specific strengths, weaknesses, opportunities, and threats (SWOT) associated with the situation will bring about desirable insights.

Goal/Objectives

A clear analysis of the situation leads to specifying the overarching goal and objectives that should be addressed by the campaign. Goals are broad targets, such as United Nations' Millennium Development Goal (MDG) of eradicating extreme poverty and hunger and reducing child mortality. Objectives are more specific and amenable to actual measurement such as the MDG target of halving the proportion of people with an income of less than US\$ 1.25 a day between 1990 and 2015 and reducing the child mortality rate by two-thirds between 1990 and 2015. Good statements of objectives will be directly related to the situation, realistic and achievable, with clear reference to completion time and evaluation. Whereas some objectives are stated in terms of program achievements or outcomes, others are meant to refer to communication output or activities. The true value of health communication campaigns should be sought in their impact or outcomes and not just in the communication activities or tactics undertaken. It bears pointing out that communication effects are not necessarily dependent or determinable from specific interventions, and so in some situation, the communication professional prefers to be held responsible for delivering the message.

Target Audience

The third element in the campaign planning process is delineating the target audience. Health communication campaigns, even when they appear to address the general public, actually are directed toward specific and particular segments of the population. Some campaigns often include more than one target audience and can include both upstream and downstream groups. A detailed description of each of these groups should be provided. The goal of this section is to make the case for the audiences or publics that you intend to reach with your campaign efforts. Attention should be paid to primary and secondary audiences as well as opinion leaders and influencers within social groups. Many health behaviors are related to peer pressure and social group influence. Research is necessary to identify key publics by their demographic and psychographic characteristics as well as by who or what influences their choices.

Strategy

A good strategy is critical to the success or failure of any health communication campaign because it provides the linkage between the how and why components. It provides a roadmap and sense of direction for generating the essential messages while also offering a rationale for the various actions that are proposed. According to Schultz and Barnes (1995), another way to explain strategy in a campaign is to see it as a roadmap that tells the whole "team what direction the campaign is going to take. It points the way in terms of what is important; what messages, information, or benefits need to come through; what is valuable; and what must be done if the campaign is to succeed" (p. 149). Part of the strategy may involve identifying and working with strategic partners. Health campaigns are often deeply rooted into communities where many groups express interest. Having the support of such partners as local media, government, and other organizations is essential. Working with such partners can help to engage the community and foster local awareness for the health initiatives by providing opportunities for unpaid media placement and contact with opinion leaders.

Tactics

Whereas strategies refer to broad roads on the map, tactics are the small alleys or specific activities that must be undertaken to address the objectives of the campaign. Being specific activities, they are the most visible aspects of the plan. Wilcox and Cameron (2012, p. 156) explain tactics as the "various methods to reach target audiences with key messages" and listed the following as the popular tactical communication tools: the World Wide Web, Web sites, Web casts, blogs, YouTube, Flickr, Texting, Twitter, Wikis, Podcasts, news releases, media kits, e-kits, mat releases, media alerts and fact sheets, electronic news releases, online newsrooms, media interviews, news conferences, media tours and press parties, public service announcements, video news releases, talk shows, magazine shows, product placements, issue placements, open houses, conventions, promotional events, etc. A tactic is a health communication activity or event or occasion designed to achieve a specific effect on target usually for the purposes of realizing a health communication objective. In this age of digital communication, it is easy to combine both traditional mass media and new social media tools in a convergent manner to increase campaign effectiveness. Campaign managers should not be carried away in their choice of tactics and must be guided by the characteristics of the target audience and the nature of the campaign strategy.

Media of Choice

Health communication campaigns require the use of the mass media, interpersonal channels, small group meetings, and one-on-one discussions, as the case may be. A good delineation of the target audience makes it easy to identify the best media of choice to reach them and the best time too. A correct media strategy maximizes reach while minimizing costs to yield optimal results. This addresses the efficiency and effectiveness questions in media selection. An effective media plan addresses the traditional media concerns of reach and frequency with the gains and downsides associated with them. Timing can be an important consideration and can refer to seasonality or time of day or "consumer aperture" a term that addresses the question: "when, where and under what circumstances is the customer's mind most receptive to the selling message?" (Schultz and Barnes 1995, p. 301). Media selection is closely related to tactics and the two can have the same meaning in some situations. In addition to the traditional media of television, magazines, radio, newspapers, outdoor, direct mail, and others such as newsletters and notice boards, we now have to add the new social media of blogs, Twitter, YouTube, and podcasts. The abundance of media at the disposal of the campaign planners necessitates the development of a media flowchart.

The media flowchart provides the timing of all the media and promotions for the entire campaign from its launch to its conclusion. Some media and promotions are planned to span the entire campaign. However, other media might be pulsed or appear incrementally throughout the campaign. The flowchart shows when and where various messages and promotions will appear. In addition, the media are often phased. Often there is a launch phase where the campaign is being initiated. It is common for the launch to involve the greatest media presence. The second phase is often the body of the campaign. Media are often used incrementally to remind the audience of the message. But, fewer media and promotions are present at this time. The third phase is usually the final media push before the campaign ends. Sometimes, there are special events that mark the end of a campaign or celebrate its success. Campaigns can last any length of time. However, most campaigns run from one to three years. Successful health campaigns can last indefinitely.

Calendar/Timeline

The seventh element in the campaign design is the calendar of events or the timeline for implementing the various activities. Depending on the goal, objectives and selected activities, the entire campaign can take as little as 1 week or as long as two years or more. Some campaigns are seasonal or perennial and should be repeated every so often while others are once and for all. A comprehensive calendar shows what should be done, when, by whom, where, and with whom. Calendars and timelines can be expressed in different formats some of which may require daily updating of individual responsibilities and tasks. Gantt charts and Microsoft Excel designs are popular for scheduling and monitoring purposes of timelines.

Budget

Health communication campaigns often involve the production of communication materials and the purchase of space and airtime in the media, in addition to paying for consulting services. Cost is a serious element in campaign planning, especially these days of increasing financial problems for health and social services programs all over the world. Many health communication departments have established funding patterns and histories that allow budgets for personnel and production expenses. The challenge is in providing acceptable justification for budget requests and taking full advantage of all possible free media, as long as this does not compromise the results. Campaign planners need to prove that they have allocated the funding efficiently. The budget is often broken down into categories such as promotional expenses, social media and Internet promotion, and traditional media. Campaign planners often leave 5–10 % of the budget for contingency purposes in case an unexpected expense or opportunity arises. In addition to showing how the money was spent, campaign planners need to defend their choices. For instance, campaign planners can show that their choices of media reached more of their target audience than another medium for the price. For instance, cost per thousand or CPM is often used to demonstrate that the choice of media vehicle was efficient. In addition, campaign planners need to estimate how many times an audience is exposed to a message to learn the message and then show that their plan will present the audience with the health message enough times for message learning to occur.

Evaluation

The last step in the campaign process is evaluation, which relates back directly to the situation analysis, goal, and objectives of the program. The measures of performance must relate directly to the objectives of the campaign and should use valid and reliable methods. Distinction must be made between output (communication products) and outcome (results and impact of actions taken).

Before a campaign is launched, campaign planners need to show their plans for evaluating the success of their campaign. Usually, research evaluating the campaign is done throughout the course of the campaign to catch any problems as early as possible. All messages must be copy tested to ensure that they are understood and that they resonate with the audience. *Copy testing* involves presenting audience members with the messages and creative executions before the campaign launches. This can be done with focus groups and surveys. Then, campaign planners need to survey the audience during the campaign to make sure that they are learning the message and that the message is having the desired outcome. Finally, when the campaign ends, the campaign can be evaluated to see if it had the desired result and if it should be continued or if major changes should be made to the communication approach.

Process research assesses the campaign as it unfolds to ensure that the messages and the media connect with the target audience (Atkin and Freimuth 2013). If there is a problem with a message or a medium during the course of a campaign, certain aspects can be tweaked to ensure that there is a good fit between the audience and the message.

Campaigns can be evaluated in a variety of ways that may include memory tests, persuasion or motivation tests, and inquiry tests that measure the number of responses to a campaign. In addition to testing the messages, campaign evaluation can assess media effectiveness and return on investment or ROI (Moriarty et al. 2009).

Health Campaign Strategies

There are a variety of popular strategies for promoting healthful habits in a target audience. Some health campaigns focus on *upstream approach* to target their audiences, such as community leaders, government officials, and other influential individuals. The opposite method is the *downstream approach,* two examples of which are social marketing and social norms campaigns. The two approaches can be used interchangeably or exclusively.

Upstream Approaches

Instead of directly targeting a particular audience, sometimes health campaigns target individuals that have *interpersonal influence,* or those who can create change through their relationship with the target audience. Another benefit of targeting this group is that opinion leaders or interpersonal influencers are more likely to have the ability to reform environmental factors that can shape behavior or influence policy and groups that work at the national or community level (Atkin and Rice 2013). Another benefit of influencing opinion leaders first is that the campaign can be more proactive because it causes something positive to happen instead of simply responding to a problem or crisis after it has occurred. It also encourages policy makers to take responsibility for health issues that affect the public (Lavack et al. 2008).

However, upstream initiatives might be necessary for downstream efforts to be effective (Kelly et al. 2005). In addition, many campaigns target the upstream audience first and then focus their attention on the downstream audience. It is often best when campaigns involve both upstream and downstream elements.

Urban Nutrition Campaign in Oakland, CA: A group of public health professionals were concerned about nutrition in urban areas of Oakland, California. To increase local awareness of healthy eating habits, they designed an educational program to increase fruit and vegetable consumption. However, when the campaign planners realized that the audience could not buy healthy food owing to the lack of grocery stores and farmers' markets in the targeted neighborhood, the health professionals decided to work with the local government. The local officials convinced Safeway to open a large grocery store (Bournhonesque and Mosbaek 2002). The public health professionals needed to focus upstream first to create the community change that would allow the neighborhood access to healthy food. After creating this environmental change, public health officials could focus on educating the community about nutrition. A health campaign targeting local residents would have been wasted if the upstream audience had not been reached first.

International Urban Wellness Campaign: Urbanization is one of the biggest health challenges for the twenty-first century. Since 2007, half of the world's population has been living in cities. By 2030, six out of ten people will be living in urban areas. Urbanization is related to many health issues such as clean water and environment, injuries and violence, disease, unhealthy diet and inactivity, and substance abuse. To help create a healthier urban environment, the World Health Organization (WHO) developed the campaign "1000 Cities, 1000 Lives" in 2010 to address issues related to urbanization and health. For the "1000 Cities" portion of the campaign, the WHO called upon city officials to open public spaces to health for one day in April. Cities around the world were encouraged to promote activities in the parks, conduct town hall meetings, engage in clean-up campaigns, and close off streets to motorized vehicles. Individual citizens were then encouraged to provide stories of urban health champions for the "1000 Lives" portion of the campaign (WHO 2010).

Downstream Approaches

A *social marketing* or public communication approach focuses on a health organization's need to be aware of and responsive to the audience's needs and relies on more public relations efforts to promote its messages. While initiatives can be launched by public health professionals, the efforts are made in response to specific needs, designed to meet those needs, effectively satisfy the needs, and are monitored to ensure that they continue to meet those needs (Lefebvre and Flora 1988). Social marketing campaigns work to impact voluntary behavior and change attitudes in order to improve personal and public welfare. To achieve this goal, the campaigns focus on the benefits of adopting a given behavior and reducing barriers that impede an audience members' ability to change a particular behavior (Glanz et al. 2008). Social marketing adopts the 4Ps (product, price, placement, and promotion) to address behavior, costs, location, and method, respectively (Glassman and Braun 2010).

As useful as the social marketing approach is, it can also have drawbacks that may include lack of clearly defined objectives, poor definition of target audience, and some health organizations focusing more on their own needs instead of the audience's needs (Lefebvre and Flora 1988).

According to the *social norms* approach, a person's social environment provides important cues related to health behaviors. Most people easily reject behaviors that jeopardize others; however, certain negative health-related behaviors can be adopted because they only jeopardize the self. Social norms campaigns are designed specifically to reduce undesirable behaviors among members of a target audience and they can be helpful in reducing those behaviors that cause self-harm.

A social norms approach is based on two principles, which are that many people overestimate the popularity of certain undesirable behaviors among their peer group and then use their perception of peer norms as a standard by which they can evaluate their own behavior. Social norms health campaigns work to reduce unhealthful behaviors by correcting the audience's perception of the occurrence of certain behaviors. Although norms are not laws that govern society, they have significant power over individuals and their social groups. For instance, *descriptive norms,* or the perception of prevalence of a behavior or group of behaviors, are the primary norming devices that social norms campaigns use to influence their target audiences (Cialdini et al. 1991). Descriptive norms are especially influential in motivating decisions to engage in decisions that adversely influence health such as high-risk drinking.

In spite of the popularity of social norms campaigns, they often achieve mixed results. In fact, some research shows that social norms campaigns can actually increase the undesirable behavior that they intended to reduce (Perkins et al. 2005). One reason for this is that people want to adopt the normative behavior. In the case of alcohol consumption, many college students do overestimate the prevalence of drinking on campus. However, between one-fifth and one-half of the college students underestimate the occurrence of drinking behavior. Therefore, a social norming campaign could increase drinking among these students (Schultz et al. 2007). On many American campuses, there are illustrative health communication campaigns that encourage responsible drinking choices using campus media such as newspaper ads, posters, electronic bulletin boards, flyers, banners, carabineers, and radio (Dartmouth College Health Services 2013). A social norms campaign approach as employed by the state of New Jersey, Hobart and William Smith Colleges, and the US Departments of Education on selected middle school (grades 6 to 8) students using print media posters as the primary communication vehicle resulted in significant reduction in school bullying. The results from this campaign demonstrate that social norms campaigns could be a promising approach for reducing bullying at school (Perkins et al. 2011).

Conclusion

Although creating effective health communication campaigns can be challenging, an understanding of the campaign planning process, health campaign research and theory, and the target audience can increase the odds of success. In addition, integrating research throughout the campaign process can help campaign planners develop messages that will resonate with the public and ensure proper coordination among sources, channels, audiences, and communication content.

References

Atkin, C. K. (1981). Mass media information effectiveness. In R. E. Rice & W. J. Paisley (Eds.), *Public communication campaigns* (pp. 256–280). Beverly Hills: Sage.

Atkin, C. K., & Freimuth, V. S. (2013). Guidelines for formative evaluation research in campaign design. In R. E. Rice & C. K. Atkin (Eds.) *Public communication campaigns* (4th ed.). Thousand Oaks: Sage.

Atkin, C. K., & Rice, R. E. (2013). Theory and principles of public communication campaigns. In R. E. Rice & C. K. Atkin (Eds.) *Public communication campaigns* (4th ed.). Thousand Oaks: Sage.

Berg, B. L. (1989). *Qualitative research methods for the social sciences*. Needham Heights: Allyn & Bacon.

Bournhonesque, R., & Mosbaek, C. (2002). Upstream public health: A proactive view. http://www.willamette.edu/centers/publicpolicy/projects/oregonsfuture/PDFvol3no2/F2Mosbaek7.pdf. Accessed 9 May 2013.

CDC (2011). Gateway to health communication and social marketing practice, http://www.cdc.gov/healthcommunication/HealthBasics/WhatIsHC.html. Accessed 9 May 2013.

Cialdini, R. B., Kallgren, C. A., & Reno, R. R. (1991). A focus theory of normative conduct. *Advances in Experimental Social Psychology*, 24, 201–234.

Dartmouth College Health Services (2013). Social norms campaign. http://www.dartmouth.edu/~healthed/focus/aod/norms.html. Accessed 9 May 2013.

Eze, C. (2013). The polio eradication campaign in Nigeria. Unpublished manuscript, Ahmadu Bello University, Zaria.

Glanz, K., Rimer, B. K., & Viswanath, K. (2008). Theory, Research, and Practice in Health and Health Education. In K. Glanz, B.K. Rimer, and K. Viswanath (Eds.) *Health Behavior and Health Education Theory, Research and Practice* (4th edition). San Francisco: Jossey-Bass, 23–62.

Glassman, T., & Braun, R. (2010). Social norms vs. social marketing: Confusion surrounding social marketing strategy and social norms theory: To prevent high-risk drinking among college students. *Social Marketing Quarterly*, 16, 94–103.

Kelly, M. P., McDaid, D., Ludbrook, A., & Powell, J. (2005). Economic appraisal of public health interventions. *NHS Briefing paper*, 1–8.

Lavack, A. M., Magnuson, S. L., Deshpande, S., Basil, D. Z., Basil, M. D., & Mintz, J. H. (2008). Enhancing occupational health and safety in young workers: The role of social marketing. *International Journal of Nonprofit Voluntary Sector Marketing*, 13, 193–204.

Lefebvre, C. R. & Flora, J.A. (1988). Social Marketing and Public Health Intervention. *Health Education Quarterly*, 15(3), 299–315.

Moriarty, S., Mitchell, N., & Wells, W. (2009). *Advertising: Principles and practice*. Upper Saddle River: Pearson.

Morrison, M. A., Haley, E., Sheehan, K. B., & Taylor, R. E. (2002). *Using qualitative research in advertising: Strategies, techniques and applications*. Thousand Oaks: Sage.

NHS Health Development Agency (2004, June). Consumers and markets: The effectiveness of public health campaigns. *HDA Briefing*, 7, 1–4.

Paisley, W. (1989). Public communication campaigns: The American experience. In R. E. Rice & C. K. Atkin. *Public communication campaigns* (2nd ed., pp. 15–38). Newbury Park: Sage.

Perkins, H. W., Haines, M. P., & Rice, R. (2005). Misperceiving the college drinking norm and related problems: A nationwide study of exposure to prevention information, perceived norms and student alcohol misuse. *Journal of Studies on Alcohol*, 66, 470–478.

Perkins, H. W., Craig, & Perkins, J. M. (2011). Using social norms to reduce bullying: A research intervention among adolescents in five middle schools. *Group Processes & Intergroup Relations*, 14(5), 703–722.

Rogers, E. M., & Storey, J. D. (1987). Communications campaigns. In C. Berger & S. Chaffee (Eds.), *Handbook of communication science*. Newberry Park: Sage.

Schultz, D. E. & Barnes, B. E. (1995). *Strategic Advertising Campaigns* (4th edition). Lincolnwood, IL: NTC Business Books.

Schultz, P. W., Nolan, J. M., Cialdini, R. B., Goldstein, N. J., & Griskevicius, V. (2007). The constructive, destructive, and reconstructive power of social norms. *Psychological Science*, 18, 429–434.

Wilcox, D. L. & Cameron, G. T. (2012). *Public Relations: Strategies and Tactics* (10th Edition). Upper Saddle River, NJ: Pearson.

World Health Organization (2010). World Health Organization 1000 Cities, 1000 Lives Brochure. http://www.who.int/world-health-day/2010/1000cities_1000lives_brochure_blue.pdf. Accessed 9 May 2013.

Chapter 3
Urbanization, Population, and Health Myths: Addressing Common Misconceptions with Strategic Health Communication

Kristine Berzins, Holly Greb, Malea Hoepf Young and Karen Hardee

Introduction

As the world becomes increasingly urbanized, health-care officials and policy-makers face challenges of providing services and education to poor populations in cities and semiurban areas. Today, more than half of the world's population lives in urban areas with some variation by region. In 2011, fully 3.6 billion people lived in urban areas. The United Nations projects that the world's population will grow by 2.3 billion between 2011 and 2050, from 7.0 to 9.3 billion. All of that growth is expected to be in urban areas, which are projected to grow by 2.6 billion, from 3.6 billion in 2011 to 6.3 billion in 2050 (United Nations 2012). "Thus, the urban areas of the world are expected to absorb all the population growth expected over the next four decades while at the same time drawing in some of the rural population" (United Nations 2012, p. 1). Africa is expected to be 50 % urban in 2035.

Megacities with populations over 10 million and sprawling slums have captured the world's imagination, but the health challenges of urbanizing areas are not confined to Lagos or Dhaka. Significant urban growth also occurs in smaller cities and towns that lack planning capacity and resources to respond to current growth and prepare for future strains. Health-care challenges in poor urban areas are different from those in poor rural or rich urban areas and often encompass the risks of both. For example, urban slum areas often put people at risk of not only infectious diseases that are common in rural areas but also to the environmental risks (pollution,

K. Berzins (✉)
Ecologic Institute, Berlin, Germany

H. Greb
PATH, Hamilton, Canada

M. H. Young
Catholic Charities, Alexandria, VA, USA

K. Hardee
Hardee Associates LLC, 5330 26th St N,
Arlington, VA 22207, USA
e-mail: Karen.Hardee@hardeeassociates.com

C. C. Okigbo (ed.), *Strategic Urban Health Communication,*
DOI 10.1007/978-1-4614-9335-8_3, © Springer Science+Business Media New York 2014

crime, diet) of urban life (WHO 2010). These unique difficulties can be addressed with education and health-care services. Misconceptions about urbanization are prevalent both among local policymakers and health program planners, as well as in the international development community. The oversimplification of rural versus urban issues precludes effective health-care policy and often downplays the needs of the poor, particularly in the area of sexual and reproductive health.

Strategic health communication interventions will be critical to improving health outcomes for the urban and semiurban poor. This chapter presents a guide to strategic health communications, discusses six common misconceptions about urbanization, and explores how innovative health communication strategies can be used to identify diverse needs and mobilize people to use available services within urban environments. The myths and suggestions presented in this chapter are derived from a review of literature on urbanization and health communications, as well as an analysis of communications methods used to address access to and use of health-care services in urban and rural areas in developing countries. Many examples are drawn from the field of sexual and reproductive health, a broad health-care sector in which public communications campaigns play a critical role.

Strategic Communication

Strategic communication is used in many fields, including private industry, but is newer to public health. A UNICEF expert consultation on Strategic Communication for Behavior and Social Change in South Asia defined strategic communication as "an evidence-based, results-oriented process, undertaken in consultation with the participant group(s), intrinsically linked to other programme elements, cognisant of the local context and favouring a multiplicity of communication approaches, to stimulate positive and measurable behaviour and social change" (UNICEF Regional Office for South Asia, 2005, p. 6). This definition has been used in the context of HIV/AIDS and will be used in this chapter.

Strategic health communications target disparate urban groups with separate but complementary interventions to ensure that the larger goal of improved urban health care is accomplished. These communications should engage all relevant stakeholders from community leaders to community members.

Strategic health communications methods can encompass a broad range of innovative techniques including the following:

- *Information, education, and communication and behavior change communication (IEC, BCC)*: "IEC is a process of working with individuals, communities and societies to develop communication strategies to promote positive behaviors which are appropriate to their settings"; and BCC adds to IEC by providing "a supportive environment which will enable people to initiate and sustain positive behaviors" (UNESCO, n.d.).

- *Social marketing*: "Social marketing applies traditional commercial marketing tools and concepts such as the 4 P's—product, price, promotion, and place (distribution)—to achieve the objectives of public health and other social programs. Social marketing programs involve products [...] or may focus only on health practices or on influencing health-seeking behaviors" (AED, n.d.b.).
- *Social change*: "Social change approaches involve strategies to shift societal norms and other environmental factors to bring about large-scale behavior change. Strategies address communities, organizations, policies, laws, and popular culture, as well as individuals" (AED, n.d.).
- *Advocacy, communication, and social mobilization (ACSM)*: Developed to address TB, the strategy of combining advocacy, communication, and social mobilization is relevant for other health areas also. "In the context of wide-ranging partnerships for TB control, advocacy, communication and social mobilization (ACSM) embrace: advocacy to influence policy changes and sustain political and financial commitment; two-way communication between the care providers and people with TB as well as communities to improve knowledge of TB control policies, programmes and services; and social mobilization to engage society, especially the poor, and all allies and partners in the campaign to Stop TB" (WHO, n.d.).

Strategic communication can be accomplished through various methods, ranging from traditional education to entertainment education, multimedia campaigns, and social media. Although many of the aforementioned communications techniques are used in urban areas, their coordinated application, when built to address specified goals through evidence-based interventions, can contribute to improved health outcomes in cities. These approaches can foster empowerment for personal and collective self-efficacy, including promoting social capital.

Common Myths and Misperceptions About Urbanization and Strategic Health Communications Opportunities

Six common misperceptions about urbanization and health (Box 1) hamper initiatives to health outcomes among poor urban and semiurban residents. Understanding and correcting these misperceptions will focus health programming in urban areas to meet the needs of poor urban residents, including through strategic health communication initiatives.

Box 1: Six Myths about Urbanization and Health

Myth 1: Urban growth is fueled by unwanted internal (rural to urban) and international migration.

Myth 2: Urban areas provide better access to essential services such as education and health, and thus have better health indicators than their rural counterparts.

Myth 3: Megacities are the sites of most urban growth in the developing world.

Myth 4: Poverty is greater in rural areas than in cities, and should thus be the focus of development efforts.

Myth 5: Cities facilitate the spread of the HIV/AIDS epidemic.

Myth 6: Urban populations have a more damaging impact on the natural environment than small rural settlements.

Myth 1: Urban growth is fueled by unwanted internal (rural to urban) and international migration, which should be curbed by government policy
While many policymakers look to the prevention of rural to urban migration to reduce urbanization, a significant portion of growth lies in natural increase among those already living in cities, with the rest attributable to migration and the reclassifications of rural residents as urban areas sprawl and engulf rural settlements. Between 1950 and 2000, natural growth within cities accounted for half of the population growth in cities in India, Pakistan, the Democratic Republic of Congo, and the Philippines (United Nations 2012). Approaches to stabilizing urban growth that emphasize reproductive rights and education of girls, respect individual human rights, and contribute to poverty reduction are critical.

The United Nations Population Fund (UNFPA) asserts that migrants have an equal right to the benefits of the city, that they are not a negative force in and not the dominant cause of urbanization, emphasizing instead the need for equitable and affordable access to reproductive health and family planning services for both old and recent residents of cities (UNFPA 2007). High fertility in rural areas can accelerate rural–urban migration, making access to family planning services and supplies important in both rural and urban areas (UNFPA 2007).

Slowing rates of urbanization give city governments flexibility and additional time to develop infrastructure and plan for the future. An evidence- and rights-based approach to managing the growing rate of urbanization requires informed city planning, empowering women and couples and providing them with tools to achieve their desired family size, and evaluating the most efficient and sustainable use of resources, rather than pejorative policies solely focused on discouraging migration.

Health Communications Policy Recommendation: Reproductive Health and Family Planning Health communication strategies need to be designed in a manner which addresses not only the immediate urban health needs of women and families, but should define long-term goals which take into account the potential growth within the urban population. Strategic health communication should incorporate a rights-based approach aimed at empowering women to make informed decisions about their desired family size, as well as how to access available reproductive health resources. Community mobilization involving men needs to be an integral part of any strategy that is implemented.

Planners should utilize a multisectored approach to achieve women's empowerment in an urban setting. Strategic health communication must cut across multiple sectors including, but not restricted to, vocational capacity building, improving education systems, and access to justice and legal rights, bolstering and communicating through community organizations, and improving infrastructure and the environment.

Certain examples of success with such efforts include studies from Nigeria, Tanzania, Nepal, and Mali that indicate both direct and indirect associations between increased family planning messages in the media and voluntarily decreasing family size (Gupta et al. 2003). In Tanzania, a study found that "the more types of media sources of family planning messages, the greater the likelihood of contraceptive use" (Gupta et al. 2003, p. 4). A similar effect was reported in Mali.

Additionally, infrastructure is often slightly better in urban areas, and consolidated social groupings and networks provide unique opportunities for communication programs to serve as starting points for national health campaigns. One such example is the Yellow Flower Campaign in Uganda, where the Ministry of Health utilized multimedia tools to communicate the benefits of modern family planning to married urban couples. Following the intervention, 50 % of the country's population could identify the Yellow Flower symbol as an indicator of family planning and increased their intentions to use it (JHUCCP 2003).

Myth 2: Urban areas provide better access to essential services such as education and health, and thus have better health indicators than their rural counterparts While many economic and health indicators are better in urban than rural areas, this often masks disparities within cities between the rich and poor. Poor individuals in urban areas generally have greater access to reproductive health services than the rural poor, but reproductive health indicators among poor urban residents tend to fall behind those of their wealthier urban counterparts (UNFPA 2007). In some cases, health indicators are worse for the urban poor than the rural poor. The child mortality rate in the Nairobi slums is 151 deaths per 1,000 births, which exceeds the rural child mortality rate of 113 per 1,000 births. Some have suggested that the better rural indicators are a result of the lower population densities and reduced risk of certain communicable diseases (Montgomery 2009, p. 8).

Urban populations are exposed to health problems unique to urban environments. These urban health issues include reduced psychological health and greater exposure to violence, traffic accidents, and outdoor pollution. For example, being poor in a city often makes residents feel socially excluded, which may lead to a lack of self-efficacy, inability to seek necessary health care, and depression (Montgomery 2009, pp. 8–9). Cities also increase the risk of certain infectious diseases: in 2010, the World Health Organization highlighted the increased incidence of tuberculosis in urban areas, noting that in the Democratic Republic of the Congo, 83 % of tuberculosis patients live in urban areas (WHO 2010).

Urban residents usually live closer to health-care providers than do rural individuals, but the low quality of health-care services and their high financial cost often precludes poor urban residents from using nearby services. While health care is often free and public in rural clinics, urban health systems are largely private and of varying quality. A study in Delhi found that the health-care providers in poor neighborhoods generally had very low knowledge. Private, highly skilled health-care services were, in turn, prohibitively expensive (Montgomery 2009).

Lastly, even where health-care services are affordable and effective, proximity does not necessarily lead to better outcomes. Health communications should concentrate on education campaigns to teach individuals how to use services. Although urban residents have better access to contraception than rural residents, high rates of abortion in urban areas in developing countries indicate that access to contraceptives does not equate proper use. In poor settlements in Karachi, for example, women have, on average, between three and four abortions, and "over 20 percent of young women in Yaoundé, Cameroon reported having had abortions" (Montgomery 2009, p. 11).

Health Communications Policy Recommendation: Addressing Diverse Urban Needs Strategic health communications interventions should specifically target the urban poor in health programming to address health-care inequalities. Strategic health communication can tailor health messages for specific audiences in order to improve demand for health-care services and educate people to take preventative measures to improve their health. Health messages can also equip communities with an understanding of how environmental factors in poor urban areas can continue to undermine their health. Effective outreach to poor urban populations should be included in comprehensive health program planning so that communities are empowered to fully utilize the available health infrastructure.

One example of this strategy can be seen in an urban youth condom use study in South Africa. Sayles and colleagues (2006) called for using health communication theories to identify how planners can ensure that urban populations utilize the services available to them. Study results showed that condoms and health facilities were generally perceived to be available, but condom use was low. The results differed based on gender, indicating a need to reach out to men and women with separate messages. The study determined that participants' self-efficacy (believing they could use an available condom with their partner) was a significant indicator of actual condom use. Regarding women's condom use, the study stated: "Factors significantly associated with low self-efficacy for young women included: not using condoms the first time they had sex, a history of having sex when they did not want to, and believing that condom use is a sign of not trusting one's partner" (Sayles et al. 2006, p. 231). Men stated that access to condoms was not a problem for them, however, the degree to which they believed themselves to be susceptible to HIV affected their self-efficacy to use a condom. Therefore, programs focused on accessibility and correct use of condoms may not be effective strategies for this population (Sayles et al. 2006). This case study reflects a need for urban health officials and implementers to collaborate with health communications research efforts to ensure that interventions are based on evidence of desired outcomes. This is important in order to design not only accessible health facilities for the urban poor, but help ensure that they are utilized.

Myth 3: Megacities are the sites of most urban growth in the developing world The number and size of megacities, cities of over 10 million people, are staggering: as of 2011, the latest year that the UN has compiled the data, the world has 23 megacities, most of which are in developing countries (United Nations 2012). But the trend of urbanization is not confined to megacities such as Dhaka, Lagos or São Paulo. Only 9.9 % of the world's urban population lived in megacities in 2011 (United Nations 2012). Key to an accurate picture of the modern urban world is that approximately half of the world's urban population lives in smaller cities and towns under 500,000, and this share is likely to increase over time (United Nations 2012). Such localities have concerns different than the megacities, as small cities have fewer resources and fewer economic opportunities for their residents, and generally do not reach the economies of scale in provision of infrastructure that promote health and quality of life observed in the largest cities.

Health Communications Policy Recommendation: Improving Health in Semiurban Areas Targeted urban strategic health communications strategies should be based on needs assessments to help identify specific entry points for improving overall urban health. These efforts should also incorporate sensitization and mobilization of local governments, in combination with capacity building, to achieve sustainable and cost-effective results.

Communications strategies should be formed in close collaboration with all local stakeholders in smaller urban areas, specifically as many smaller urban municipalities are gaining increasing responsibilities through rapid decentralization of health systems. Strategies should open communication channels that build community partnerships and empower local NGOs, faith-based groups, and private sector stakeholders to contribute to improving health outcomes. Collaboration in low-resource urban areas will aid in promoting a sense of ownership, localizing health messages, and mobilizing local leaders to identify specific health problems.

Disparities between cities of different sizes and within cities must be taken into account when planning for improvements in public health and overall community development. An example of using health communications to improve the health of semiurban areas is the case of Gabarone, Botswana. The UNFPA highlights Botswana's approach to urban planning in the rapidly growing town of Gabarone as relevant to the growth issues faced by emerging towns. To regulate settlements, the government provided plots of land for relatively low rent and allowed plot holders to own their land for a 99-year term. While first thought to be a novel approach, the government later realized that this approach left out the poorest of the poor in Gabarone, who then flooded squatter settlements on the outskirts of town, aggravating the spread of disease. The report recommends directly involving the poorest of the poor as key stakeholders in planning. Strategic health communication strategies can aid in meeting the needs of these poorer populations, for example, by better identifying the barriers low-income women face to managing household sanitation before sanitation and health programs are put in place (UNFPA 2007).

Myth 4: Poverty is greater in rural areas than in cities, and should thus be the focus of development efforts It is undisputed that the majority of the world's poor reside in rural areas, which have long been the focus of economic development programs. But a 2007 study from the World Bank found that while poverty rates will be higher in rural areas for several decades to come, the urban share of poverty is increasing over time, and that poor individuals are moving to cities in greater numbers than the general population. On average, an urban poverty line is approximately 30 % higher than that in rural areas (generally pegged at US$ 1 a day; Ravallion et al. 2007). This increased cost is due to multiple factors in urban life, including greater dependence on cash income for goods and services and less access to free education in rural areas.

Solving the problems of urban areas, including slums, is critical to reaching those made most vulnerable by urbanization. While some efforts to improve the quality of life in slums have been successful, they have not been uniform in their success and are not keeping up with the global growth of slum areas. Since 2000, fully 227 million people have left slums because of improvements in living conditions. But these improvements have been isolated to the more economically prosperous countries, and in 2010, more people than ever before were living in slum areas (830 million), primarily in sub-Saharan Africa (UN News Centre 2010).

Health Communications Policy Recommendation: Targeting Critical Overlaps of Urban Poverty and Health Needs Growing urban areas require a combination of messaging techniques which can serve the needs of diverse populations within the city and assist residents with navigating their options. Rural and urban health communication strategies should be combined to equip populations who have recently transitioned from rural to urban settings. Taking a proactive approach to specifically target new migrants in cities will strengthen vulnerable communities overall.

Health policies should ensure that funding and resources for urban health and community development are allocated according to needs assessments in both urban and rural areas. Growing urban areas are often comprised of migrants from rural areas, young people looking for work and urban lifestyles, and others with their own unique health needs. Strategic health communications strategies can utilize different messaging techniques to specify a target audience for a specific intervention as well as better inform people of what urban health services are available.

An example of using health communication to meet diverse health needs within urban populations is efforts to target migrant men. Migrant men living in urban areas represent one important group in need of health services. HIV/AIDS incidence has increased along migratory routes in many regions. Migrant men may have varying levels of acculturation to urban life and require services tailored to the specific cultural and health-related barriers they face. In a successful effort, the HIV/AIDS Awareness for People on the Move 2002, a partnership between CIDA and the Ministry of Railways in Shanxi, China, disseminated health messages targeted at migrant men by utilizing communication channels provided by the railways. The project was later expanded to other provinces and incorporated reproductive health education campaigns at railway stations and through radio and poster campaigns. This example suggests that the transportation sector can collaborate with health promotion programs to better reach specific subgroups of the urban population (Marie Stopes International Australia, n.d.). These sorts of nontraditional partnerships can provide a strategic advantage in health care.

Myth 5: Cities facilitate the spread of the HIV/AIDS epidemic Although cities have elements that facilitate HIV transmission (breakdown of social norms, vulnerability of women to gender-based violence, access to illegal drugs, and access to multiple sexual partners), higher population density can make HIV prevention messages and products easier to disseminate and can improve access to condoms. City life may also make traditional norms more flexible, providing a leverage point for programs to fight harmful gender norms that promote the spread of HIV, such as having multiple sexual partners among young men, and passivity in sexual decision making among young women (see http://www.whatworksforwomen.org). Urban areas also allow greater access to HIV treatment and care, and can facilitate networks of people living with HIV/AIDS (PLHA) that can empower individuals and combat stigma and discrimination (UNFPA 2007).

Health Communications Policy Recommendation: Mobilizing Urban Resources to Facilitate Health Communication Interventions in HIV/AIDS Strategic health communications should use all relevant communications channels, from the mass media to the new social media networks and eHealth, to educate people about HIV and promote behavior change. Media and mass communication advocacy channels should be used to educate the public on what HIV/AIDS is, what specific methods can be used to prevent it, and where to obtain testing services. Various forms of media can also disseminate community endorsements. Individual and group counseling can reinforce mass media messages. Separate methods can be used to reach diverse groups: married couples, young people, sex workers, and men who have sex with men, among others.

An example of mobilizing urban resources to facilitate health communication interventions in HIV/AIDS comes from Malawi. As part of the United Nation's Urban Management Program, the city of Blantyre, Malawi has worked to utilize urban resources for HIV/AIDS prevention programming. With a 21.7 % HIV prevalence in urban Malawi, Blantye implemented innovative City Consultations with civil society, local government, businesses, and others to develop a comprehensive AIDS profile of the city. Later, targeted seminars were used to reach women and girls specifically to increase knowledge of HIV and provide treatment (UN-Habitat, n.d.). As many governments decentralize HIV/AIDS efforts to local authorities, localized health communication campaigns can reach women and girls previously underexposed to health education and services.

Myth 6: Urban populations have a more damaging impact on the natural environment than small rural settlements Planned cities have important potential in preventing environmental degradation. Concentrating population in relatively small areas (50 % of the earth's population on 3 % of its land) relieves pressure on fragile ecosystems and minimizes agriculture on marginal land. However, urban sprawl can undermine these benefits. Sprawling cities can take up needed agricultural land, biodiverse land, and other needed green space. This occurs through periurbanization (growth along the edge of a city, or along transportation routes between cities), which is often unplanned, and frequently occurs as the poor are pushed from the center to peripheries of cities. Peripheral settlements are frequently not served by city sanitation and water, and are far from health and education facilities, and are subject to destruction by governments due to their illegal status. Better city planning can mitigate the effects of sprawl, as well as minimize the impact of pollution produced by cities (UNFPA 2007).

While urban residence has the potential to minimize negative impact on the environment, urban residents (particularly the poor) face multiple threats from the environment, such as pollution, and will face impact from climate change, such as natural disasters and rising sea levels, disproportionate to their relatively low carbon emissions. These threats will have an impact on their health outcomes. Coastal cities, particularly those in low-income countries, are highly vulnerable to the effects of climate change, in terms of rising sea levels and stronger storms, as well as salt water invasion of aquifers providing vital water resources to urban residents (UNFPA 2007). Increasing temperatures and urban living conditions also increase the risk of emerging and reemerging infectious diseases, as evidenced by urban dengue outbreaks in Latin America and Asia (Campbell-Lendrum and Corvalán 2007).

Health Communications Policy Recommendation: The Case of Clean Water and Sanitation A social marketing intervention designed to develop safe water products that were both produced and marketed locally in Peru and Nicaragua was successful at helping people in both periurban and rural areas make the link between disease and the quality of their water as well as empowering them with tools to correct the situation. The communications component of this program was significant in that the population was more responsive to locally branded products. This example demonstrates the need for policymakers and health officials to include those living on the outskirts of cities in water and sanitation planning, so that health communication interventions can work simultaneously to educate and motivate residents to improve the surrounding environment and health of the community (Armand et al. 1998).

Conclusion

In the coming decades, policymakers and health program planners will have to address the health needs of an increasingly urban world. The needs of smaller cities and towns should be at the center of policies and campaigns to address urbanization. In addressing these efforts, policymakers should be sure not to oversimplify urban contexts. It is important to keep in mind that:

- Urban growth is fueled by internal growth in addition to migration.
- Smaller cities are sites of the most urban growth in the developing world.
- Urbanization poses health-related challenges and opportunities related to environmental degradation and climate change.

- People living in cities have many obstacles to health education and services.
- Urban areas should increasingly be a focus of poverty alleviation programs.
- Cities provide opportunities for improved health outcomes, including for HIV/ AIDS prevention and treatment and sexual and reproductive health.

Through targeted and evidence-based programs, policymakers and health-care officials can use strategic health communications to anticipate and address the needs of their growing cities. Urbanization can provide many opportunities, such as access to education, widened economic choices for men and women, increased access to health care, access to a wide range of media, and new social networks for the urban poor. The successes of the strategic health communication described in this chapter can help guide efforts to make the most of these new prospects. As the examples in this chapter show, a range of strategic communication approaches are appropriate. Indeed, all forms of communication will be needed to tackle the challenges.

The demand for access to high-quality health services will continue to increase. As policymakers and health officials make these services more available, strategic health communications techniques designed to engage the public are needed to help populations understand and utilize services. The urban poor, recent migrants, women, young people, and married couples represent just a small sample of groups within growing urban areas who require specific messaging and engagement to meaningfully improve their health outcomes.

References

Academy for Educational Development (AED). (n.d.a). "Social Change." http://www.globalhealthcommunication.org/strategies/social_change. Accessed 13 July 2010.
Academy for Educational Development (AED). (n.d.b). "Social Marketing." http://www.globalhealthcommunication.org/strategies/social_marketing. Accessed 13 July 2010.
Armand, F., Crowley, H., & Faura, P. (1998). Social marketing for household disinfection of water. Population Services International. http://www.bvsde.paho.org/bvsacg/i/fulltext/symposium/ponen5.pdf. Accessed 13 July 2010.
Campbell-Lendrum, D., & Corvalán, C. (2007). Climate change and developing country cities: Implications for environmental health and equity. *Journal of Urban Health, 84*(1), i109–117.
Gupta, N., Katende, C., & Bessinger, R. (2003). Association of mass media exposure on family planning attitudes and practices in Uganda (Working Paper 03-67, Page 4). MEASURE Evaluation. www.cpc.unc.edu/measure/publications/pdf/wp-03-67.pdf. Accessed 13 July 2010.
Johns Hopkins Bloomberg School of Public Health, the Center for Communication Programs (JHUCCP) (2003). A field guide to designing a health communication strategy. Uganda's DISH Project: A case study of an integrated communication strategy. http://www.jhuccp.org/pubs/fg/02/13-appendix2.pdf. Accessed 13 July 2010.
Marie Stopes International Australia. (n.d.) Problems Facing Internal Migrants Accessing Sexual and Reproductive Health Services [PDF document]. http://www.pgpd.asn.au/documents/SOWP%20seminar%20presentations/MSISeminarSpeech.pdf. Accessed 13 July 2010.
Montgomery, M. (2009). Urban poverty and health in developing countries. Population Bulletin, 64.2. Population Reference Bureau. 8.
Ravallion, M., Chen, S., & Sangraula, P. (2007). The urbanization of global poverty. World Bank Research Digest Vol. 1(Number 4).

Sayles, I., Pettifor, A., Wong, M., MacPhail, C., Lee, S., Hendriksen, E., Rees, H., Coates, T. (2006). Factors associated with self-efficacy for condom use and sexual negotiation among South African Youth. *JAIDS Journal of Acquired Immune Deficiency Syndromes, 43*(2), 226–233.

UN News Centre. (18 March, 2010). Over 200 million escape slums but overall number still rising, UN report Finds. http://www.un.org/apps/news/story.asp?NewsID=34119 & Cr=mdg & Cr1. Accessed 13 July 2010.

The United Nations Children's Fund (UNICEF) Regional office for South Asia. (2005). Strategic communication—for behaviour and social change in South Asia. Kathmandu, Nepal. http://www.unicef.org/rosa/Strategic_Communication_for_Behaviour_and_Social_Change. pdf. Accessed 13 July 2010.

United Nations Educational, Scientific and Cultural Organization (UNESCO). (n.d.). "HIV coordination, adolescent reproductive and school health: Advocacy, IEC & BCC." http://www.unescobkk.org/education/hivaids/projects/adolescent- reproductive-sexual-health-arsh/information-resources-publications/advocacy-iec-bcc/. Accessed 13 July 2010.

United Nations Human Settlements Programme (UN-Habitat). (n.d.). Fighting HIV/AIDS in Blantyre, Malawi. http://ww2.unhabitat.org/programmes/hiv/malawi.asp. Accessed 13 July 2010.

United Nations Population Fund (UNFPA). (2007). Smaller cities: Home to half the urban population. In state of world population 2007: Unleashing the potential of urban growth. New York. http://www.unfpa.org/swp/2007/english/chapter_1/smaller_cities.html. Accessed 13 July 2010.

United Nations. Department of Economic and Social Affairs/Population Division. (2012). *World urbanization prospects: The 2011 Revision.* New York.

World Health Organization (WHO). (2010). Urbanization and health. http://www.who.int/bulletin/volumes/88/4/10-010410/en/index.html. Accessed 7 May 2010.

World Health Organization (WHO). (n.d.). Tuberculosis (TB). Advocacy, Communication and Social Mobilization (ACSM). http://www.who.int/tb/people_and_communities/advocacy_communication/en/index.html. Accessed 29 May 2012.

Chapter 4
"Soaps" for Social and Behavioral Change

Kriss Barker

Over the past 20 years, health communicators have come to realize that communication strategies need to do more than simply "tell." Prior to this, it was commonly believed that "if we tell them what's good for them, people will just naturally adopt healthy behaviors." But, we all know that none of us likes to be told what to do. We want to choose for ourselves. As health communication has become increasingly more behavior-change-oriented, it has of necessity evolved to include the voices of the target audiences themselves in not only identifying the problem, but in crafting the solution.

Such strategic communication requires the participation of audience members in the design of content, themes, and messages. Strategic communication shifts away from communicating *to,* and instead focuses on communicating *with* target groups in order to establish solutions.

In this chapter, we will explore a unique and highly successful approach to the use of entertainment-education for strategic communication. This approach is termed as the Sabido Methodology, named for its creator, Miguel Sabido of Mexico.

The Sabido methodology is an approach to development of mass media serial dramas (often referred to as "soap operas"). However, unlike typical "soap operas," Sabido-style serial dramas are not used to sell soap, but rather, social and behavioral change.

The Sabido methodology for development of mass media serial dramas has been proven to be highly effective in motivating positive behavior change in the numerous countries where it has been used.

K. Barker (✉)
Population Media Center (PMC), 145 Pine Haven Shores Road,
#2011, Shelburne, VT 05482, USA
e-mail: krissbarker@populationmedia.org

C. C. Okigbo (ed.), *Strategic Urban Health Communication,*
DOI 10.1007/978-1-4614-9335-8_4, © Springer Science+Business Media New York 2014

In 1973–1974, Miguel Sabido was General Director for Research at Televisa in Mexico. In 1974, he was named Vice President for Research at Televisa, commissioned to prepare a plan to reorganize Mexican television along more socially responsible lines in the face of criticisms from the president of Mexico, who objected to the imported US television shows that were being broadcast.

While at Televisa, Sabido developed a theoretical model for eliciting prosocial attitudinal, informational, and behavioral changes through commercial television programming.

Between 1973 and 1981, Sabido produced six social content serial dramas in Mexico. During the decade, when many of these Mexican soap operas were on the air, the country underwent a 34 % decline in its population growth rate. As a result, the United Nations Population Prize was awarded to Mexico as the foremost population success story in the world.

Here are the six social content serial dramas:

- *Ven Conmigo* ("Come with Me") provided specific information about a study program offered by the Secretary of Public Education in 1975. Role models were used to motivate viewers to register for literacy classes.
- *Acompáñame* ("Accompany Me"), Sabido's second entertainment-education soap opera, contained a family planning message (broadcast from August 1977 through April 1978). Role models were used in this serial drama to motivate women to use contraceptive methods, and to show wives how to negotiate contraceptive use with their spouses.
- *Vamos Juntos* ("Let's Go Together") promoted responsible parenthood and the active development and integration of children in the family and in society (July 1979 through March 1980). Role models were used in this program to teach parents about family integration behaviors and family life planning.
- *El Combate* ("The Struggle") promoted an adult education program launched in several communities outside of Mexico City (April through September 1980). Behavior models were used in this program to inform rural audiences how to dispel the myth that adults cannot go back to school.
- *Caminemos* ("Going Forward Together") tackled the theme of sex education for adolescents (September 1980 through April 1981). Role models in this program were used to model responsible sexual behavior for teenagers.
- *Nosotros las Mujeres* ("We the Women") ran from April to October 1981. Through the effective use of role modeling, this program was designed to counter traditions associated with machismo and to encourage women to become aware of their important role in the family and society.

In 1997–1998, Sabido produced one additional social content serial drama before retiring from Televisa in 1998:

- *Los Hijos de Nadie* ("Nobody's Children") addressed the issue of street children. This program used role models to change opinions among audience members about the "silent conspiracy" surrounding the problem of street children in Mexico.

How the Sabido Methodology Addresses Principles of Strategic Communication

According to the Center for Communication Programs at Johns Hopkins University (Center for Communication Programs 2002), strategic health communication has the following specific characteristics:

1. Results-oriented
2. Science-based
3 Client-centered
4. Participatory
5. Benefit-oriented
6. Service-linked
7. Multichanneled
8. Technically high quality
9. Advocacy-related
10. Expanded to scale
11. Programmatically sustainable
12. Cost-effective

The Sabido methodology addresses each of these principles as follows:

Results-oriented The Sabido methodology requires both ongoing monitoring and summative (impact) evaluation. The summative evaluation is based on a number of criteria related to the design and goals of the communication project and is based on measurable changes in knowledge, attitude, and behavior among audience members. Classical forms of media evaluation, such as the numbers of episodes produced and broadcast, or the size of the audience, are not enough to satisfy the Sabido methodology, because they give little indication of changed behaviors on the part of the audience members. In the Sabido methodology, evaluation is based on the numbers of people who have accessed health or social services (such as family planning clinics or HIV testing centers). To the extent possible, the Sabido methodology seeks to document how the serial drama led to such behavior change (often through the use of control or comparison groups who did not watch or listen to the drama).

Science-based Sabido-style dramas are developed using elements of communication and behavioral theories to reinforce specific prosocial values, attitudes, and behaviors. Every detail of a Sabido-style drama is developed according to a theoretical and empirical research-based formula in order to reinforce a coherent set of interrelated values that is tied to specific prosocial behaviors. The Sabido methodology is a replicable methodology that, although formularized, is still adaptable to the individual values and cultures of each country where it is used (Singhal and Rogers 1999).

Client-centered Many communication programs fail to conduct a systematic examination and analysis of the audience and the cultural and societal factors that form and affect it. The Sabido methodology requires extensive audience research—generally known as formative research—in order to design culturally appropriate settings, story lines, and characters.

Participatory Of necessity, Sabido-style programs involve the audience at every stage of development from identification of the issues to be addressed, to design of characters and story lines, to refinement of the program during broadcast to ensure that the program is both entertaining and educational, to final evaluation to determine if the program achieved its goals in terms of behavior change among audience members. Significant audience involvement in the design, revision, and evaluation of Sabido-style programs through extensive formative, monitoring and evaluation research throughout the life cycle of the project is critical.

Benefit-oriented The audience must perceive a clear benefit in taking the action promoted by the communication effort. Through the formative research that is conducted during the design phase of a Sabido-style program, the audience determines the values that are to be promoted through the program; thus, the benefits of the social and behavioral change are not simply *understood* by the audience, the benefits of the values promoted by the program are actually *dictated* by the audience.

Service-linked The goal of Sabido-style dramas is to motivate audiences to seek the service infrastructure. A Technical Advisory Committee is generally created in order to ensure that the technical content of the program is accurate. The Advisory Committee, which comprises representatives of relevant ministries, NGOs, UN agencies, and other institutions working on the issues to be addressed, also provides coordination to guarantee the availability of services, demand for which may be generated by the program. Epilogues, which are a special characteristic of Sabido-style programs, inform the audience about available services (such as clinic locations, phone numbers, addresses, and hot lines).

Multichanneled Population Media Center (PMC) has taken the Sabido methodology to a new level by introducing what is called the "Whole Society Strategy." The Whole Society Strategy combines print, television, radio, music, and new media with training for health workers, journalists, and television reporters to reweave a country's mythology concerning issues such as sexuality, the role of women in society, and family size. The Whole Society Strategy begins with audience research to target each language, cultural, tribal, and economic segment of a national population with the media they utilize. That information is combined with sophisticated audience targeting and cross-promotions, audience analysis, and advertising and public relations. The result is an integrated, nationwide, or region-wide message that can impact the context of thinking about all aspects of health and other social issues.

Technically High Quality Because audiences have choices, communication programs have to be of the highest possible quality. First and foremost, Sabido-style programs must be entertaining. As Sabido insists, the program must be at least as good (if not better!) than any other program on the air.

Advocacy-related As the Center for Communication Programs states, "advocacy occurs on two levels: the personal/social level and the program or policy level. Personal and social advocacy occurs when current and new adopters of a behavior acknowledge their change and encourage family members and friends to adopt a similar behavior. Policy or program advocacy occurs when the advocacy is aimed at change in specific policies or programs. Seeking to influence behavior alone is insufficient if the underlying social factors that shape the behavior remain unchanged" (Center for Communication Programs 2002).

Sabido-style programs advocate change at the individual and normative levels, thus not only motivating adoption of prosocial or healthy behaviors, but creating the social climate that will allow for these behaviors to be practiced.

Expanded to Scale Because they are designed for mass media, Sabido-style programs reach large audiences. Although costly to implement, mass media interventions provide a cost per beneficiary effectiveness unrivaled by interpersonal communication campaigns.

Programmatically Sustainable Mass media serial dramas are a unique tool in strategic health communication because they are infinitely adaptable. As the audience changes, as the audience's needs change—the drama can change with them. Mass media serial dramas are also commercially viable. For example, a long-running radio serial drama in Tanzania, *Twende na Wakati* ("Let's Go With The Times") was largely financed by commercial advertising. Radio Tanzania, who broadcast the program, was able to sell advertising to Ply Foam Limited, a company that markets foam mattresses, after a survey of the program in 1994 showed that half the adult population in Tanzania was listening (Singhal and Rogers 1999).

Cost-effective Sabido-style programs are extremely cost-effective. For example, the cost per new adopter of family planning in Tanzania, following the broadcast of *Twende na Wakati* was 34 US cents. The cost per person who changed behavior to avoid HIV/AIDS as a result of the same program was 8 US cents (Ryerson 2010).

Ethiopia: A Case Study Using the Sabido Methodology for Sexual Health

Anguach and Demlew are the main characters in an Ethiopian serial drama. They are a loving young couple with a bright future. But Demlew's mother, who doesn't like Anguach, begins to meddle and pushes a neighbor to seduce her son. He succumbs, sleeps with the neighbor, and is infected with HIV. Anguach is devastated, but forgives him, and cares for him until he dies. Although she is terrified that she might be HIV-positive, Anguach gets tested and finds out that she is negative. Anguach eventually marries again (this time, a man without a meddling mother!) and lives happily ever after. Touching story—but did it have any impact?

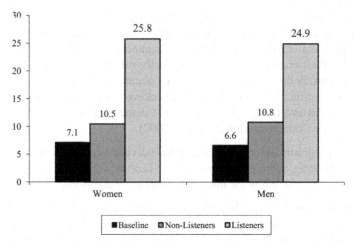

Fig. 4.1 Percentage of Respondents Who Had Taken a Blood Test for HIV (Source: Birhan Research 2005).

Ethiopia has the second largest population in Africa—82.8 million in mid 2009—and, given its annual growth rate of 2.7% (Population Reference Bureau 2009), its population is estimated to double in approximately 26 years. Ethiopia's fertility rates are among the highest in Africa, at 5.3 children per woman (Population Reference Bureau 2009). In addition, Ethiopia has one of the world's highest numbers of HIV cases: in 2007/2008, there were an estimated 1.5 million Ethiopians living with HIV/AIDS (Geneva Global 2009). The estimated HIV prevalence among adults aged 15–49 in 2007/2008 was 2.1% (Population Reference Bureau 2009).

To respond to these issues, PMC produced a radio serial drama, *Yeken Kignit* ("Looking over One's Daily Life"), which was broadcast over Radio Ethiopia in 257 episodes between June 2002 and November 2004. *Yeken Kignit* addressed issues of reproductive health and women's status, including HIV/AIDS, family planning, marriage by abduction, education of daughters, and spousal communication.

Yeken Kignit was extremely popular. More than 15,000 letters poured in from inside and outside Ethiopia, and the media ran more than 100 stories on the show. Scientific research conducted by an independent research firm in Ethiopia showed that listeners included 47% of all the men in the country and 45% of all the women. But the impact went far beyond letters, news stories, and a loyal audience. As shown in Fig. 4.1, nationwide surveys conducted before and after the broadcast showed significant increases in the percentage of listeners who actually got tested for HIV. In fact, male listeners got tested at 4.3 times the rate of nonlisteners, and female listeners got tested at four times the rate of nonlisteners. The postbroadcast survey revealed that listeners had "fallen in love" with Anguach and followed her example of getting tested for HIV. There was also a significant reduction in prejudice against those living with HIV/AIDS among listeners than among nonlisteners.

Why was *Yeken Kignit* so Popular? Sabido-style serial dramas are popular because they: (1) are entertaining; (2) address issues of concern to the target audience, and (3) reflect real-life situations and lifestyles of members of the target audience. Extensive formative research is conducted to determine the key issues that will be addressed by the serial drama and to gather information about the characteristics, needs, and preferences of the target audience. This information is used to design the characters, settings, and story lines of the serial drama.

How Do Sabido-Style Serial Dramas Achieve Impressive Behavior Change Results?

Relying on the formative research, the show's developers create characters for the serial drama that reflect the lives of the audience members so that the show is in harmony with the culture. Through the gradual evolution of characters in response to problems that many in the audience are also facing, the serial drama can model the adoption of new, nontraditional behaviors in a way that generates no negative response from the audience. Because of the bonds that are formed between audience members and characters and because of the commonality of problems between characters and the audience, audience members tend to accept these changes, even though they may challenge some cultural traditions.

The Sabido methodology is adaptable to the individual values and cultures of each country where it is used. The process of formative research provides culture-specific information to assist the writing and production team to design characters, settings, and story lines that are specific to each audience.

Research over the past 30 years has repeatedly demonstrated the effectiveness of the methodology. Since its inception in the 1970s and 1980s, the approach has been used in more than 200 health intervention programs in more than 50 countries in Latin America, Africa, and Asia, dealing mainly with reproductive health issues such as HIV/AIDS prevention, family planning, environmental health, teenage pregnancy prevention, and gender equality (Singhal et al. 2004).

The Sabido Methodology: An Empirical and Reproducible Approach to Entertainment-Education

The design of the serial drama is critical to its potential success in terms of behavior change. Sabido-style serial dramas achieve results because they are developed using an empirical and reproducible approach to behavior change communication via mass media. In fact, every detail of a Sabido-style serial drama is developed according to a theoretical and empirical research-based formula in order to reinforce a coherent set of interrelated values that is tied to specific prosocial behaviors. The

Sabido methodology is also a replicable methodology that, although formularized, is still adaptable to the individual values and cultures of each country where it is used.

One of the advantages of using serial dramas, rather than documentaries or single-episode dramas, is that they allow time for the audience to form bonds with the characters and allow characters to evolve in their attitudes and behavior at a gradual and believable pace in response to problems that have been well illustrated in the story line. Entertainment programs forge emotional ties to audience members that influence values and behaviors more forcefully than the purely cognitive information provided in documentaries.

Entertainment, whether via a nation's airwaves, popular magazines, or newspapers, is the most pervasive mass media genre. It can also be extremely persuasive, influencing how we dress, speak, think, and behave. We are "educated" by the entertainment media, often unwittingly.

The major tenet of the Sabido methodology is that education can be compelling and that entertainment can be educational. Sabido originally termed his approach "entertainment with proven social benefit," and, since then, many communication professionals and scholars have applied the term "entertainment-education" to the Sabido approach. However, the Sabido methodology is more than mere entertainment-education.

What Makes Sabido-Style Programs so Different from Other Forms of Entertainment-Education?

Successful use of the Sabido methodology hinges on two key factors: (1) use of the serial drama format and (2) rigorous adherence to the theories underlying the methodology. Also, most entertainment-education programs are devoted to sending messages, whereas the Sabido methodology uses characters as vicarious role models to demonstrate the desired behaviors. The use of these vicarious role models is a critical element of successful application of the Sabido approach.

First and foremost, the Sabido methodology requires the use of serial drama. In serial dramas, the story is carried over days and months, with story lines developing over time and characters remaining fairly constant. The fact that the serial drama continues with these characters for several months or years is an extremely powerful form of entertainment-education that can influence both specific health behaviors and related social norms. This is because:

- Serial dramas capture the attention and the emotions of the audience on a continual basis.
- Serial dramas provide repetition and continuity, allowing audiences to identify more and more closely over time with the fictional characters, their problems, and their social environment.

Table 4.1 Theories underlying the Sabido methodology. (Source: Nariman 1993)

Theory	Function in Sabido-style soap opera
Communication model (Shannon and Weaver)	Provides a model for the communication process through which distinct sources, messages, receivers, and responses are linked
Dramatic theory (Bentley)	Provides a model for characters, their interrelationships, and plot construction
Archetypes and stereotypes (Jung)	Provides a model for characters that embody universal human physiological and psychological energies
Social learning theory (Bandura)	Provides a model in which learning from soap opera characters can take place
Concept of the triune brain (MacLean) and Theory of the tone (Sabido)	Provide a model for sending complete messages that communicate with various centers of perception

- Serial dramas allow time for characters to develop a change in behavior slowly and to face the hesitations and setbacks that occur in real life.
- Serial dramas have various subplots that can introduce different issues in a logical and credible way through different characters, a key characteristic of conventional soap operas.
- Serial dramas can build a realistic social context that mirrors society and creates multiple opportunities to present a social issue in various forms (Piotrow and de Fossard 2004, p. 51).

By modeling the process of change gradually, serial dramas are less likely to result in backlash, or negative reactions by the audience, than are programs that try to bring about behavior change too quickly. Ideally, Sabido-style serial dramas should continue for at least 104 to 208 episodes (over the course of several years).

Second, the Sabido methodology is based on various communication theories, each of which plays an essential role in the development of a Sabido-style serial drama (see Table 4.1). The application of these theories is critical to the success of the Sabido methodology in achieving behavior change.

Communication Model: Shannon and Weaver 1949

Modern communication theory is based on mathematical theorems developed by Claude Shannon, an engineer and researcher at Bell Laboratories, in 1948. Shannon's original theory (also known as "information theory") was later elaborated and given a more popular, nonmathematical formulation by Warren Weaver, a media specialist with the Rockefeller Foundation. In effect, Weaver extended Shannon's insights about electronic signal transmission and the quantitative measurement of information flows into a broad theoretical model of human communication, which he defined as "all of the procedures by which one mind may affect another" (Shannon and Weaver 1949).

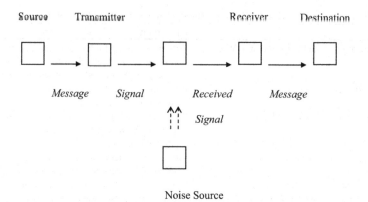

Fig. 4.2 Shannon and Weaver's model of communication. (Shannon and Weaver 1949)

Fig. 4.3 Sabido's circular model of communication. (Institute for Communication Research 1981, used with permission)

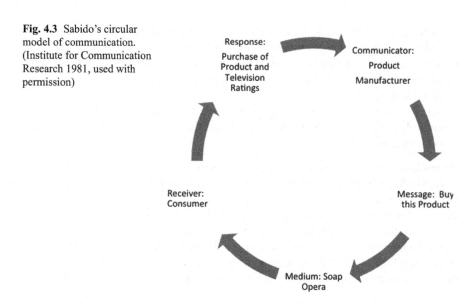

The original model consisted of five elements, arranged in a linear fashion (Fig. 4.2).

Shannon and Weaver's transmission model is the best known example of the "informational" approach to communication. The major problem with Shannon and Weaver's model is that there is no provision for *feedback* (reaction from the receiver). Sabido adapted Shannon and Weaver's linear diagram and formed a communication circuit that depicted the circular nature of the communication process. He then applied this circuit to a serial drama. In the case of a commercial soap opera on television, the communicator is the manufacturer of a product, the message is "buy this product," the medium is the soap opera, the receiver is the consumer, and the response is the purchase of the product and television ratings (see Fig. 4.3).

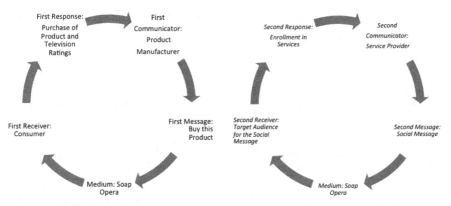

Fig. 4.4 Additional circuit for a social content soap opera. (Communication Research Department 1982, used with permission)

In the design of a social content serial drama, Sabido left the communication circuit of a commercial serial drama intact; however, he added a second communicator, a second message, a second receiver, and a second response. These additions to the communication circuit did not impede the function of the first communicator, which is still the product manufacturer, as shown in Fig. 4.4.

Dramatic Theory: Bentley 1967

A second key element of the Sabido methodology is the use of melodrama. Melodrama is one of the five genres of theater (tragedy, comedy, tragicomedy, farce, and melodrama) described by Eric Bentley in 1967. Among these genres, melodrama presents reality in a slightly exaggerated sense in which the moral universes of good and evil are in discord. Sabido, originally a dramatic theoretician himself, employed Bentley's structure of the melodrama genre as a basis on which to design characters and plots. "Good" characters in Sabido-style serial dramas accept the proposed social behavior, and "evil" characters reject it. Plots are then constructed around the relationships between good and evil characters as they move closer to or farther away from the proposed social behavior. Their actions encourage the audience to either champion or reject these characters accordingly.

The tension between the good and evil characters evoked by the melodrama places the audience between the forces of good and evil. But, in a twist on the typical audience role in melodrama, where audience members simply watch or listen to the battle between good and evil, Sabido inserted the audience into the heart of the action—by representing audience members through a third group, one that is uncertain about the social behavior in question. These "uncertain" characters are intended to be those with which the target audience most closely identifies. It is also these "transitional" characters who guide the audience members through their own evolution toward adoption of desired behavior changes.

Archetypes and Stereotypes   Theory of the Collective Unconscious: Jung 1970

Jung's theory states that there are certain scripts or stories with familiar patterns and characters that people play out throughout history. These universal scripts or stories appear in myths, legends, and folktales around the world. Jung posited that these universal scripts or stories are the "archetypes of a collective unconscious" and share common characters such as "Prince Charming," "the mother," and "the warrior." Jung further suggests that these archetypes are expressions of a primordial, collective unconscious shared by diverse cultures (Jung 1970).

Sabido-style serial dramas rely on extensive formative research to identify the culture- or country-specific versions of these archetypes and to identify local archetypes that represent the prosocial values (or the antithesis of these values) that will be addressed in the serial drama. If the formative research upon which the serial drama is based is done properly, the scriptwriters will be able to develop archetypical characters with which audience members will be able to identify. The formative research is used to develop a grid of positive and negative social values that these positive and negative characters will embody.

Social Learning Theory: Bandura 1977 and Social Cognitive Theory: Bandura 1986

Social Learning Theory, as articulated by Stanford University psychologist Professor Albert Bandura, explains how people learn new behaviors from vicariously experiencing the actions of others (Bandura 1977). Bandura postulates that there are two basic modes of learning. People can learn either through the direct experience of trial and error and the rewarding and punishing effects of actions or through the power of social modeling. Trial-and-error learning by direct experience is not only tedious but harmful when errors produce costly or injurious consequences. So, many people short-cut this process by learning from the successes and mistakes of others. This shortcut, called vicarious learning or modeling, is a key tenet of Bandura's Social Learning Theory (Bandura 1977).

A key to the use of Social Learning Theory in Sabido-style serial dramas is the use of appropriate models that are visibly rewarded (or punished) in front of the audience in order to convert the values being promoted by the serial drama into behavior. Social Learning Theory postulates that positive rewards have a vicarious effect upon the observer (in this case, the audience) and can motivate audience members to practice similar behavior(s). Punishing a role model for practicing a socially undesirable behavior likewise provides a vicarious experience for the observer and can inhibit his or her practice of the same behavior. This adoption is called modeling because it is based on the role model's conduct. Through modeling, it is possible to acquire new forms of behavior and to strengthen or weaken certain behaviors. In

Sabido-style serial dramas, characters "teach" audience members via modeling so that they are able to make a recommended response.

Sabido determined that three types of characters are fundamental to successful modeling by audience members. The first two types of characters are positive and negative role models. They embody positive and negative behaviors related to the social issues addressed in the serial drama (and are based on Jung's theory of archetypes and stereotypes, described earlier). These characters do not change during the course of the serial drama but are repeatedly rewarded or punished for their behaviors. The consequences of these positive or negative behaviors must be directly linked to the behavior in question; for example, a truck driver character that is practicing at-risk sexual behavior should suffer from a sexually transmitted infection or even contract HIV but should not be the victim of a traffic accident.

The third type of character is the "transitional character." These characters are neither positive nor negative but somewhere in the middle. These transitional characters play the pivotal role in a Sabido-style serial drama and are designed to represent members of the target audience. The transitional characters' evolution toward the desired behavior is like that which the audience members will use to model their own behavior change.

Triune Brain Theory: Maclean 1973, and Theory of the Tone: Sabido 2002

The Sabido methodology is based on conveying a holistic message that is perceived by audience members on several levels of awareness. Prior to his work at Televisa, Sabido was a theater director and dramatic theoretician. In his work in the theater, Sabido discovered that actors can have different effects on their audiences by channeling their energy through three different body zones. If actors focused their energy behind their eyes, the tone of the production would be conceptual. If the actor focused energy in the base of the neck, the tone of the production would be emotive. If the actor focused energy in the pubic area, the tone of the production would be primal (Sabido 2002). Sabido instinctively understood that in order to motivate or persuade, it is necessary to provide a complete message that speaks to these three levels of perception.

At first, Sabido lacked a theoretical explanation for what he was observing. He eventually discovered Paul MacLean's concept of the triune brain, which presents a model of human brain structure with three levels of perception—cognitive, affective, and predispositional (MacLean 1973).

Thus, MacLean's theory gave Sabido the scientific basis he needed for focusing on the emotional (second) and the instinctive/impulse (first) zones as the basis for his serial dramas, with the third (cognitive) zone used primarily to reinforce the first and second zones' messages in the drama.

These theories form the basis for construction of Sabido-style dramas. Though the nature of the interaction of the theories in motivating behavior change among audionooo momborn is still not completely understood, the interplay of each of these theories is critical to successful application of the methodology, as has been proven in the numerous settings and contexts in which the methodology has been used.

Conclusion

Sabido-style serial dramas are one of the most cost-effective communication strategies for motivating behavior change. The ultimate measure of cost-effectiveness is the cost per person among those who changed their behavior in a positive direction. Sabido-style serial dramas are highly cost-effective because of the huge audiences they attract and the strong impact they have on the public. In Ethiopia, *Yeken Kignit* cost just 4 US cents to reach each listener. Cost per listener of a similar program in Tanzania was 3 cents per year. The annual cost per new adopter of family planning in Tanzania was 34 US cents, while the cost per person among those who reported that they changed behavior to avoid HIV infection as a result of hearing the serial was 8 cents.

In summary, the Sabido methodology for development of mass media entertainment-education serial dramas is unique in that it is designed according to elements of communication and behavioral theories. These confirm specific values, attitudes, and behaviors that viewers can use in their own personal advancement.

References

Bandura, A. (1977). *Social learning theory*. Englewood Cliffs: Prentice Hall.
Bandura, A. (1986). *Social foundations of thought and action: A social cognitive theory*. Englewood Cliffs: Prentice Hall.
Bentley, E. (1967). *The life of drama*. New York: Atheneum.
Center for Communication Programs (2002). A field guide to designing strategic health communication. Baltimore: Johns Hopkins University.
Communication Research Department (1982). *Handbook for reinforcing social values through day-time T.V. serials*. Paper presented at the International Institute of Communication. Strasbourg, France.
Geneva Global (2009). http://www.genevaglobal.com/docs/focused_funds/Ethiopia_HIV-AIDS_ Fund_2009.pdf. Accessed 14 June 2012.
Institute for Communication Research (1981). *Towards the social use of commercial television*. Paper presented at the Annual Conference of the International Institute of Communications. Strasbourg, France: September 1981.
Jung, C. G. (1970). *Archetypes and the collective unconscious*. Buenos Aires: Editorial Paidos.
Kincaid, D. (2002). Drama, emotion, and cultural convergence. *Communication Theory, 12*(2), 136–152.
MacLean, P. (1973). A triune concept of the brain and behavior, including psychology of memory, sleep, and dreaming. In V. A. Kral, et al. (Eds.), *Proceedings of the Ontario Mental Health Foundation Meeting at Queen's University*. Toronto: University of Toronto Press.
Nariman, H. (1993). *Soap operas for social change*. Westport: Praeger.

Piotrow, P. T., & de Fossard, E. (2004). Entertainment-education as a public health intervention. In A. Singhal, et al. (Eds.), *Entertainment-education and social change: history, research and practice* (pp. 39–60). Mahwah: Lawrence Erlbaum.

Population Reference Bureau (2009). http://www.prb.org/Datafinder/Geography/Summary.aspx?region=38 & region_type=2. Accessed 14 June 2012.

Ryerson, W. (2010). *The effectiveness of entertainment education.* Burlington: Population Media Center.

Sabido, M. (2002). *The tone, theoretical occurrences, and potential adventures and entertainment with social benefit.* Mexico City: National Autonomous University of Mexico Press.

Shannon, C. E., & Weaver, E. (1949). *The mathematical theory of communication.* Urbana: University of Illinois Press.

Singhal, A., et al. (2004). *Entertainment-education and social change: History, research and practice.* Mahwah: Erlbaum.

Singhal, A., Rogers, E.M. (1999). Entertainment-education: A communication strategy for social change. Mahwah, NJ: Lawrence Erlbaum Associates.

Chapter 5
Strategic Health Communication in Urban Settings: A Template for Training Modules

Renata Schiavo

Introduction

Strategic health communication interventions in urban settings present many similarities with health communication planning, implementation, and evaluation in other settings. In fact, interventions in all settings should be firmly grounded in communication theory and rely on strategic and research-based planning frameworks that aim at behavioral, social behavior, and organizational change/results (Schiavo 2013). "However, a specific set of issues, trends and challenges may influence interventions in urban settings and should be addressed as part of training modules and sessions intended for public health professionals and non-profit organizations" (Schiavo and Ramesh 2010).

Training of public health, community development, and healthcare professionals on strategic health communication and its integrated action areas—including interpersonal communication/community dialogue, mass media and new media communication, public advocacy, community engagement and mobilization, constituency relations, professional medical communication and others (Schiavo 2013)—is an increasingly vital requirement for effective public health communication interventions that aim at generating improved public health outcomes (Schiavo and Ramesh 2010). This chapter focuses on an overview of distinguishing features of urban settings and their implications for communication training efforts in such context. It also identifies sample needs, special topics, and emerging trends that should be considered as part of training modules and sessions on strategic health communication

This chapter was written during R. Schiavo's tenure with Strategic Communication Resources (SCR).
Twitter: renatasNYC
Webpage: www.renataschiavo.com

R. Schiavo (✉)
Health Equity Initiative, New York, NY, USA
Mailman School of Public Health, Columbia University, New York, USA

C. C. Okigbo (ed.), *Strategic Urban Health Communication,*
DOI 10.1007/978-1-4614-9335-8_5, © Springer Science+Business Media New York 2014

intended for public health, healthcare, community development, and other professionals who operate or intend to operate in urban settings. Key topics covered in
this chapter were informed—among others—by a 2009 online survey of "public
health and/or health communication professionals from a variety of settings—non-
profit organizations, community organizations, foundations, government agencies,
and academia," (Schiavo and Ramesh 2010) as well as other published work and the
author's own practical and teaching experience in this field.

Key Distinguishing Features of Urban Settings: Implications for Health Communication Interventions and Training Efforts

Urban health settings present many similarities but also several distinguishing features from other geographical, cultural, and/or physical contexts. Several authors
have dwelled on the key characteristics of urban environments and their implications for public health interventions and outcomes. While some of these factors
include social determinants of health that are not unique to urban environments,
they are often "transformed when viewed through the characteristics of cities such
as size, density, diversity, and complexity" (Vlahov et al. 2007, p. 16) and contribute
to health challenges that may be unique to or exacerbated by urban environments,
including "poverty, violence, social exclusion, pollution, substandard housing, the
unmet needs of elderly and young people, homeless people and migrants, unhealthy
spatial planning, the lack of participatory practices and the need to seriously address
inequality and sustainable development" (Waelkens and Greindl 2001, p. 18). Such
differentiating factors include but they are not limited to (Hynes and Lopez 2009;
Vlahov et al. 2007):

- *Physical Environment* such as access (or lack of) to clean air, safe drinking water,
  garbage collection, etc. This also includes the *built environment*, which includes
  the quality and structure of buildings and transportations, access to facilities for
  physical activity and other indoor and/or recreational activities, etc.
- *Social Environment* which is defined by different authors both as differences
  in socioeconomic status (and resultant health inequalities, potential segregation,
  neighborhood violence, etc.) as well as the social structure and characteristics of
  people's relationships within their communities, which may result in different
  levels and quality of the social support individuals and families may rely upon.
- *Population Composition/Diversity* as a result of migration, culture, gender and
  age distribution, language diversity, genetics, epigenetics, etc.
- *Influences on People's Health* including government, health and social services,
  and civic society (including community and nonprofit organizations, and related
  community-based services and events).

Implications for Health Communication Interventions and Training Efforts

All the above factors—and many others that may be specific to one urban setting—influence public health and community development outcomes and interventions. As expected, they also influence or should influence the planning, implementation, and evaluation and refinement of strategic *health communication* interventions for behavioral, social, and/or organizational change/results. (Strategic *health communication* for behavioral, social, and organizational change/results is an area of theory, research, and practice that relies on the integrated, strategic, and programmatic use of multiple communication areas and platforms. More specifically, "health communication is a multifaceted and multidisciplinary field of research, theory, and practice. It is concerned with reaching different populations and groups to exchange health-related information, ideas and methods in order to influence, engage, empower, and support individuals, communities, health care professional, patients, policymakers, organizations, special groups and the public, so that they will champion, introduce, adopt, or sustain a health or social behavior, practice, or policy that will ultimately improve individual, community, and public health outcomes" (Schiavo 2013, p. 9.).

Because of the diversity and complexity of urban environments, health communication interventions often need to take into account the unique characteristics of the different communities that share the urban space. As for other contexts, "the term *community* can indicate a variety of social, ethnic, cultural, or geographical associations, and it can refer to a school, workplace, city, neighborhood, or organized patient or professional group, or association of peer leaders, to name a few" (Schiavo 2013, p. 181). In urban settings, the broader urban or city community is divided in many other communities, each tending "to share similar values, beliefs, and overall objectives and priorities." According to UN-AIDS (2005), a community is a "group of people who have shared concerns and will act together in their common interest" (Schiavo 2007, p. 150). Within urban contexts, "equity, intersectoral cooperation, and community involvement and sustainability" are key guiding principles to achieve healthy cities (World Bank 2010), which is something that requires the efforts and commitment of many different communities. Since health communication aims at achieving behavioral, social, or organizational results that would lead to improved public health outcomes, all differentiating characteristics of urban health settings apply—or should apply—to health communication interventions. In fact, health communication is an "evidence-based" and "people-centered" discipline (Schiavo 2013), so the need for understandings contributing factors, situations, needs, and preferences that shape a health issue is not unique to urban settings. Training modules on health communication in urban settings should focus on the entire communication cycle (Schiavo 2013) in order to equip participants with practical knowledge and tools they may apply to their areas of interest.

Yet, "when asked to identify key factors that may differentiate health communication interventions in urban health settings from those in other settings, respondents to an online survey chose *social environment* (and more specifically the component that refers to social support and social networks, potential isolation of people and groups, etc.), *disparities in the availability and access to health and social services, diversity,* and *population density"* as the top four differentiating factors that distinguish health communication interventions in urban and nonurban settings (Schiavo and Ramesh 2010). Following is a brief description of how each of these factors influence or should influence the "health communication cycle—planning; implementation and monitoring; and evaluation, feedback and refinement" (Schiavo 2013, p. 28) in urban settings. Still, all these topics should be covered within comprehensive training modules on health communication theory, methods, and case studies.

- Social environment (and more specifically the component that refers to "the level and quality of social support and social networks, or potential isolation of people and groups, etc." (Schiavo and Ramesh 2010), which may affect people's ability to adopt and sustain positive health and social behaviors. For example, school and parental support have been shown to be protective against the effects of peer victimization, such as maladjustment, psychological problems, etc. (Stadler et al. 2010). Moreover, smoking cessation programs that include social support and the resulting enhancement of people self-esteem are "usually more effective than those that ignore these elements" (Ma and Agarwal 2006). Social support is usually provided by significant others, such as family, friends, colleagues, teachers, spiritual leaders, and other groups with whom people interact in their everyday life. In addition to its well-documented impact on emotional and psychological wellbeing, "the presence of social support has been implicated in alleviating the negative effects of several physical and health-related ailments" (Ma and Agarwal 2006). Several existing communication models, e.g., Communication for Behavioral Impact (Hosein et al. 2009), P-Process (Bertrand 2008), Communication for Development (UNICEF 2010), Communication for Social Change (Figueroa et al. 2009), already recognize the importance of key "influencers" and stakeholders on individual and community behavior (Schiavo 2013). Key influencers are also referred to as "secondary audiences" or "secondary participant groups" in different planning models. Regardless of the terminology being used, communication planning should always include an in-depth analysis of the level of social support being received by different groups in urban cities as well as a profile of the key characteristics, values, attitudes, behaviors, and social norms of key influencers, so that communication interventions could be also effective in helping create and maintain social support as well as influencing attitudes and behaviors of those who may help achieve health and social behaviors results among key groups (for example, grandmothers or healthcare providers who may both influence the behavior of new mothers in reference to breastfeeding). Training efforts should include an overview of different ethnic, cultural, and socioeconomic groups as well as the level of social support or isolation they may experience within urban contexts at different times (for example, recent immigrants versus immigrants who have been already working and living in a new country for a few years). This should help raise awareness of the importance of social support among trainees, and increase the likelihood that this topic would be covered as part of the research being conducted to analyze situations and to profile key groups during early phases of communication planning (Schiavo 2013).

- *Disparities in the availability and access to health and social services:* This relates both to the physical and social environments (see definitions earlier in this section). In fact, while availability and access to health and social services is often related to the physical presence of adequate institutions and infrastructures within a given neighborhood (the physical environment), too often access is also conditioned by awareness (or the lack) of existing resources and/or health literacy levels that may create differences in the way such services are utilized. Both resource awareness and health literacy levels are influenced by socioeconomic conditions (which are part of the social environment). Since this is a very complex and multifaceted topic that may be influenced by different factors in different groups and neighborhoods, special attention should be given to a careful analysis of situations and needs (Schiavo 2013) and to structural interventions that aim at modifying both the physical and social environments. Moreover, changes in the policy environment, which is critical to removing physical barriers to access (for example, by creating structure and services within a given neighborhood), would further bolster impact. Training efforts on health communication in urban settings should dwell—among others—on several topics that influence availability and access to health and social services—including but not limited to:

  - Strategies to communicate with policymakers to achieve behavioral change within this important group and encourage them to prioritize and act upon specific public health issues (Schiavo 2013).
  - Health literacy and its influence on: (1) provider–patient communication; (2) patients' ability to navigate the health system; and (3) levels of community participation and engagement on key health issues.
  - Sample strategies and tools to inform vulnerable and low socioeconomic populations and other key groups about existing resources and include and engage them in the health communication process.

- While the above topics are not unique to urban settings, they may gain added complexity in such a context and therefore should be considered for inclusion as part of case studies or interactive exercises during training sessions.
- *Diversity:* The importance of culture, socioeconomic conditions, age, geographical location, ethnicity, and other key factors that affect people's concepts of health and illness as well as their ability to act upon the health information they receive from a variety of source is a well-established concept both in public health and health communication literature in a variety of settings. Health communication planning relies on an in-depth understanding of all these factors so that interventions can be tailored to address and engage specific groups within planning frameworks, activities, and materials that are specific to their needs and preferences. In urban settings, the impact of diversity is magnified because of

cities' appeal to a variety of ethnic and socioeconomic groups and migrant popu
lation. Therefore, it is important that training interventions provide participants
with skills and methods to segment relevant audiences/key groups of health
communication interventions so that such segmentation not only informs health
communication programs but also allows organizations to evaluate their ability
to reach and engage different groups vis-à-vis past experiences, organizational
capacity, budgets, and other key items to be considered as part of communication
planning.

- *Population density* is an increasingly important factor in planning and managing
  health communication interventions. In fact, "cities are exerting growing influence on the health of both urban and non-urban residents" while at the same time
  are shaped by "municipal determinants and global and national trends" (Galea
  et al. 2005, p. 1017). For example, population density is a key factor affecting
  rehospitalization and outcomes of people with severe mental illnesses (Husted
  and Jorgens 2000). Because of the limited number of support services and day
  hospitals, high population density has been associated with relapse of severe
  and persistent mental illnesses (Muijen et al. 1992). Moreover, "as Scott and
  Dixon pointed out, one of the difficulties in treating individuals with serious and
  persistent mental illness may be the lack of similarity between the stimuli that
  occur in treatment and those that occur in everyday living. In rural areas, where
  there is a relative absence of distracting stimuli in daily life, whatever happens in
  therapy may be assimilated more effectively" (Husted and Jorgens 2000 p. 604).
  Outside of mental health, population density may also affect the ability of people
  to adopt and sustain health and social behaviors promoted by health communication programs during outbreaks of infectious diseases. For example, high
  population density—which may result in crowded living conditions and high
  patient numbers in hospitals and other clinical facilities—may be an obstacle to
  the implementation of public health emergency measures such as social distan-
  cing and/or may undermine the adoption of safety behaviors in taking care of
  patients and loved ones (Schiavo 2009). Therefore, population density should be
  explored as one of the topics to be featured as part of case studies and other relevant sections of training modules and efforts on health communication in urban
  settings.

Health Communication Training in Urban Settings: Key Issues and Emerging Trends

This section provides an overview of sample areas and emerging trends that should
inform health communication training in urban contexts. Training modules and sessions should be customized to the specific needs and previous experiences of different professional groups (for example, public health professionals, communication
practitioners, healthcare workers, and community leaders) as well as the unique

characteristics of specific urban cities if training efforts have a regional or city-specific connotation.

Health Communication Theory: Focus on Behavioral and Social Results

Since the alleviation and prevention of health-related ailments is often related to the adoption and sustainability of individual, community, social, and organizational behaviors that support changes in health outcomes, health communication—with its focus on behavioral, social, and organizational results (Schiavo 2013)—has been contributing over the years to a variety of public health goals. While the scope of this chapter does not include a discussion of communication theory and models, it is still worth to remember here that health communication is a "multidisciplinary and multifaceted field" (Schiavo 2013, p. 9). Some of the main theoretical influences of health communication include, but are not limited to, social and behavioral sciences theories and models, marketing, mass communication theories, "and other theoretical influences, including medical models, sociology and anthropology. In addition several planning frameworks and models have been developed to reflect or incorporate key principles from some or all of these categories" (Schiavo 2007, p. 32). While planning frameworks may evolve over time to incorporate lessons learned and to reflect the organizational culture, brand, strengths, areas of expertise, and/or terminology of the organizations or leaders that develop them, there are some commonalities in many communication models and lessons learned that are reflected or should be reflected in training efforts and inform their content and key messages. These include but are not limited to (Schiavo 2013; USAID, UNICEF and AI.COMM 2009; Hosein et al. 2009):

- Increased awareness and knowledge on a given health issue among key groups are important but not sufficient outcomes of health communication interventions. Increases in knowledge do not always translate into effective behavioral and social change.
- Regardless of the framework being used, behavioral outcomes at different levels of society (individual, community, policymakers, health workers, organizations, etc.) are the ultimate results of health communication interventions and also lead to social outcomes.
- Health communication planning is a systematic and strategic process that leads to tailored and evidence-based interventions and not a miscellaneous of activities and materials that are designed as an afterthought. Early integration of communication teams with other public health and healthcare teams is important to take advantage of program's synergies.
- Community participation and mobilization are key components of well-designed health communication interventions since they encourage community investment in recommended health and social behaviors as well as help create societal

ownership of all programs, which may lead to the sustainability of behavioral and social results.

- The integration of different communication areas, channels (for example, mass media, community-based/traditional, interpersonal, and new media), and other platforms is more likely to reproduce the kind of environment in which people actually communicate in their everyday life.
- Monitoring and evaluation components should be considered and included early in program planning (including a detailed plan of action and related budget).

Key Training Needs and Areas

Communication capacity is increasingly recognized as an important focus of training interventions intended for public health and community development professionals from a variety of organizations, settings, and health and social areas. For example, "there is a need to incorporate communication training into the curriculum for all stakeholders involved in preparedness and response activities. This would include strategies for communicating the needs of relevant communities to policy-makers. There is a need to educate all relevant stakeholders on how to communicate risk before, during, and after an emergency with the general public" (Berger et al. 2009). Moreover, respondents from a UNICEF study on community- and household-based communication to prepare and respond to pandemic flu (Schiavo 2009) identified capacity building on key communication areas (for example, interpersonal communication, community dialogue, advocacy, and the overall communication planning, implementation, and evaluation cycle) as a key priority for pandemic flu preparedness among key groups including governments, social mobilization partners (for example, local nonprofit organizations, schools, community, and religious leaders), and other key influencers (for example, health workers).

However, building adequate communication capacity may still be an ongoing process in many organizations and settings, including urban contexts. For example, it can be deducted from the responses to a 2009 survey on health communication in urban settings of those participants who reported having received some training on urban health communication that the training did not adequately cover the entire health communication planning, implementation and evaluation cycle, but instead focused on specific topics, such as risk communication, cardiovascular disease, social networking, public relations, language barriers, communicating with adolescents about sexual health, etc. This points to a very fragmented level of knowledge and training among the professionals who completed the survey. Most importantly, there was no reference to any training on understanding, engaging and mobilizing relevant groups and publics—one of the key pillars of strategic health communication planning (Schiavo 2007). This is instrumental to addressing issues of diversity and disparities, as it allows average citizens and communities to become involved and participate in program development as well as in achieving health and social results (Schiavo and Ramesh 2010). Respondents also identified a few

Table 5.1 Key training needs on health communication in urban settings

Communication topics	Sample respondent responses
Diversity: tailoring communication to diverse audiences	Developing interventions for diverse groups (e.g., as defined by ethnicity and socioeconomic level)
	Dealing with culturally diverse audiences
	Tailoring communication to specific populations
	Development of effective communication strategies for racially/ethnically diverse communities that are credible and trustworthy
Technical guidance: communication planning and evaluation methods	Message development
	Grassroots communication
	Use of new media
	Measuring communication uptake
	Behavior change communication methods
	Impact assessment
	How to conduct formative research
	How to evaluate findings and modify program
	How to tap social networks
Health disparities	Learning about racial and ethnic health disparities/racism
	Environmental issues (asthma in public housing, lack of access to fresh food/vegetables, unsafe neighbourhoods)
	Addressing health disparities in urban settings
Other	Challenges and specific problems associated with urban health settings
	Cost-effectiveness of interventions
	Funding of communication interventions
	Key issues in health literacy

topics and key training needs (see Table 5.1). While training interventions should be tailored to the specific urban settings and needs of the participants, Table 5.1 may serve as preliminary guidance on some of the areas to be covered as part of more comprehensive training interventions and modules on health communication in urban settings. Of notice, many of the questions and needs highlighted by respondents could be easily addressed if professional development programs and other training interventions had adequately focused on the overall health communication process. Therefore, while the topics in Table 5.1 should be considered for inclusion as part of case studies, interactive exercises, special sessions, or training updates, the main focus of training interventions should be on the overall communication cycle and not on select aspects of planning, implementation, and evaluation.

Training Venues

The advent of new media has provided trainers with additional venues for capacity building interventions. Several studies and organizations are in the process of analyzing the effectiveness and suitability of new media-based training sessions (for example, Webinars and online courses) for a variety of audiences. While conclusive evidence may not be available in relation to health communication training, results on other kinds of training (for example, research update courses) "indicate that online and face-to-face courses can be equally effective in delivering professional development materials" (Dillon et al. 2008). However—in addition to effectiveness—cultural- and group-specific preferences as well as cost-effectiveness analyses should also be taken into account in selecting adequate training venues. For example, "94% of respondents" to a 2009 survey of public health and health communication professionals who work or plan to work in strategic health communication in urban settings "favored in-person interactive training and 69% preferred a mentoring program (that may include in-person or online training, followed by periodic update sessions and follow up during the first 6 months to 1 year after training). Only 44% of respondents preferred webinars and 31% voted for online training, revealing that while new media and social media-based interventions are increasingly allowing communities and professionals to overcome geographical, cost- and time-related barriers and ultimately have access to some training, interpersonal communication settings and strategies may continue to be the preferred training modality" (Schiavo and Ramesh 2010). While these findings would need to be validated by larger studies and group-specific observations, some of the criteria that more generally apply to channels selection (for example, task appropriateness; cost-effectiveness; audience characteristics, needs, and preferences; cultural relevance; and access.) should also apply to the selection of training venues and channels so that training interventions could be customized to specific participant groups.

Summary

In conclusion, this chapter emphasizes the need for capacity building and training on health communication in urban settings and describes examples of key factors, emerging trends, issues, and topics that may need to be considered as part of relevant training modules on specific communication planning frameworks and/or the overall health communication planning, implementation, and evaluation cycle. Ideally, training interventions should be designed to include case studies and special topics that would provide participants with strategies and tools to address issues related to the complexity, diversity, size, and population density of urban cities.

Acknowledgments The author wishes to thank Radhika Ramesh, MA who served as freelance project coordinator at Strategic Communication Resources, and is also a former student and graduate of New York University, for her dedication and assistance with references, tables, and other research needs related to this chapter.

References

Berger, K. M., Pinard, W., Frankel, M. S., & Lee, E. C. (2009). *Workforce development: Preparing the next generation for infectious disease threats*. Workshop report. Washington DC: American Association for the Advancement of Science. http://cstsp.aaas.org/files/Preparing%20the%20 Next%20Generaltion%20for%20Infectious%20Disease%20Threats.pdf. Accessed 29 June 2010

Bertrand, J. (2008). *P-Process*. Paper presented at the American Public Health Association (APHA) 136th Annual Meeting & Expo, San Diego, CA

Dillon, K., Dworkin, J., Gengler, C., & Olson, K. (Sept. 2008). Online or face to face? A comparison of two methods of training professionals. *Journal of Family and Consumer Sciences, 100*(3), 28–33.

Figueroa, M. E., Kincaid, D. L., Rani, M., & Lewis, G. (2002). *Communication for social change: An integrated model for measuring the process and its outcomes*. New York: The Rockefeller Foundation and Johns Hopkins University Center for Communication Programs.

Galea, S., Freudenberg, N., & Vlahov, D. (2005). Cities and population health. *Social Science & Medicine, 60*(5), 1017–1033.

Hosein, E., Parks, W., & Schiavo, R. (2009). Communication-for-behavioral-impact: An integrated model for health and social change. In R. J. Di Clemente, R. A. Crosby & M. C. Kegler (Eds.), *Emerging theories in health promotion practice and research: Strategies for improving public health* (pp. 535–550). San Francisco: Jossey-Bass.

Husted, J., & Jorgens, A. (2000). Best practices: Population density as a factor in the rehospitalization of persons with serious and persistent mental illness. *Psychiatric Services, 51,* 603–605.

Hynes, H. P., & Lopez, R. (2009). *Urban health: Readings in the social, built, and physical environments of U.S. cities*. Sudbury: Jones and Bartlett.

Ma, J., & Agarwal, R. (2006). With help from strangers: Social support and smoking cessation in technology-mediated communities. *Decision and Information Technologies, 1*(1B), 1–4.

Muijen, M., Marks, I. M., Connolly, J., Audini, B., & McNamee, G. (1992). The daily living programme. Preliminary comparison of community versus hospital-based treatment for the seriously mentally ill facing emergency admission. *The British Journal of Psychiatry, 160,* 379–384.

Schiavo, R. (2007). *Health communication: From theory to practice*. 1st edition. San Francisco: Jossey-Bass.

Schiavo, R. (2009). *Mapping & review of existing guidance and plans for community- and household-based communication to prepare and respond to pandemic flu: Research report*. New York: UNICEF. http://www.influenzaresources.org/files/Mapping_and_Review_of_Guidance_and_Plans_to_PI.pdf. Accessed 28 June 2010

Schiavo, R. (2013). *Health communication: From theory to practice*. 2nd edition. San Francisco: Jossey-Bass.

Schiavo, R., & Ramesh, R. (2010). *Strategic communication in urban health settings: Taking the pulse of emerging needs and trends*. http://www.renataschiavo.com/surveyresultsnew.html. Accessed 18 May 2010

Stadler, C., Feifel, J., Rohrmann, S., Vermeiren, R., & Poustka, F. (2010). Peer-victimization and mental health problems in adolescents: Are parental and school support protective? *Child Psychiatry and Human Development, 41*(4), 371–386.

United Nations Children's Fund (UNICEF). (2010). *Communication for Development*. http://www.unicef.org/cbsc/index.html. Accessed 29 June 2010

United States Agency for International Development (USAID), United Nations Children's Fund (UNICEF), & AI.COMM. (2009). *Social mobilization and behavior change communication for pandemic influenza response: Planning guidance*. New York: Author.

UNAIDS. "Community Mobilization." www.unaids.org/en/Issues/Prevention_treatment/community-mobilization.asp. Retrieved Sept. 2005.

Vlahov, D., Freudenberg, N., Proietti, F., Ompad, D., Quinn, A., Nandi, V., & Galea, S. (2007). Urban as a determinant of health. *Journal of Urban Health*, *84*(Suppl. 1), 16–26

Waelkens, M., & Greindl, I. (2001). *Urban health: Particularities, challenges, experience and lessons learnt*. Germany: Deutsche Gesellschaft fur. http://lnweb90.worldbank.org/CAW/ Cawdoclib.nsf/vewCrossCountryStudies/AFEB5AC26082735E85256CF5006BD326/$file/ urban_health_2001.pdf. Accessed 28 June 2010

World, B. (2010). *Urban health: Overview*. http://web.worldbank.org/WBSITE/EXTERNAL/ TOPICS/EXTURBANDEVELOPMENT/EXTURBANHEALTH/0,,contentMDK:20485964~ menuPK:1090912~pagePK:148956~piPK:216618~theSitePK:1090894,00.html. Accessed 28 June 2010

Chapter 6
Risk, Crisis, and Emergency Communication in Developing Countries: Identifying the Needs of Urban Populations

Kenneth A. Lachlan, Patric R. Spence and Christine A. Eith

Crisis Communication

Media images of recent events such as war and genocide in sub-Saharan Africa, earthquakes in Haiti and Chile, and the 2004 tsunami in the Indian Ocean have made salient the devastating potential of natural disasters in the developing world, as well as the difficulties inherent in alerting people of impending crises and responding to their needs in the aftermath. Numerous government agencies and NGOs alike have argued that devastating events such as these are occurring with greater frequency, and that this increase in frequency and severity will continue for years to come. The developing world is especially vulnerable to incidents of this type, due to increasing population density, settlements in high-risk areas, increased technological risks, greater international travel, and an international upturn in war and terrorism, to name a few (Auf der Heide 1996).

Given this uptick in major disasters and crises, government communication efforts have received increased scrutiny, as have those of first responders and community organizations. Communication scholars have honed in on *crisis communication*–the construction and dissemination of public messages in the event of natural disasters, accidents, and other incidents likely to induce fear, anxiety, or unrest. Although crisis communication efforts are garnering increased attention from both scholars and practitioners, little consideration is given to the effectiveness of mediated emergency messages across different subpopulations. This lack of consideration is evident in the undifferentiated nature of emergency messages. Specific, predictable differences in audience responses associated with race and socioeconomic status are given even less attention.

K. A. Lachlan (✉)
University of Massachusetts, Boston, USA
e-mail: Ken.Lachlan@umb.edu

P. R. Spence
University of Kentucky Lexington, USA

C. A. Eith
Johns Hopkins University, Washington, USA

C. C. Okigbo (ed.), *Strategic Urban Health Communication,*
DOI 10.1007/978-1-4614-9335-8_6, © Springer Science+Business Media New York 2014

While we have a somewhat limited knowledge base concerning intercultural dif
ferences in crisis response to emergency messages across subpopulations in North
America, almost nothing is known about the intercultural differences across international audiences, and the specific vulnerabilities, cultural factors, and information
needs that may be germane to urban populations in the developing world. This chapter aims to discuss the problematic lack of consideration of diverse subpopulations—
specifically differences across race and class—in the construction of crisis and emergency messages. It begins by outlining what is known from past research concerning
the psychological responses to emergency messages that are ideal in the induction
of effective remedial and prosocial behavior on the part of those affected by a crisis
or disaster. It then goes on to discuss some known differences in these responses
across ethnicity and class and offers recent data pertaining to a number of crisis and
incidents. The chapter then goes on to explore challenges to emergency management
that may be expected in urban audiences in sub-Saharan Africa, the Caribbean, and
Southeast Asia, with particular emphasis on the challenges posed by urban conditions in developing nations. The chapter concludes by addressing the potential consequences of ignoring diverse audiences under these conditions, and offers tangible
suggestions for emergency planners and responders in addressing these concerns.

Risk and Crisis Communication

The word crisis is derived from the Greek, Krinein, meaning "to separate." Crises
have been defined as "a specific, unexpected, and non-routine event or series of
events that create high levels of uncertainty and threaten or are perceived to threaten
high priority goals including security of life and property of the general individual
or community well being" (Seeger et al. 1998, p. 233). Weick (1988) describes
crises as "low probability/high consequence events that threaten the most fundamental of goals of the organization. Because of their low probability, these events
defy interpretations and impose severe demands on sensemaking" (p. 305). Communication efforts—whether mediated or disseminated through interpersonal channels—before, during, and after crises in order to manage these negative responses is
typically defined as crisis communication.

Communication efforts surrounding crises and emergencies were once only examined in terms of postincident responses. More contemporary thinking on the matter suggests that communication efforts are a continual process, rather than merely
a postcrisis response (Coombs 1999). This expansion in thinking has somewhat
blurred the lines between crisis communication and *risk communication*, or communication efforts designed to inform the public of hazards, preventative measures,
and ideal responses *before* a crisis or emergency occurs. In a broader sense, crisis
and risk communication can both be viewed as subcomponents of strategic health
communication, as they can be viewed as components of large scale communication plans—before, during, and after crisis events—that are designed not only to
deal with negative psychological responses but to minimize the harm experienced
by those affected.

Ideally, effective risk and crisis messages meet the public's need for control. The messages must outline tangible steps that individuals can take in order to minimize their susceptibility to risk. The inaccurate communication of risk will compromise the ability of individuals to make rational choices in a potentially volatile and dangerous situation. Equally important is proper message placement: messages cannot be acted upon if they are not heard, and failure to deliver risk and crisis messages will therefore impede the ability to make appropriate decisions. Communication efforts during emergencies and crises should ideally serve as agents of uncertainty reduction for an affected audience, offering them procedural advice and other information necessary to avoid or minimize harm.

During crises or high-risk events, the mass media will emerge as the dominant source of information to satisfy the need of individuals to return their environment to an orderly system (Murch 1971; Brashers et al. 2000; Spence et al. 2005, 2006). This information seeking brings about a sense of order, reducing uncertainty and (rightly or wrongly) creating a sense of some control over the situation (Brashers et al. 2000; Berger 1987). The acquisition of information instigates several remedial processes (Seeger et al. 2003), one of which is the observation of how others behave in the situation; essentially, this is a type of learning or that provides the ability to take some action and fosters a sense of empowerment and control.

When uncertainty is connected to danger, people can be relied upon to seek information in a very active and engaged manner (Brashers et al. 2000). Typically, they seek out this information from specific, trusted sources and attempt to constantly update their knowledge base as the parameters of the crisis change. Under these conditions, mass media has been the dominant source of information (Murch 1971), likely because it is thought to be an immediate and valuable source during crisis events (Heath et al. 1995). Thus, when audiences are compelled to seek information about impending and occurring emergencies, they typically turn to mediated information.

Although knowledge derived from uncertainty reduction theory explains this desire to immediately seek initial knowledge, theoretical support for the processes that follow can be found in media dependency theory. Media dependency theory (Ball-Rokeach and DeFleur 1976) predicts that audiences depend on mediated information to meet certain goals, but have very specific preferences in terms of where they will turn for information concerning specific subject matter. Thus, while initial alerts and information may come from any one of a variety of sources, audiences will still likely turn to mediated information that they find trustworthy for further information as the crisis unfolds.

Media dependency is especially relevant to crisis and emergency communication. DeFleur and Ball-Rokeach's (1989) assertion that dependency processes become far stronger under conditions in which either audiences are highly invested in the information presented, or find themselves in scenarios in which conflict and ambiguity are present. Crises and emergencies clearly satisfy both these criteria. Indeed, research has demonstrated empirical evidence of increased media dependency under crisis conditions, and that increased dependency is closely tied to attitudinal and behavioral changes in the wake of a crisis event (Hirschburg et al. 1987; Loges 1994).

Given this turn to mediated information, primacy then becomes a critical con
cern. The initial alert message that is received will set expectations for any subsequent crisis messages (CDC 2002). In order to avoid antisocial behavior, panic,
inaction, or other negative responses by the audience, initial alerts need to be as
accurate as possible and placed in appropriate channels.

This is, of course, assuming that the audience in question has access to their
preferred source. The physical and social conditions typically of crises and emergencies may inhibit media access (see Lachlan et al. 2007). While the Internet may
be widespread and well utilized in the developing world, access may be limited
by widespread poverty, language barriers, and the deficient communication infrastructure often associated with congested urban areas. In recent years, development
efforts have helped global media outlets, such as CNN, BBC, and Reuters, achieve
a presence across all continents and in developing countries. At the same time, telecommunication infrastructure can be extremely fragile, particularly in the developing world, and the physical characteristics of a crisis or disaster may inhibit their
availability. This was the case during the 2004 tsunami in the Indian Ocean. Loss of
power, phone lines, and satellite availability rendered communication efforts in the
wake of the tsunami difficult, if not impossible. Less forgivable, despite advanced
seismic warnings indicating that a tsunami was imminent, no communication infrastructure was in place to alert local government and media outlets in affected areas; a standing system of information dissemination regarding this type of incident
could have saved thousands of lives (Townsend and Moss 2005). Assuming the individual has access to the information, they will also not only find that information
satisfying, but are more likely to be persuaded by that source to engage in behavior.
However, in the absence of information from preferred sources, individuals will be
left to make decisions based on whatever information—good or bad—avails itself.

Ethnicity and Responses to Mediated Warnings

Previous research examining culture and crisis has examined inequalities in terms
of evacuation (Gladwin and Peacock 1997; Peacock 2003) and accesses to basic
necessities. While scant research has explored differences in response to crisis messages, there is evidence of differences in terms of message needs, comprehension,
and reaction. Hohm (1976) and Van Ardosol et al. (1965) found evidence for intercultural differences in concern about environmental risks, even when statistically
controlling for income and education. Similar research has suggested that disadvantaged groups may be less likely to accept a risk or warning message as credible without further confirmation of the information though interpersonal networks
(Spence et al. 2007). This need for confirmation impedes response time (Fothergill
et al. 1999; Lindell and Perry 2004). These results are troubling when one considers that adherence to government directives may be essential to ensuring health and
safety (Braveman et al. 2004; Quinn et al. 2005). Further, it may be the case that
centralized messages fail because not all members of an affected audience speak the

same language or dialect as those producing the messages. Crisis communication practitioners in developing nations should, before anything else, gain a sense of the extent to which messages should be constructed in multiple languages and the best outlets for those messages in attempting to reach different cultural subgroups that may be differently affected by a crisis or disaster.

Socioeconomic Differences in Access to Information

Of equal concern is the notion that in developing nations, there may be large segments of the population with limited or no access to mediated information concerning crises and emergencies, The likely outcome of this scenario is the existence of subpopulations who have not received adequate information, have not been appropriately motivated in terms of response, and/or who may not be aware of pragmatic steps to take to avoid the threat presented by a given crisis.

The traceable relationship between access to appropriate crisis messages and socioeconomic status may be indicative of Knowledge Gap processes. Tichenor et al. (1970) first explicated the knowledge gap process, using data concerning public knowledge of a newspaper strike (Samuelson 1960). In the 40 years since the Knowledge Gap hypothesis was put forward, over 70 studies have supported its central argument: that there are differences in obtained knowledge between those in higher and lower socioeconomic strata (Viswaneth and Finnegan 1996). However, only a handful have attempted to identify knowledge gap processes in crisis or public health concerns. Of note, Kahlor et al. (2004) found that those of a high education level were more likely to both acquire and comprehend information concerning a local parasitic outbreak in drinking water. Lachlan et al. (2007) found that hurricane refugees of lower socioeconomic strata may have had limited access to necessary information, less understanding of evacuation messages, and were less satisfied with the information they received. Given these findings, it may be the case that during crises and disasters, emergency planners should not only tailor messages to these groups, but should prioritize them, since they are also less likely to have extensive social networks that will disseminate information through interpersonal channels. Given well-documented accounts of the vulnerable populations endemic to urbanization in the developing world, including the elderly and urban poor, the ramifications of these differences may be even direr in an international context.

Sub-Saharan Africa, the Caribbean, and Southeast Asia

Numerous examples of the ramifications of overlooking these concerns can be envisioned. For purposes of illustration, this chapter will now detail likely emergencies, infrastructure concerns related to urban development, and intercultural factors in audience needs and response that may be expected in sub-Saharan Africa, the Caribbean, and Southeast Asia.

While little is known about the impact of these factors on urban crisis communi cation in an international context, sub-Saharan Africa is one region where this lack of understanding may be especially problematic. Especially salient in this region is the role of war and unstable government in the crisis communication and management process. Twenty-eight of 53 African states have been at war at some point since 1980, many of whom have suffered through repeated turnover in ruling parties, political structure, and forms of governance (Buve et al. 2002). This constant instability in government makes its role in crisis management difficult to determine in many instances. Furthermore, it casts doubt upon the extent to which citizens may trust their news media, as during these dramatic periods of upheaval news media are often used to voice extremist political arguments, or as propaganda devices for new rule (Putzer and van der Zwan 2005). Despite the limitations associated with the use of broadcast media in sub-Saharan Africa, low literacy rates almost mandate its use. The judicious use of radio and television for the dissemination of crisis information seems critical, while a relative lack of access makes the Internet and email virtually useless.

Scholars have identified the Caribbean as another region that may pose unique challenges to crisis management and crisis communication in particular. While the Caribbean is especially vulnerable to natural disasters such as earthquakes, tsunamis, and hurricanes, knowledge management systems in the Caribbean tend to be largely underdeveloped and poorly managed (Clerveaux 2009). For example, while governments of Caribbean nations typically rely solely on the news media for disseminating crisis and risk information, little regard is given for multicultural interpretation of this information or language differences; varying dialects of the same languages also generate concerns in terms of interpretation and response. Furthermore, while some national authorities in the Caribbean publish newsletters related to emergency management, they often focus on intellectual endeavors with very little regard for everyday risk preparation and response. Compounding these difficulties, we find a general lack of understanding and awareness on the part of the general public in many Caribbean countries; there is almost a complete absence of risk reduction training in the formal education systems of these nations (Clerveaux 2009). Thus, while knowledge gaps likely exist between the educated and uneducated in terms of best practices, even those fortunate enough to obtain an education may not be receiving appropriate training in risk management and basic disaster planning. This lack of preparation and the failure to have a risk management plan in place was seen in the aftermath of the 2010 Haiti earthquake, in which contingencies for large-scale infrastructure collapse and telecommunication failure had not been anticipated by the general public or by emergency managers.

Unique challenges also present themselves when considering crisis communication efforts in Southeast Asia. The urban centers of Asia are highly interconnected, dependent upon technology and rapid innovators of new technology. Ironically, Asia's rural landscape is quite the opposite, with a stark digital divide existing between the countryside and densely populated urban areas. Even within urban areas, a similar gap can be seen across economic status. This creates unique challenges in terms of message placement, while little exists correspondingly examining the relationship between different media outlets and perceived credibility. For instance, during the political unrest in Bangkok, Thailand in 2010, the conflict was centered in a wealthy urban community. Individuals affected by the strife were well informed, as was the rest of the world that received global media. However, the emergency messages mechanism during and after the tsunami in Phuket, Thailand, a small, rural community, was not as effective in communicating the crisis and options for evacuation.

Like the Caribbean, migration patterns present difficulties for disaster communication in Asia. For example, in China scholars agree that the number of temporary migrants is rising (Shen and Tong 1992); similar patters can be found in Thailand, Vietnam, and India. A temporary migrant is an individual who is present but not registered at the place of destination (Zou 1996). This is usually because the individual has made a temporary migration from a rural to urban environment, with the goal of making money and eventually returning home. Such temporary migration patterns make the targeting of specific populations difficult because emergency managers are either unaware of their presence, or underestimate the number of temporary migrants in a region. Such patters of temporary migration also make disaster warning difficult due to cultural and language barriers, as temporary migrants may not speak the same language or use the same media.

Given the above concerns in these especially vulnerable parts of the world, future efforts in emergency management should look at using both new media technologies and network mapping at the interpersonal level in these fragile regions. Through networking mapping, emergency mangers can develop plans to disperse emergency messages to migrant populations through both the appropriate media outlets and interpersonal channels. Furthermore, in these diverse regions reliance on one centralized message is not going to be useful or effective, especially in regions where distrust of centralized government or media may exist. It is naive to assume that one centralized crisis message will effectively inform, motivate, and calm all possible subpopulations especially with the range distribution of income, access, and ethnicity seen in these locales. Yet, emergency communication efforts in the developing world continue to rest on this assumption, with little regard for the differences in response across demographics apparent in empirical research conducted elsewhere in the world.

Consequences of Failing to Consider Audience Diversity

It is clear that in the developing world there are unique circumstances and concerns related to culture, infrastructure, and the likelihood of emergency that create unique circumstances for emergency communication efforts. Despite these demonstrated and theorized differences between these and North American audiences in terms of informational needs and response, and likely differences across multiple groups within these cultures, little is known about crisis communication in the developing world and in urban contexts in particular. Most disturbing, in many instances the failure to consider differences in audience needs and response is equivalent to the failure to consider those most at risk by an impending crisis or disaster. In failing to address these differences, crisis practitioners and first responders run the risk that responses to these messages will be ineffective or even antisocial.

Poorly constructed messages can produce scenarios in which members of varying publics are confused, and may actually increase the potential harm posed by the crisis. Peter Sandman (1998) has argued that ideally crisis messages should serve to both alert and reassure people. Further, he posits that crisis and risk communication should establish a certain degree of manageable fear in order to adequately motivate at-risk audiences, while at the same time presenting a realistic depiction of the level of harm posed by the crisis. If people are responding negatively due to a lack of information concerning the hazard, then they should be provided with additional information concerning the nature and extent of the crisis. If hazards are clearly understood, then outrage must then be addressed. Within the Sandman model, if the appropriate messages are followed with specific behavioral advice, audiences will likely follow suit. This consideration is critical, as the ability to make reasoned decisions may be greatly reduced by fear and apparent threats to safety. Providing information concerning concrete, behavioral responses will likely lead to a sense of empowerment, creating the impression (rightly or wrongly) that the individual has control over the situation (Seeger et al. 2002).

Let us consider a major ecological disaster, such as the Chilean earthquake of 2010. Emergencies of this scope can and will lead to uncertainty and fear, and will both present direct risks (high hazard) and induce fear (high outrage). Messages following an event of this nature would then ideally focus on this outrage, as well as remedial actions that would be appropriate. Induced outrage would ideally be strong enough to motivate people to act in the most positive way possible (such as seeking shelter or supplies), yet ensure that they do not lose their ability to engage in sense-making, panic, or resort to antisocial behavior. Sadly, this was not the case in Chile, as areas affected by failure in media infrastructure received little information concerning tangible remedial actions that could be taken. In the panic that resulted, extensive looting and rioting took place in Concepcion and other cities. In the absence of information concerning relief efforts and steps that could be taken by the public, citizens began bypassing the law in order to ensure their own survival by stealing what they could.

Under this model, message primacy is another critical consideration. The initial message received by members of a given group will set expectations for subsequent crisis messages (CDC 2002). In order to minimize negative outrage, initial alerts should be as accurate as possible, even if this means stating that there is a large amount of information that is unknown. The rush to break a story and provide information can sometimes lead to the erroneous reporting of information concerning a crisis. Such was the case with the 2008 terror attacks in Mumbai. In this particular terrorist event, a militant Pakistani organization known as Lakshar-e-Taiba killed over 170 and injured at least 380 in a series of coordinated shootings and bombings. In the hours that followed, numerous erroneous theories and attributions were made by the Indian press concerning the number of attackers, the probability of additional attacks, the national origin of the attackers, the organizational affiliations of the attackers, and the extent of the casualties. This likely led to needless panic and confusion on the part of the general public, which could have been avoided by more cautious fact checking.

In addition to timeliness and accuracy, behavioral recommendations during these first alerts should ideally be framed in an active, positive manner (CDC 2002). For instance, if earthquake victims are instructed to shelter-in-place, the message should be framed as "stay in the safety of your home," as opposed to "don't go outdoors."

While Sandman's (1998) considerations make sense logically and have received increased attention in recent research on emergency communication and crisis management, they also illustrate further the potential ramifications of failing to consider differences in informational needs and response across diverse audiences. If assessing risk perceptions and motivation to act are critical considerations in the effectiveness of emergency messages, yet emergency messages are completely undifferentiated in terms of their target audiences, then these factors will vary greatly from subpopulation to subpopulation. If they do in fact vary from group to group, then this in itself begs the need for multiple campaign efforts targeted at different cultural and ethnic groups, and different social strata as they seek additional information. Indeed, past research indicating differences in source preference, access, and response across subpopulations, coupled with striking case studies in which crisis communication efforts in developing efforts have failed in their efforts, mandate the consideration of multiple messages for varied affected publics. Issues of language, access, infrastructure fragility, and cultural differences in response must be considered *well in advance* of the onset of a crisis or emergency, in order to ensure that swift, effective, and accurate information reaches those adversely affected by incidents of this kind.

Conclusions

This synthesis of research findings and examples from recent crises and emergencies in the developing world indicates that media use, informational needs, and psychological response vary greatly across different audiences. The conditions of urban communities in developing nations present a varied and largely unexplored tapestry of scenarios and intercultural differences. Given the current—albeit incomplete—data, there are clear lessons for first responders and emergency managers.

Despite a wealth of research detailing variability in informational needs, messages used, and responses to mediated information during times of crises, current crisis and risk messages in the developing world are essentially undifferentiated in terms of specific, diverse target audiences. These risk messages are typically part of much larger campaigns that use multiple outlets to disseminate messages; yet, they typically focus on maximizing positive behaviors in the overall population. These campaigns fail to consider differences in needs, use, and response across varying subpopulations. Further, specific differences in audience responses associated with race, status, and location are given even less consideration, despite the fact that recent research on best practices in crisis communication in the developed world literally *mandates* that these factors be taken into account in terms of message design and placement

Caution must also be used in regard to the use of new media during disasters. It would be unwise to expect new media technologies to be reliable means of communicating during crises in the developing world. It is also unwise to view technology as the only means of reducing inequalities that exist in access to messages. The earthquakes of Haiti and Chile and other disasters outlined the potential use of new media in disaster response. New technologies allow the public to obtain crisis information faster and in circumstances that a few years ago seemed unlikely. Various services are emerging that utilize cell phones and mobile devices for emergency messages. However, many problems exist with these services, adoption maybe slow, and economic factors may render them unavailable to poorer urban populations.

Some new media technologies may prove useful to those who can access them. Moreover, although Twitter was not designed for emergency response or crisis communication, the medium appears to be diffusing to aid in disaster response. The applicability of social media such as Twitter and Facebook seems more apparent in the face of a crisis, when pleas for help can spread across the world in a matter of minutes. Although most online users still rely on traditional media for coverage of the crises, the potential exists to use Twitter to share information, react to the situation, and rally support. Therefore, social media can be seen as a tool that is emerging to disseminate information throughout the crisis lifecycle. Again though, a divide exists between users and adopters of such technologies and the most vulnerable in society. Because of this, message design, placement, primacy, cultural norms, and technology response must all be taken into consideration, but no one aspect should solely drive decision regarding message design and placement.

What is ultimately necessary for understanding best practices in crisis communication is an ongoing dedication on the part of government organizations, emergency responders, and members of the media to consider differences in access, informational needs, and psychological response within their coverage areas. These considerations should include ideal locations for diverse emergency messages and appropriate placement before, during, and after the eventuality of a crisis. They should also include the consideration of potential communication infrastructure failures, the implications of these failures for reaching at-risk audiences in a timely manner, and contingency plans that can be made to offset these vulnerabilities. It cannot be stressed enough that patterns of media use across diverse subpopulations within these cultures should be taken into consideration when implementing risk and crisis communication campaigns. While the study of message placement will not solve larger issues related to poverty in the developing world and failing infrastructure in urban locations, we have learned time and time again in recent history that the simple implementation of message campaigns targeted at general audiences is bound to fail.

It is hoped that this review and subsequent recommendations will help to highlight the work that needs to be accomplished in the study of emergency messages targeted at urban audiences in the developing world. This review provides evidence that further research is needed and that new directions must be taken to limit the harm, duration, and severity of a crisis, and that the role of the media in these processes is not adequately understood in developing nations.

References

Auf der Heide, E. (1996). Disaster planning, Part II: Disaster problems, issues and challenges identified in the research literature. *Emergency Medicine Clinics of North America, 14*(2), 453–480.

Ball-Rokeach, S. J., DeFleur, M. L. (1976). A dependency model of mass-media effects. *Communication Research, 1*, 3–21.

Berger, C. R. (1987). Communicating under uncertainty. In M. E. Roloff & G. R. Miller (Eds.), *Interpersonal processes: New directions for communication research* (pp. 39–62). Newberry Park: Sage.

Brashers, D. E., Neidig, J. L., Haas, S. M., Dobbs, L. K., Cardillo, L. W., & Russell, J. A. (2000). Communication in the management of uncertainty: The case of persons living with HIV or AIDS. *Communication Monographs, 67*(1), 63–84.

Braveman, P., Egerter, S., Cubbin, C., & Marchi, K. (2004). An approach to studying social disparities in health and health care. *American Journal of Public Health, 94*, 2139–2148.

Buve, A., Bishikwabo-Nsarhaza, K., & Mutangadura, G. (2002). The spread and infection of HIV-1 in sub-Saharan Africa. *The Lancet, 359*, 2011–2017.

Centers for Disease Control and Prevention (CDC) (2002). *Crisis and emergency risk communication*. Atlanta: CERC.

Clerveaux, V. I. (2009). *Risk information and communication for hazard risk reduction in Carribbean multicultural societies*. Unpublished doctoral thesis: Gunma University.

Coombs, W. T. (1999). *Ongoing crisis communication: Planning, managing, and responding*. London: Sage.

DeFleur, M. L., & Ball-Rokeach, S. (1989). *Theories of mass communication* (5th ed.). White Plains: Longman.

Fothergill, A., Maestas, E. G. M., & Darlington, J. D. (1999). Race, ethnicity, and disasters in the United States: A review of the literature. *Disasters, 23*(2), 156–173.

Gladwin, H. & Peacock, W. G. (1997). Warning and evacuation: A night for hard houses. In W. G. Peacock, B. H. Morrow, & H. Gladwin (Eds.), *Hurricane Andrew: Ethnicity, gender and sociology of disasters* (pp. 52–74). London: Routledge.

Heath, R. L., Liao, S., & Douglas, W. (1995). Effects of perceived economic harms and benefits on issue involvement, information use and action: A study in risk communication. *Journal of Public Relations Research, 7*, 89–109.

Hirschburg, P. L., Dillman, D. A., & Ball-Rokeach, S. J. (1987). Media system dependency theory: Responses to the eruption of Mt. St. Helens. In S. J. Ball-Rokeach & M. G. Cantor (Eds.), *Media, audience and social structure* (p. 117–126). Beverly Hills: Sage.

Hohm, C. (1976). A human-ecological approach to the reality and perception of air pollution: The Los Angeles case. *Pacific Sociological Review, 19*, 21–44.

Kahlor, L. A., Dunwoody, S., & Griffin, R. J. (2004). Accounting for the complexity of causal explanations in the wake of an environmental risk. *Science Communication, 26*, 5–30.

Lachlan, K. A., Spence, P. R., & Eith, C. A. (2007). Access to mediated emergency messages: Differences in crisis knowledge across age, race, and socioeconomic status. In R. Swan & K. Bates (Eds.), *Through the eye of Katrina: Social justice in the United States* (pp. 203–219). Durham: Carolina Academic.

Lindell, M. K., & Perry, R. W. (2004). *Communicating environmental risk in multiethnic communities*. Thousand Oaks: Sage.

Loges, W. E. (1994). Canaries in the coal mine: Perceptions of threat and media system dependency relations. *Communication Research, 21*(1), 5–23.

Murch, A. W. (1971). Public concern for environmental pollution. *Public Opinion Quarterly, 35*, 100–106.

Peacock, W. G. (2003). Hurricane mitigation status and factors influencing mitigation status among Florida's single-family home owners. *Natural Hazards Review, 4*, 149–158.

Putzer, J., & van der Zwan, J. (2005). *Why templates for media development do not work in crisis states: Defining and understanding media development strategies in post-war and crisis states*. London: London School of Economics.

Quinn, S. C., Thomas, T., & McAllister, C. (2005). Postal workers' perspectives on communication during the anthrax attack. *Biosecurity and Bioterrorism, 3*, 207–215.

Samuelson, M. E. (1960). *Some news-seeking behavior in a newspaper strike*. Unpublished dissertation: Stanford University.

Sandman, P. M., Weinstein, N. D., & Hallman, W. K. (1998). Communications to reduce risk underestimation and overestimation. *Risk Decision and Policy, 3*(2), 93–108.

Seeger, M. W., Sellnow, T. L., & Ulmer, R. R. (1998). Communication, organization and crisis. In M. E. Roloff (Ed.), *Communication Yearbook* (Vol. 21, pp. 231–275). Thousand Oaks: Sage.

Seeger, M. W., Vennette, S., Ulmer, R. R., & Sellnow, T. L. (2002). Media use, information seeking and reported needs in post crisis contexts. In B. S. Greenberg (Ed.), *Communication and terrorism*, (pp. 53–63). Cresskill: Hampton.

Seeger, M., Sellnow, T. L., & Ulmer, R. R. (2003). Communication and organizational crisis. Westport: Praeger.

Shen, Y., & Tong, C. (1992). *Population migration in China: Historical and contemporary perspectives*. Bejing: China Statistics.

Spence, P. R., Westerman, D., Skalski, P., Seeger, M., Ulmer, R. R., Venette, S., & Sellnow, T. (2005). Proxemic effects on information seeking after the September 11th attacks. *Communication Research Reports, 22*(1), 39–46.

Spence, P. R., Westerman, D., Skalski, P., Seeger, M., Sellnow, T., & Ulmer, R. R. (2006). Gender and age effects on information seeking after 9/11. *Communication Research Reports, 23*(3), 217–223.

Spence, P. R., Lachlan, K. A., & Griffin, D. (2007). Crisis communication, race, and natural disasters. *Journal of Black Studies, 37*(4), 1–16.

Tichenor, P. J., Donohue, G. A., & Olien, C. N. (1970). Mass media flow and differential growth in knowledge. *Public Opinion Quarterly, 34*, 159–170.

Townsend, A. M., & Moss, M. L. (2005). *Telecommunication infrastructure in disasters: Preparing cities for crisis communications*. New York: NYU Centre for Catastrophe Preparedness and Response.

Van Ardosol, M., Sabagh, G., & Alexander, F. (1965). Reality and the perception of environmental hazards, *Journal of Health and Human Behavior, 5*, 144–153.

Viswaneth, K., & Finnegan, J. R., Jr. (1996). The knowledge gap hypothesis: Twenty-five years later. *Communication Yearbook, 19*, 187–227.

Weick, K. (1988). Enacted sensemaking in crisis situations. *Journal of Management Studies, 25*(4), 305–317.

Zou, L. (1996). *The floating population in Beijing*. Beijing: China Population.

Chapter 7
Strategic Health Communication
for Cancer Prevention

Jennifer J. Edwards, Chuka Onwumechili and Carol A. Stroman

Introduction

Increasing urbanization has exacerbated health problems globally and its impact
on African populations has led to several concerns. Urbanization has led to sedentary living, increased consumption of processed foods, obesity, diet lacking in fresh
fruits and vegetables, poor drinking water, chemical hazards, and contact with industrial wastes. These result in increased prevalence of noncommunicable diseases
(NCD), including, but not limited to, cardiovascular disease, diabetes, high blood
pressure, stroke, or communicable diseases such as AIDS and tuberculosis. Urbanization problems such as overweight, sedentary living, dietary fats, and less breast
feeding are also among causes of cancer. More troubling is that cancer has become
a leading cause of death in the world in 2010 and breast cancer is the most prevalent
type of cancer worldwide.

Cancer is an NCD with risk awareness overshadowed by diseases such as AIDS
and tuberculosis due to their immediate health consequences and immediate impact
on economic development in South Africa because individuals cannot earn wages
when affected by these often fatal communicable diseases. The diseases also affect
the number of available laborers and family structures in an apparent short time
period. However, awareness concerning NCD prevention, specifically cancer,
should still be addressed through interventions because the long-term effects of a
chronic illness can have a similar impact. Two-thirds of NCD deaths occur in low-
and middle-income nations (Health Systems Trust 2011).

African countries are rapidly experiencing urbanization along with its associated
health problems. While strategic health communication programs designed in the
west have been successful in ameliorating some urban health problems, those programs may not be effective for African countries because of differences in cultural
dynamics and health-care infrastructure. Each country is unique and has its own

J. J. Edwards (✉) · C. A. Stroman
Howard University, Washington, DC, USA

C. Onwumechili
School of Communications, Howard University, Washington, DC, USA

C. C. Okigbo (ed.), *Strategic Urban Health Communication,*   77
DOI 10.1007/978-1-4614-9335-8_7, © Springer Science+Business Media New York 2014

social constructs, such as defined gender roles and a cultural context that governs the planning of cancer prevention efforts. For example, health interventions in a highly patriarchal society should greatly consider the role of males as facilitators or barriers to women engaging in breast cancer screening versus interventions in a society that is less patriarchal and has highly independent women who are not exposed to subjective norms that may require a male's approval for health decisions. Therefore, the goal of this chapter is to explore and explain how the social constructs of a country can shape health communication for cancer prevention. Our goal in the subsequent sections is to discuss the cultural uniqueness of South Africa and the importance of addressing breast cancer problems, and the operationalization of culturally competent measures to shape intervention objectives.

Urbanization and Health Problems

While black and colored South Africans form nearly 90% of the country's population, they were prevented from living in the cities under apartheid laws. These groups face the most danger from health problems that result from increasing urbanization. At the time, most South Africans from these cultural groups lived in shanty towns or squatter camps just outside the city boundaries while others resided in the countryside. However, the repeal of apartheid rules and the 1994 multiracial elections drove an increasing number into urbanized areas. As many as 57% are believed to reside in urban areas. This makes South Africa one of the countries with a high urban concentration of population in Africa. It is therefore more susceptible to urban-related health problems, where 90% of cancers are caused by environmental and lifestyle-related factors (CANSA 2013).

Cultural Issues

Several scholars acknowledge the role of culture in public health, citing its impact on how a disease is defined, perceptions of such disease and how health-care consultation takes place (Peterson et al. 2002; Wood et al. 1997). Peterson et al. (2002) note that some African cultures, including South Africa, believe that cancer is a "White man's disease," meaning a disease of the western world. Increased urbanization has not prevented significant reliance on traditional healers who prescribe muti (traditional medicine) and may misdiagnose the disease, attributing it to a human cause or spiritual curse. The significance of these healers is exacerbated by a collectivist culture where close family members, particularly the elderly, prefer traditional healing methods. Invariably, these elders wield immense influence providing support and recommendation to an ailing relative. These cultural characteristics most likely contribute to the alarming data from the South African Health Department which reports a paltry 6% screening rate for cancer in a country where 100% of primary health-care clinics have professionals trained in cancer screening

(Health Department 2006). Furthermore, social forces actively create and shape patterns of disease, and these forces connect social interactions and human activities to health outcomes (Link et al. 1998).

Cancer Issues Among South African Women

While communicable diseases like HIV and tuberculosis often receive greater attention, particularly in developing countries, breast cancer is the most prevalent type of cancer diagnosed in women, and unfortunately black South African women experience late-stage diagnosis disparities that decrease the likelihood of survival although the women are at lower risk. South Africa has increasing NCD mortality rates, cancer included, that are often attributed to lifestyle and environment. Breast cancer represents the most common cancer site diagnosed in South Africa (American Cancer Society 2011a, b). Risk factors for female breast cancer include: aging, early menarche, hormones, diets high in fat (especially animal fats), not giving birth or giving birth after the age of 35, and around 5 % of breast cancers represent individuals at an increased risk attributed to family history and are typically diagnosed before age 55 (MSKCC 2013; South Africa Department of Health (DOH) 2009). Cancer also has shared risk factors with other conditions such as cardiovascular diseases.

The National Cancer Institute of Cairo University in Egypt noted that overall annual age-standardized incidence rates of breast cancer is low in sub-Saharan Africa at 22 per 100,000 women. Comparatively, North America is 90, western Europe is 78, and north Africa/western Asia is 28 per 100,000 women. However, based on the gross national income per capita, South Africa is an upper-middle-income nation (World Bank 2013), a nation that is on a health trajectory similar to that of high-income nations like Canada, the UK, and the USA. South African women experience a cancer death rate of 123.9 per 100,000 in the population, representing 22.3 % of all NCD deaths (Health Systems Trust 2011). In 2008, breast cancer deaths in the region of southern Africa exceeded 19 per 100,000 (Cancer Research UK 2013). Southern Africa already stands as the region with the highest breast cancer mortality rates in the world (International Agency for Research on Cancer 2013). Slightly lower rates of deaths were reported in 2008 in western Africa (18.9), western Europe (17.5) and northern Africa (17.8). Nevertheless, Fregene and Newman (2005) find that although breast cancer is relatively infrequent among black women, however, the consequence is more severe leading to higher mortality rates. Disease prevention within health-care systems is often segmented along the lines of race, class, and gender. Compounding the effects of these social constructs, marginalized groups are typically those who are at higher risk of disease mortality. For instance, the disease is a serious threat to women in South Africa. While men have also been diagnosed with the disease, such diagnoses are in smaller numbers. As a result, culturally competent interventions, considering marginalized populations, are necessary to equitably improve health status across diverse populations affected by disease, particularly women.

Cancers and cardiovascular diseases are often preventable and treatable, and health interventions that address social constructs within a culture as well as risk factors are most effective. Approximately one-third of cancers can be prevented and another third can be cured, but as a result of late diagnosis and other factors, South Africa's rates will be part of 804,000 new cases of cancer and 626,400 cancer-related deaths that are anticipated by 2020 if prevention and treatment interventions are not put into place (WHO 2008). Unfortunately, the percentage of women who get screened for breast cancer in South Africa is significantly less than the percentage of women who get screened in the UK and the USA, at 6, 76.5, and 76.2%, respectively.[1] Screening rates are high in North America and Europe, but low in large portions of Africa (American Cancer Society 2011a, b). This conveys a need for health communication interventions; however, there is also a significant difference in life expectancy that may impact the health priorities of women in South Africa compared to women in the USA (WHO 2009). Additionally, lower health worker densities in South Africa can limit access to services, efficiency of clinical and laboratory services, and perceptions concerning accessibility of breast cancer screening resources based on patient experience. Therefore, culturally competent interventions for black South African women can increase awareness of screening resources to decrease late-stage diagnoses.

Culturally Competent Interventions

Culturally competent health interventions tailored to a priority population have the opportunity to inspire changes in health behaviors, such as seeking cancer screening, when they integrate intercultural communication with intervention planning. When macrolevel social constructs of a culture are operationalized as microlevel, measurable qualities, strategic points of health communication intervention can be targeted to promote behavior change among the priority population.

This can be done by considering the macrolevel constructs and transition to how they are manifested in everyday life among individuals. As a result, a comprehensive intervention that considers strategic points at a policy, community, and individual level can effectively support cancer prevention within the appropriate cultural context where access and available resources for screening are considered. This level of social assessment serves as the foundation for behavior change and must be understood in order to implement a planning model that exercises strategic points of intervention that will have the greatest impact to promote positive health behaviors like increased breast cancer screening, for example.

---

[1] For women ages 50–64 in the USA, 50–69 in South Africa, and 53–70 in the UK.

National Health Policy

Ideal health communications interventions for cancer control will not only target the perceptions of the individual in the context of his or her culture to promote behavior change, but will also incorporate national, state, and/or local policy advocacy, local institutions (e.g., NGOs, CSOs), and community groups in supporting culturally competent cancer prevention efforts that influence perceptions toward screening.

The presence of relevant health policies, strategies, and guidelines demonstrate that South Africa recognizes that cancer and other NCDs are emerging health issues of the nation. National guidelines specifically relating to cancer prevention in South Africa include: National Guideline on NCDs, National Guideline on Cervical Cancer Screening, and National Guideline on Testing for Prostate Cancer at Primary Level and Hospital Level. Additionally, the South African Department of Health presents information online regarding breast cancer screening recommendations. Unfortunately, these guidelines only broadly address socioenvironmental factors and do not provide a means to address socioeconomic barriers, social determinants for health, and health disparities for populations, regions, and communities that impact how these guidelines are fulfilled. Influencing behavioral intent and promoting positive behavior change to obtain screening and live a healthy lifestyle ultimately depends on the health-care infrastructure. This infrastructure must include policies that specifically address social constructs like gender relations as well as environmental factors like health-care access to facilitate the impact of health interventions.

Strategic Points of Health Communication Intervention Based on Cultural Factors

Strategically planned health communication interventions follow defined planning models; and the added consideration of culture can acknowledge and support marginalized populations and populations in low-income nations in the global context. Operationalizing a multidimensional concept such as culture into practical measures for intervention planning and evaluation can be difficult; however, incorporating the practical cultural considerations during the diagnostic steps in planning serves as a background for shaping a culturally competent intervention that yields positive health outcomes (Green and Kreuter 1991).

Unfortunately, South Africa's public health sector is underresourced and overused, while the private sector caters to middle- and high-income earners, 15 % of the population; however, the private sector receives 60 % of health-care resources (Sanders and Chopra 2006). Therefore, a disproportionate number of financially disadvantaged South Africans do not have access to appropriately staffed health-care services and advanced treatment; and black South Africans comprise the majority of the financially disadvantaged population. In addition to the government-funded health-care system founded under western principles, many South Africans practice traditional healing. While the western medicine culture may be accepted for treatment, perceptions concerning traditional healing must be considered during culturally competent intervention design and health policies as well.

Gender Relations as a Social Construct that Influences Health Behavior

Social relationships influence health behaviors through subjective norms and pressures that govern individual perceptions (Pasick and Burke 2008). The subjective norms that govern the manner in which men and women in South Africa relate are shaped by cultural identity; and this identity influences health decisions such as seeking breast cancer screening as well as the manner in which the community orients itself and engages itself concerning the health issue (Airhihenbuwa 2009).

Using the Ecological Framework

The social, behavioral, and policy assessments that inform health communication interventions can be represented using the ecological framework. This framework represents the various levels at which an intervention can be planned to comprehensively address the issue of breast cancer screening. To achieve a comprehensive, culturally competent intervention, the applicable levels of the ecological framework should be considered within the South African cultural context. The complete ecological framework is based on five factors: (1) intrapersonal or individual factors; (2) interpersonal factors; (3) institutional or organizational factors; (4) community factors; and (5) public policy factors (National Cancer Institute 2007).

Each ecological level interacts with each other bidirectionally and concurrently, where, "two key concepts of the ecological perspective help to identify intervention points for promoting health: first, behavior both affects, and is affected by, multiple levels of influence; second, individual behavior both shapes, and is shaped by, the social environment (reciprocal causation)" (National Institutes of Health 2005). Health-care access and gender relations correspond to the organizational and community levels, respectively, and perceptions reside on the intrapersonal level. Once these have been established as relevant and valid cultural components, strategic points of intervention can be established.

Applying these cultural variables in an operationalized format allows them to be defined in terms of measurable qualities that are useful during the impact evaluation phase of the health intervention. This phase considers whether the priority population changed their perceptions or behaviors concerning seeking breast cancer screening (see Table 7.1 for details).

Now that health-care access and gender relations in the South African culture have been conceptualized from the macrolevel of social constructs to the microlevel

Table 7.1 Culturally competent measures to shape intervention objectives

Ecological level	Socioenvironmental level	Measures
Intrapersonal	Perceptions	1. Intention to conduct breast self-examination (BSE) monthly (NCI, MSKCC)
		2. Intention to seek mammography yearly if over age 40 (NCI, ACS)
		3. Intention to request a clinical breast exam yearly if over age 25 (ACS, MSKCC)
Organizational	Health-care access	1. Geographic access to health-care workers (GEWE)
		2. Location of health facility that offers mammograms (GEWE)
		3. Use of traditional healers, spiritual and religious overlaps with health-care treatment
		4. Health insurance coverage (AHRQ)
		5. Regular/usual source of health-care (AHRQ)
		6. Referrals owing to limited screening resources (AHRQ; Gouge et al. 2009)
Community	Female empowerment	1. Participation in decision making concerning breast cancer screening (GEWE)
		2. Perceived control over her health decisions regarding breast cancer screening (GEWE)
		3. View of significant male others' responsibility for her health decisions regarding breast cancer screening (GEWE)
		4. Perceived significant male others' support of breast cancer screening (DOH)

of specifically defined behaviors, how can these behaviors be targeted for intervention planning from a culturally relevant perspective?

The cultural relevance of the measures extracted from the previous definitions can be validated by examining South African documents and research to determine measures while considering the cross-cultural application of any local measures used from other countries. The measures serve as strategic points of intervention where one or more specific behaviors can be targeted to promote health behavior change among black South African women. Measures identified in South Africa's National Policy Framework for Gender Equality and Women's Empowerment (GEWE), South Africa Department of Health National Guideline for NCDs, NCI Division of Population Control and Population Sciences Measures Appendix, American Cancer Society (ACS) Guidelines for the Early Detection of Cancer, MSKCC Guidelines, and Agency for Healthcare Research and Quality can be used as resources for measurable behaviors within the cultural context of the priority population. Comprehensive interventions address multiple ecological levels to achieve maximum effectiveness. Following a similar process of discerning social constructs, these measures or others depending on the targeted culture can be used to shape strategic objectives for interventions that effect behavior change. Once the objectives have been identified, planning an intervention with measurable impact outcomes is possible.

Although the measures in Table 7.1 are designed considering the cultural context of South Africa, they can be applied in other countries. The specific intervention objectives will differ by country based on how the priority population responds to the measures.

Strategic Health Communication Cases

Effective strategic health communication campaigns usually have a culturally competent component and there are numerous examples in Africa. AIDS, for example, has been a major concern in the continent with 1.4 million dead from AIDS in 2008 and another 1.9 million becoming newly infected in the same year. Yet, effective AIDS-prevention campaigns have taken place in Uganda, Senegal, Zambia, and Burkina Faso. Below we describe the successful campaign in Uganda and other health campaigns in South Africa.

The Ugandan Case

One of the remarkable turnaround in the African AIDS epidemic is the Ugandan case. The AIDS scourge in Uganda was in epidemic proportions in the mid to the late 1980s when, with the support of the government, several NGOs began various health promotions designed to reduce the prevalence of the disease among Ugandans (Hogle 2002). By 2002, remarkable successes were recorded with decline of HIV prevalence from 30 % and 14 % in 1992 in Kampala and other sites to 12 % and 5 %, respectively. Additionally, prevalence of AIDS among pregnant women fell from 30 % in the early 1990s to 10 % in 2001. What happened? The ecological framework suggested in this chapter provides answers. First, the government enacted several policy structures for change including establishing the Uganda AIDS Commission (UAC) among others. The national President, Museveni, along with top leaders conducted community visits urging behavioral changes and these were supported at all levels by religious leaders, traditional healers, schools, nongovernmental agencies, and peer educators, among others. All these percolated to the intrapersonal level where individuals reported less sexual involvement with multiple partners, delayed sexual debut, and increased condom use among other behavior changes.

The Cape Town Case

Perceptions toward breast cancer screening directly relate to sociocultural factors, as discussed in this chapter, including interpersonal and organizational factors as well as health policy for comprehensive cancer prevention. Based on a survey of

163 Capetonian women plus 12 interviews, knowledge of screening services and accurate information provided through strategic, culturally competent health programs was determined to be at the heart of shaping positive perceptions regarding breast cancer screening in Cape Town, South Africa. This knowledge and information subsequently impact interpersonal relationships where husbands and boyfriends can become comfortable and supportive of discussing breast cancer screening with the women in their lives. The information also empowers women to be readily able to navigate the government health-care system to obtain screening such as breast exams from their physicians and mammography.

The cultural diversity within Cape Town, which includes diverse ethnicities, languages, and religions, necessitates health programs and policies that target each priority population. Any differences in health-care system perceptions between the colored and black populations, for example, should be recognized while simultaneously considering income and access to health services. A risk exists in grouping persons from these cultural groups together who have differing perceptions of the health-care system although they share similar cultural experiences of marginalization. These cultural groups also have differing primary languages that shape the most fundamental levels of health program targeting as well as cultural competence for programs and policy.

Other Examples from South Africa

The Cancer Association of South Africa (CANSA), Cancer Research Initiative of South Africa (CARISA), the Medical Research Council of South Africa (MRC), the Radiological Society of South Africa, and the South African Oncology Forum are among organizations that host breast cancer prevention efforts in the nation. The CANSA has developed an impressive array of cancer prevention initiatives for the entire family.

The Healthy Living Schools Program delivers health messages via dramas, music, and entertainment to South African children and youth. The messages encourage youth to avoid smoking, to eat healthy foods, to get regular exercise, and to monitor direct exposure to sunlight—all practices associated with cancer prevention.

In an effort to encourage men to detect cancer early, CANSA developed the Men Health and Awareness Campaign. Fact sheets and survivor stories are among the tools used to educate South African men about the benefits of early detection of cancer, especially prostate cancer.

Focusing on women's health, CANSA's Breast Health Awareness Campaign distributes information through a number of channels, including a leaflet designed to increase knowledge about breast cancer and video clips demonstrating how to do self-examination of the breasts. These messages are personal, emotional, and socially contextualized as well as motivational for behavior changes. This campaign is especially appropriate because it utilizes the specific discursive practices of South African women. In short, this health campaign is based on awareness of local culture, norms, and behaviors.

Efforts present in South Africa to increase breast cancer screening can be expanded by including culturally relevant points of intervention at the various ecological levels to comprehensively address breast cancer screening at the social, behavioral, and policy levels will add to this foundation. The following two cases represent organizations that can consider additional levels of the ecological framework and the measures previously mentioned for the assessment phases of intervention planning to facilitate strategic health communication.

Case 1 *Organization A* has broader research goals for improving the health status of the South African population; and is part of the agreement with two other cancer prevention organizations. Its intervention efforts include issuing technical reports and policy briefs, and publicizing health information on its Web site, such as upcoming health awareness days.

Ecological levels considered: public policy (policy briefs), individual (Web site).

Strategic health communication recommendations: ensure cultural relevance of Web site information (individual), examine whether policies address social constructs or will they be difficult to implement due to larger societal factors (public policy), consider whether the priority population has equal access to resources to participate in the awareness days (organizational).

Case 2 *Organization B* promotes breast cancer awareness and plans breast cancer awareness month intervention activities. It leads a mammography initiative for nearly 100 medical practices in the county; and works toward cost-effective cancer treatment and engages in advocacy for cancer prevention. The advocacy includes policy documents, guidelines, and value propositions for the health-care industry.

Ecological levels considered: individual (mammograms for patients), public policy (advocacy).

Strategic health communication recommendations: consider whether the priority population has access to the medical practices (organizational), consider whether the priority population has spiritual or religious practices that may affect whether they visit the medical practices (organizational), consider whether the value propositions consider the social constructs that affect the priority population, such as gender relations and health-care access (community/organizational).

To increase the cultural competence of the interventions planned by the organizations above, the measures from Table 7.1 for the ecological levels covered in the intervention should be considered during the early planning phases. Cognizant of the notion that health interventions are "understood by professional and laypersons alike in terms of preexisting, culturally determined health-related schemas" (Landrine and Klonoof 1996), health researchers and professionals have attempted to develop culturally appropriate health communication interventions for South Africa. Moreover, effective interventions must be directed to the person, the extended family, and the neighborhood and the community (Airhihenbuwa 1992).

Conclusion

The progression from macrolevel cultural considerations to measurable microlevel concepts can facilitate identifying strategic points for culturally competent health interventions. Operationalizing cultural factors such as female empowerment and health-care access into measurable qualities of these social and behavioral constructs can be used during the planning and evaluation process. Asking what cultural factors may have a relationship with the priority population's perceptions toward a given health behavior, then identifying what elements of daily life signify these cultural elements corresponding to ecological levels, and then deciding strategic methods based on health communication behavioral theory to design a culturally competent health communication intervention can prevent cancer in the affected population.

Program planners must understand that whether the information is being communicated to breast cancer victims and their families and friends or to health professionals, traditional healers, and others, the basic approach is the same. In order to engage the various audiences, cancer prevention information must be communicated in a manner that the audience can understand and it must be viewed as credible, personally relevant, and reflective of community norms and values. Finally, comprehensive cancer prevention interventions must be multilayered, long term, and aimed across the ecological levels.

References

Airhihenbuwa, C. O. (2009). Stigma, culture, and HIV/AIDS in the Western Cape, South Africa: An application of the PEN-3 cultural model for community based research. *Journal of Black Psychology, 35*(4), 407–432.

American Cancer Society (2011a). Cancer in Africa. www.cancer.org.

American Cancer Society (2011b). Global Cancer Facts and Figures. www.cancer.org.

Cancer Association of South Africa (CANSA) (2013). Homepage. http://www.cansa.org.za/. Accessed 15 June 2013.

Cancer Research UK (2013). Breast Cancer. http://www.cancerresearchuk.org/cancer-info/cancerstats/world/breast-cancer-world/. Accessed 15 June 2013.

Fregene, A., & Newman, L. (2005). Breast cancer in sub-Saharan Africa: How does it relate to breast cancer in African American women? *Cancer, 109*(8), 1540–1550.

Green, L. W., & Kreuter, M. W. (1991). *Health promotion planning: An educational and ecological approach* (3rd ed.). Palo Alto: Mayfield.

Health Department (2006). *Annual Report 2006*. Pretoria: Government Publisher.

Health Systems Trust (2011). South African Health Review. www.hst.org.za. Accessed 16 June 2013.

Hogle, J. (Ed.). (2002). *What happened in Uganda? Declining HIV prevalence, behavior change, and the national response*. Washington, DC: USAID.

International Agency for Research on Cancer (2013). Globocan 2008 Cancer Fact Sheet. *http://globocan.iarc.fr/factsheets/cancers/breast.asp*. Accessed 16 June 2013.

Link, B. G., Northridge, M. E., Phelan, J. C., & Ganz, M. L. (1998). Social epidemiology and the fundamental cause concept: On the structuring of effective cancer screens by socioeconomic status. *The Milbank Quarterly, 76*(3), 375–402.

Memorial Sloan-Kettering Cancer Center (MSKCC) (2013). Breast cancer screening guidelines. www.mskcc.org. Accessed 15 June 2013.

National Cancer Institute (2007). National Institutes of Health, 2005: A guide for health promotion practice. http://www.cancer.gov. Accessed 23 Jan 2008.

National Institutes of Health (2005). Theory at a glance: A guide for health promotion practice. http://www.cancer.gov/PDF/481f5d53-63df-41bc-bfaf-5aa48ee1da4d/TAAG3.pdf. Accessed 14 Jan 2008.

Pasick, R. J., & Burke, N. J. (2008). A critical review of theory in breast cancer screening promotion across cultures. *Annual Review of Public Health, 29,* 351–368.

Peterson, W., Trapp, M., Vierkant, R., et al. (2002). Outcomes of training nurses to conduct breast and cervical cancer screening of Native American women. *Holistic Nursing Practice, 16*(2), 58–59.

Sanders, D., & Chopra, M. (2006). Key challenges to achieving health for all in an inequitable society: The case of South Africa. *American Journal of Public Health, 96*(1), 73–78.

South African Government (2013). South Africa's People. http://www.info.gov.za/aboutsa/people.htm. Accessed 15 June 2013.

Wood, K., Jewkes, R., & Abrahams, N. (1997). Cleaning the womb: Constructions of cervical screening and womb cancer among rural black women in South Africa. *Social Science and Medicine, 45*(2), 283–94.

World Bank (2013). Country and lending groups. http://www.worldbank.org. Accessed 15 June 2013.

World Health Organization (WHO) (2008). WHO Global InfoBase. http://www.who.int/en/. Accessed 6 Apr 2008.

World Health Organization (WHO) (2009). WHO Statistical Information System. http://www.who.org. Accessed 30 Nov 2009.

Chapter 8
Strategic Health Communication

Kiran Prasad

Introduction

The Millennium Development Goals (MDGs) adopted by several countries in 2000 were aimed to promote gender equality and empowerment of women as the core of other development goals. Several countries are improving their performance on human development goals, but there are widening gaps between socioeconomic groups, urban and rural areas, and between males and females. The urban–rural divide is pronounced in 26 African, Latin American, and Asian countries leading to skewed development. Rapid urbanization and globalization have widened the urban–rural divide. This has led to migration of populations from the rural areas to the urban areas often in search of a better quality of life, consequently giving rise to sprawling urban slums. The world slum population is estimated to grow by 6 million each year (UN 2010), which will render many slum women vulnerable. South Asia including India is home to the largest rural–urban disparities and gender inequality, which has serious implications for women's health and well-being (Prasad 2008b).

Malnourishment of girls and women is endemic in South Asia and sub-Saharan Africa due to social and cultural factors, which predispose them to ill-health and mortality. Less than 50 % of women in these regions have skilled birth attendants to attend to their deliveries. These regions are also plagued by problems of early pregnancies—more than 100 births per 1,000 women in South Asia and sub-Saharan Africa occur during the ages of 15–19 years—putting adolescent mothers and children at the greatest risk. The MDGs call for reducing maternal mortality ratio by three-quarters by 2015, increasing women's access to modern health services and also promoting equitable access to household resources for improving maternal health (World Bank 2003).

Many developing countries of South Asia have been implementing strategic health communication initiatives among women to step up their knowledge and

K. Prasad (✉)
Department of Communication and Journalism, Sri Padmavati Mahila University,
Tirupati 517 502, Andhra Pradesh, India
e-mail: kiranrn.prasad@gmail.com

C. C. Okigbo (ed.), *Strategic Urban Health Communication,*
DOI 10.1007/978-1-4614-9335-8_8, © Springer Science+Business Media New York 2014

utilization of health services toward fulfilling the MDG of reducing maternal mortality and promoting reproductive health. This chapter discusses how strategic communication goes beyond information, education, and communication (IEC) and behavior change communication (BCC) approaches to catalyze the reproductive health of urban slum women through an integrated approach of community mobilization, interpersonal communication, and capacity building of women.

Women in Urban Slums

The number of people living in slums reached 827.6 million in 2010 with sub-Saharan Africa having the most slum dwellers (199.5 million) followed by South Asia (190.7 million) and East Asia (189.6 million; UN 2010). According to UN (2010) estimates, China (28.2%) and India (27.8%) are the most populous nations that have more than one-fourth of the total population living in slum conditions. In cities with a population more than a million, nearly one-fourth (24.1%) of the population reside in slums (Registrar General of India 2003). India is the world's second fastest growing economy and slums are an integral part of urban India. Three states of India, Maharashtra, West Bengal, and Andhra Pradesh, have an estimated 25% of the urban population living in slums (NSSO 2003). Slums are characterized by poor households, poor-quality shelter, inadequate water supply, unsanitary conditions, and high incidence of sickness. Urban slum dwellers, women in particular, have limited access to basic health facilities as they are socially and economically marginalized.

The lower quality of life among women in urban slums is often associated with a decline in their reproductive health. Insecurity related to regular income, food, shelter, access to health care, and other essential services, along with poverty and difficult physical and social environments, such as exploitation and abuse in the treatment of women, have an adverse impact on the health of the urban poor women (Das and Shah 2001). Coupled with these conditions, the most potent impact of structural adjustment policies (SAP) as underlined by globalization has been on mortality, girl's schooling, prenatal health care, and child nutrition, which had previously improved, but have deteriorated as government support in these areas has been withdrawn (Purewal 2001). This has resulted in high mortality rates among the urban poor and rural women and children due to widespread malnutrition and poor infrastructure.

Indian women get married at a median age of just 17 years. Among women aged 15–19, 16% have already begun childbearing, according to the 2005–2006 National Family Health Survey (NFHS 2007). According to the NHFS (2007) study, women's food intake across South Asia must improve if the region's high maternal mortality rate (MMR) is to drop. Maternal mortality in South Asia is alarmingly high, with an average of 454 deaths per 100,000 live births (Gaye et al. 2010). More than half of the Indian women have anemia, another potential killer during childbirth. Every year, about 78,000 mothers die in childbirth and from complications of pregnancy in India. India ranks among the countries with the highest MMR; the MMR in India stood at 212 per 100,000 live births in 2007–2009 (Registrar General of India 2011). India is way behind the MDG for a reduction of MMR to 109 by 2015, which underscores the need for strategic health communication. The following section describes the quality of life of the urban poor and women in slums.

Housing and Energy Needs

In urban areas, the marginal increase in income for the poor, in itself, does not assure better living conditions due to wide disparities, which make decent accommodation and clean water and air unaffordable. Moreover, certain necessities, which existed as free goods in rural settings, are commodities in urban areas such as drinking water, cooking fuel, and housing space. The type of housing and space available is crucial in ensuring good health, particularly of women who require greater privacy to manage their health. The last National Census (Census of India 2011) revealed that 37.1 % of Indian families (325 million) live in one-room houses. Small houses with hardly any ventilation and lack of privacy to manage personal sanitation can also increase the morbidity conditions of inhabitants more often women and children who are homebound.

The 2011 Census data revealed that two-thirds of households continue to use firewood, crop residue, cow dung cakes, or coal for cooking—putting women to significant health hazards and hardship. At the same time, women in a number of households residing in urban slums are forced to rely on traditional smoky fuels to cook. Studies on carbon monoxide exposure (WHO 1991) have shown significantly high levels of the toxic gas in blood of women cooking with biomass fuel. The cooking environment also compounds this pollution as kitchens in most urban slums are poorly ventilated and prolonged exposure to high levels of pollutants has a very adverse impact on the health of women who spend more than 3 h for cooking every day with biomass fuels.

Water and Sanitation

According to the Census (Census of India 2011) data, in India only 32 % of the households use treated water for drinking. Seventeen percent households do not have access to water at home and fetch drinking water from a source located more than 500 m in rural areas or 100 m in urban areas. But much of it is not potable and the supply is not adequate to meet the daily requirements. In most cities, the water supply to homes does not average more than 4 h a day and there is acute water shortage in urban slums. Women are the water providers for families and the disappearance of water sources presents consequential burdens and drudgery. The increasing time spent on collection of water has direct effect on their health and opportunities for other fruitful activity (Prasad 2004).

The Census (Census of India 2011) also revealed that less than half of the house holds (46.9%) have toilet facilities and less than 50% of wastewater is collected and treated. The shortage of water leads to poor sanitation, especially among women, who are in the reproductive age group and are menstruating. Lack of toilet facilities also increases the chance of infections and related diseases. Women and children are particularly vulnerable to diseases due to poor sanitation and insufficient water to manage personal hygiene and health care (Rao and Somayajulu 2004). It seems absurd that families walk for miles from their homes to bathe and attend to nature's call, but would watch television within the confines of their homes (Saran 2003). Health initiatives must entail providing women with access to safe water and to basic sanitation facilities along with strategic health communication programs for empowering them to seek health services.

IEC for Health Communication

The IEC approach was widely used in the developing world to create awareness on development issues. Official recognition of women's health needs in South Asia has been singularly and significantly focused on women's childbearing functions. Most of the IEC health strategies were conceptualized and implemented around this function to bring about change in women's health-seeking behavior. This approach regarded women as mere recipients of information in a family and the "family" rather than "women" continued to be the basic unit for intervention. The result was that women continued to be at the periphery of the development process that ignored their special requirements and problems with health benefits only reaching them incidentally. Despite IEC efforts by governments and voluntary organizations, it has been found that few women are aware of availability of government health centers, which provide a range of primary health-care services. Those who were aware of the availability of health-care facilities knew more about the provision of basic health services such as immunization, malaria, antenatal and postnatal care, diarrhea, and family planning (Sinha 2009).

Behavior Change Communication

While IEC was aimed at giving people information and awareness about health issues, BCC campaigns seek to help people change behavior relating to health. BCC campaigns on reproductive health of women focused on behavior such as: delaying sexual initiation and age at marriage, encouraging using of condoms, spacing births, supporting others trying to change, supporting people living with HIV/AIDS, and seeking and adhering to health services/treatment. But BCC also could not always bring desired results because the decision to change one's behavior rests with an individual. Health educators in BCC initiatives act as facilitators and do not exert any control over an individuals' behavior change because usually only the individual understands the implication of behavior change on his/her life; the individual knows about his/her prior experience with behavior change; and the individual is better aware of his/her own abilities, strengths, and weaknesses. The Andhra Pradesh Urban Slum Health Care Project (APUSHCP) was a successful BCC initiative in improving the health status of urban slum women in India (Family Welfare Department 2001).

Andhra Pradesh Urban Slum Health Care Project

The APUSHCP was initiated and implemented in 2001, with the World Bank's assistance, in Andhra Pradesh State of India. It is the largest and most populous state in south India. The total population of Andhra Pradesh stands at 75,727,541 of which around 36 % of the population lives in slums (Census of India 2001). In spite of availability of government hospitals in the municipal towns, they are primarily curative service centers and do not render preventive health-care services to the slum population. The Post Partum Units and Urban Family Welfare Centers provide health extension services to a small proportion of urban slum population. Inability to provide neighborhood health extension such as antenatal care for pregnant women, immunization services for children, sensitization about preventive health care aspects, and regular advice on temporary or permanent methods of contraception was a major limitation of the institutions catering to the needs of the urban poor women living in the slums.

The APUSHCP was aimed to achieve the goal of improved maternal and child health among the slum community. The project used BCC to respond to the needs of the target audiences, provide a supportive environment to encourage and reinforce behavior change, and provide linkages with services using a coordinated multi-pronged approach. The following focus areas were identified for undertaking BCC: age at marriage, safe and institutional delivery, nutrition for mother and child, small family norms with male responsibility, spacing, immunization and Vitamin A administration, home-based care for diarrhea, early treatment for Acute Respiratory Infection (ARI), and prevention and treatment for Reproductive Tract Infections (RTI) and HIV/AIDS. BCC led to community mobilization and increased demand for services, while satisfactory services provided at the Urban Health Centers reinforced behavioral change. BCC through Women's Health Groups, Self-Help Women's Groups, Integrated Child Development Services (ICDS) workers, and community volunteers succeeded in enabling positive behavior change among the slum women beneficiaries to seek health care and demand quality services from the Urban Health Centers (Somayajulu 2004).

Strategic Health Communication

Strategic communication goes beyond IEC and BCC even though it incorporates elements form the two approaches. It has become central to combating the world's major complex development problems. This approach recognizes that effective communication is grounded in a particular socioecological context, includ ing enabling environments, service delivery systems, communities, husbands and wives, family members, and individuals. Strategic communication involves identifying and understanding pathways to change within these complex systems and developing bold strategies that address these behavioral pathways. It mobilizes a comprehensive array of communication approaches including digital media, broadcast media, community mobilization, interpersonal communication, advocacy, and capacity building to catalyze change.

Strategic health communication can bring about considerable change in the health-seeking behavior of the target population. It creates an environment for introduction and adoption of a health intervention. It is assumed that once the environment is created and the intervention is launched, it would have relatively better acceptability. Strategic health communication aims at creating awareness as well as creating an environment perceptive to change. Strategic health communication takes an integrated approach to maternal and childcare in the areas of nutrition, clean environment, hygiene, and family interaction and support. While health is a common concern of all age groups and gender, it became imperative for health communication experts to be conscious of gender-based perceptions about health, gender differentials in health information needs, the credibility of sources of information, and the preferred sources of information of women.

India's fight to lower MMR is failing due to growing social inequalities and shortages in primary health-care facilities. Maternal deaths can be avoided with the help of strategic health communication involving skilled health personnel, access to adequate nutrition, better medical facilities, and family planning. India has begun to implement strategic health communication to initiate positive behavior change among slum women to step up the knowledge and utilization of health services. The following section analyzes the benefits of successful strategic health communication initiatives for slum women in India and their implications for the health status of their sisters who live in urban slums of Asia and Africa.

Rights of the Girl Child

Despite women's biological advantages, the higher mortality rates in several countries of south and east Asia reveals the persistence of "missing women" who have died due to infanticide, gender-based abortion, systematic neglect, and discrimination in access to health and nutrition. Women in India constitute a population of 495.74 million with 360.52 million in the rural areas and 135.22 million in the urban areas. The human development status of women shows wide interstate and intrastate variations. In the Indian context, gender relations are determined by the complex interplay of power relations based on class, caste, ethnicity, and religion (Desai and Thakkar 2001). There is considerable variation in the social construction of gender in different parts of India, especially between the northern and southern regions (Prasad 2004).

The high preference for sons in South Asia including India has led to many girl children being annihilated even before they are born. The adverse sex ratio in India, which stands at 940 females per 1,000 males, is a reflection of this reality (Census of India 2011). Women in the developing world including India generally neglect health problems and tend to go without medical attention for a prolonged period of time. Health care for women is often regarded as a luxury rather than a necessity. Women face complicated pregnancies and related poor reproductive health, abortion, and chronic iron deficiency. They have the primary responsibility of bearing children and shouldering the household burden with little time, energy, or resources for personal health care. Women tend to neglect their health and direct their concern and attention toward the care of families. Since women are by and large silent about their health problems, the decisions regarding their health care rests with family members, particularly male members. According to the NFHS (2007), around half of the women in India are not involved in decisions about seeking health care for themselves.

The Meena Communication Initiative in South Asia developed by UNICEF (2002) and supported by the governments of Bangladesh, India, Pakistan, and Nepal is an important strategic communication initiative aimed at changing the perceptions and behavior that hamper the survival, protection, and development of female children in the region. This strategic communication initiative involves production of multimedia packages to put across gender, child rights, and educational messages using the medium of popular entertainment, which is aimed at altering the targeted persons from mere recipients of information to seekers of information to protect the health of girls and women. The Meena Communication Initiative is based on a shared need for content creation in the region to promote women's health, gender equality, and empowerment of women, which are important MDGs to be achieved in South Asia to improve the human development status in the region.

Reproductive Health Care

Reproductive health care forms an important and permanent agenda in women's health. Annually, huge investments area made in terms of money, resources, and materials to create health infrastructure and awareness among women. As in many other developing countries, unequal power relations and the low status of women, as expressed by limited access to human, financial, and economic assets, weakens the ability of women to seek health care for themselves (Prasad 2008b). The National Rural Health Mission launched by the government in 2005 was aimed at increasing the outreach of the health system to village and rural households through the provision of voluntary trained female community health activists called ASHA. It also recommends strengthening the primary or community health centers as a key step to empowering public health infrastructure.

The National Mission for Empowerment of Women (NMEW) announced on March 8, 2010 works with all the states and union territory governments and has 14 ministries and departments of Government of India as its partners with the Ministry of Women and Child Development as the Nodal Ministry. The mandate of the Mission is to bring in convergence and facilitate the processes of ensuring economic and social empowerment of women with emphasis on health and education, reduction in violence against women, generating awareness about various schemes and programs meant for women, empowerment of vulnerable women, and women in difficult circumstances (http://www.nmew.gov.in). The Mission aims to engage in strategic communication for interministerial convergence of gender mainstreaming of programs, policies, institutional arrangements, and processes of participating ministries, which have largely hitherto operated independently and in a stand-alone manner.

The child sex ratio in India has been sliding gradually over the decades from 962 to 1,000 boys in 1981, to 945 in 1991, 927 in 2001, and 914 in 2011. To address this complex issue, which lacked a national action plan, the NMEW has launched Thematic Convergence Projects in 2012 using strategic communication to tackle the declining child sex ratio in 12 gender-critical districts spread over seven states of India. It has developed a Communication Charter based on BCC through community social organizations to chalk out strategic communication action plans to address the problem of sex-selective elimination of girls in India (http://www.nmew.gov.in).

In a study of the influence of strategic health communication on health behavior change of urban slum women in two slums of Hyderabad City in Andhra Pradesh with intensive and nonintensive health communication campaigns, it was found that there is a gap between health services and the users' end in terms of information, knowledge, availability, and utilization of services (Haripriya and Prasad 2009). The intensive strategic reproductive health communication program used a variety of print media to target slum women including posters, charts, newspapers, pamphlets/leaflets and magazines. Electronic media such as TV, radio, film shows/ videos and audio cassettes were also used to expose women to intensive strategic reproductive health communication. Street plays, puppet shows and *Harikathas* or mythological/traditional stories were also used to create widespread exposure to all health messages among slum women in the intensive program area. Interpersonal/ group media were also employed to expose slum women to health messages in the intensive area through group meetings, women's clubs, child service center (*balwadi*) teachers, health officers/personnel and relatives/friends.

Haripriya and Prasad (2009) observed that slum women in the program-intensive area had better levels of awareness of reproductive health than slum women in the nonintensive area. More than two-thirds of the slum women in the intensive area had live births whereas only half of the slum women in the nonintensive area had live births. While three-fourth of pregnant women were visited by health workers and advised for regular antenatal checkup by a health worker in the intensive area, only half of the women reported such visits in the nonintensive area. Majority of the slum women (91 %) had undergone three or more antenatal checkups in the intensive area against half of the women in the nonintensive area. A great majority of slum women (94 %) utilized the free distribution of Iron or folic acid tablets in the intensive area women against less than half of the women in the nonintensive area.

More than three-fourth of the women in the intensive area had their delivery in a medical institution while more than 10 % of the slum women in the nonintensive area had their delivery at home. Most of the women in the nonintensive area were assisted by relatives/friends/others in their delivery at home, whereas a negligible number of women in the intensive area who had delivery at home were assisted by Trained Birth Attendants (TBAs). The awareness and utilization of monetary benefits from the government during first and second pregnancies and sterilization is significantly higher among women of intensive area than among women of the nonintensive area (Haripriya and Prasad 2009).

It is found that women who reside in the slums with intensive strategic reproductive health communication have better levels of exposure and awareness of reproductive health and have greater levels of utilization of health services than women who reside in the slums with nonintensive health communication programmes. Slum women exposed to intensive strategic reproductive health communication had better knowledge of antenatal, delivery and postnatal care, family planning, maternity benefits, and monetary benefit for sterilization. Slum women exposed to intensive strategic reproductive health communication expressed greater improvement in health behavior in terms of nutrition, environmental cleanliness, personal hygiene, and reproductive health. Strategic communication to increase the awareness and knowledge levels of reproductive health had positive effects on the utilization of health services and health behavior of slum women (Haripriya and Prasad 2009).

Women with HIV/AIDS

There is a growing feminization of the HIV/AIDS epidemic in India with 38.4 % of those living with the virus being women (http://www.unaids.org). The fact that more than 2 million women in India are living with HIV/AIDS has set off alarm bells in the Indian medical fraternity—especially since more than 90 % of these are married women in monogamous relationships: more married women in India are at risk of getting AIDS than sex workers. The virus is also increasingly moving toward the rural areas and slums with 57 % of the virus load being shared by the women who live in villages and slums. Several factors combine to increase the vulnerability of women to HIV/AIDS and they must also be understood in the context of the poverty and inequalities that define the daily lives of both women and men in South Asia.

Knowledge of AIDS among women has been increasing over time, but many women have still not heard of AIDS. Knowledge of AIDS is universal among men and women with 10 or more years of schooling but majority of women with no education have not heard of AIDS (Gupta et al. 2006). As part of the AIDS prevention program, the Government of India has been using mass media, television in particular, extensively to create awareness among the general public about AIDS and its prevention. In India *Breakthrough,* a human rights organization has launched a strategic media campaign titled *What Kind of Man Are You?* This strategic communication campaign highlights the rising incidence of married women infected by the AIDS virus by their husbands. Apart from this, *Breakthrough* has been organizing various workshops to provide sex education to the general public. It also has an SMS facility through which people's queries are answered, informing them about the treatment and care for the infected.

The organization has also launched an intensive multimedia campaign to focus public attention on the growing problem of HIV/AIDS. Sameer Soni and Mandira Bedi, popular television stars, who feature in a music video, *Maati,* sung by Shubha Mudgal, which talks about a pregnant woman who discovers that she is HIV-positive because of her husband's promiscuity, feel that the responsibility and the guilt that a man feels on infecting his innocent wife is brought out beautifully in the video, directed by Arjun Bali. "The fact that television and music are so popular with the masses will help spread the message much faster in a populated country like India, than workshops and prevention measures targeting small groups of people," says Soni (Khosla 2005). The message is being conveyed through music videos, eye catching advertisements in newspapers, radio, and television. The different visuals have the same theme—a woman asking her husband to protect her by using a condom. This strategic campaign aims to empower women in an exceedingly patriarchal society, enabling them to discuss sexuality freely with their husbands and encouraging the use of condoms among men with their wives.

Women living with HIV/AIDS have started strategic initiatives that would express and improve their situations. They have called for recognition of their fundamental human rights and for decision-making power and consultation at all levels of policy and programs affecting them. They have urged economic support for women living with HIV/AIDS in developing countries, support for self-help groups and networks, realistic portrayals of people living with HIV/AIDS by the media, and accessible and affordable health care. They also want their reproductive rights to be respected, including the right to choose whether or not to have children (http://www.icw.org).

Strategic communication involves many community efforts mobilized to protect women's health. A young widow who lost her husband from AIDS started a support group specifically for women to break the cultural taboo of silence among women with HIV/AIDS. She decided to fight AIDS by educating young girls and began appearing in public, speaking at schools and gatherings, and eventually on television when the media picked up on her efforts. She also began visiting other HIV-positive women, trying to get them to go public and called the first meeting of the Positive Women's Network of South India. Positive Women's Network is an organization formed by women living with HIV/AIDS (WLHA) in 1998 to address the need for a support system and to improve the quality of life of women living with HIV and their children in India (http://www.pwnplus.org/who.htm—Positive) Women's Network The network began with 18 women who showed up to talk about their lives and the impact HIV had had on them. Now the group has more than 1,000 members most of whom are housewives and meetings feature doctors, dieticians, and social workers. Members of the network can take advantage of counseling and social services as well (Warrior 2003).

Policy Implications

In countries where low literacy remains a substantial barrier to development, considering the fact that an estimated 115 million children, mostly girls remain out of school in sub-Saharan Africa and South Asia, strategic health communication can significantly impact women's development in several countries—for example, India, Indonesia, sub-Saharan Africa, and Dominican Republic. Development processes made extensive use of IEC and BCC approaches to raise awareness, to inform and encourage responsible behavior, and to publicize available services in the community. IEC and BCC programs used a variety of formats to deliver appropriate messages to targeted segments of the population and in promoting a variety of health messages including family planning, AIDS prevention, better nutrition, and reproductive health. But IEC and BCC often failed to recognize that health communication is grounded in a specific socioecological context and complex patterns of behavior in a social system. For instance, IEC and BCC projects on reproductive health and HIV/AIDS often fail to recognize that women in South Asia and Africa have weak bargaining power in the area of sexual relationships, childbearing, and childrearing. Deprivation of women's reproductive rights stems from the complex nature of social systems that reinforce women's dependence, deny them a voice in family matters, and identify the family as the most important institution that shapes women's identity.

Strategic health communication makes a difference in the reproductive health status and quality of life of women by identifying and understanding the specific courses of action needed to modify behavior that leads to lack of control over their sexuality and fertility. Some actions addressed by strategic health communication include stepping up literacy levels among slum women, educating young women on reproductive health issues such as delaying age at marriage and adoption of the small family norm, which will bring down the burden of childrearing on women leaving sufficient time for other fruitful pursuits.

Strategic health communication also engages in a dialogue with policy makers to provide infrastructure such as proper housing, toilet facility, potable water facility, and sanitation to promote health and hygiene management among slum women (Prasad 2008b). Sustained exposure to reproductive health messages through different mass media and interpersonal channels that are preferred among slum women is one of the key objectives of strategic health communication (Haripriya and Prasad 2009).

Strategic health communication goes beyond IEC and BCC approaches by intensifying measures that take health to the doorsteps of slum women rather than getting them to go health educators for information. Health workers in strategic health communication initiatives make regular visits to homes of slum women who are pregnant to distribute free iron and folic acid tablets, provide nutritional supplements, and motivate them to attend antenatal and postnatal checkups. Reproductive health care should not be equated with just family planning as in the BCC approach but women must be empowered to make informed choices through strategic health communication. Women are not to be considered passive recipients of a benevolent government or voluntary agency program as is the case in many other development programs (Prasad 2008a). Counseling for husband–wife and strategies to improve couple communication should be adopted in strategic reproductive health communication. The strategic health communication initiatives described here demonstrates that intensive information, education, and communication along with better health services can bear positive results and enable slum women in India and other developing countries to enjoy a healthy lifestyle.

Conclusion

The number of people living in slums is growing; adding 55 million over the past decade to reach 827.6 million in 2010. According to the UN (2010), the world slum population in sub-Saharan Africa, South Asia, and East Asia is estimated to grow by 6 million each year. Strategic communication initiatives in slums will be able to translate MDGs into strategic objectives to be achieved in maternal and child health. Strategic health communication can empower women in slums and the community to participate in health-care decisions.

Health care and medical personnel must be trained in strategic communication skills to interact with the community, build confidence, and motivate them to seek early treatment. The number of health service delivery points should be increased, better road and transport facilities should be established in slums, and link volunteers should be trained from the community to motivate families in slums to make the optimum use of health services.

Strategic health communication for slum women must enable women to freely express their realities and have them taken into account in the development of gender-just social systems. Positive role modeling through audiovisual communication tools will help to break the initial resistance and enable the family and community to participate in empowering women toward health care and improving their status. Strategic health communication can create a gender equitable environment in which boys and girls are equally valued, equally cared for, and equally educated, to move countries toward the MDG of sustainable development.

References

Census of India (2001). *Provisional population totals*. Paper-1 of 2001 Census, Andhra Pradesh.
Census of India (2011). *Provisional population totals*. Paper-1 of 2011 Census, Government of India.
Das, N. P., & Shah, U. (2001). *Understanding women's reproductive health needs in urban slums in India: A rapid assessment*. Paper contributed for XXIV IUSSP General Population Conference, Salvador, Brazil, 18–24, August 2001.
Desai, N., & Thakkar, U. (2001). *Women in Indian society*. New Delhi: National Book Trust.
Family Welfare Department (2001). *Reference Manual of Andhra Pradesh Urban Slum Health Care Project*. Government of Andhra Pradesh.

Gaye, A., Klugman, J., Kovacevic, M., Twigg, S., & Zambrano, E. (2010). *Measuring key disparities in human development: The gender inequality index.* Human Development Research Paper 2010/46, UNDP, New York: UN.

Gupta, R., et al. (2006). Risk factors and societal response to HIV/AIDS in India. *http://t8web.lanl. gov/people/rajan/AIDS-india/MYWORK/hivindia2001.html.* Accessed 18 Mar 2009.

Haripriya, M., & Prasad, K. (2009). Reproductive health communication and utilization of health services among slum women. In S. R. Joshi & K. Prasad (Eds.), *Feminist development communication.* New Delhi: The Women Press.

Khosla, S. (2005). Nothing positive—AIDS & the Indian woman. http://www.the-south-asian. com/June2005/AIDS-Women-in-India.htm. Accessed 27 Oct 2009.

NFHS (2007). *National Family Health Survey 2005–2006, India.* Mumbai: IIPS.

NSSO (2003) *Condition of slums 2002: Salient features*, NSS 58th Round (July 2002-December 2002).

Prasad, K. (2004). Women's health and communication policy. In K. Prasad (Ed), *Communication and empowerment of women: Strategies and policy insights from India* (Vol. 2). New Delhi: The Women Press.

Prasad, K. (2008a). Gender-sensitive communication policies for women's development: Issues and challenges. In K. Sarikakis & L. Regan Shade (Eds.), *Feminist interventions in international communication: Minding the gap.* Lanham: Rowman and Littlefield.

Prasad, K. (2008b). Women's vulnerability to HIV/AIDS in Asia and Africa. In K. Prasad & U. V. Somayajulu (Eds.), *HIV and AIDS: Vulnerability of women in Asia and Africa.* New Delhi: The Women Press.

Purewal, N. K. (2001). New roots for rights: Women's response to population and development policies. In S. Rowbotham & S. Linkogle (Eds.), *Women resist globalization: Mobilizing for livelihood and rights.* London: Zed Books.

Rao, A. P., & Somayajulu U. V. (2004). Health status of women living in the slums of Bangalore. In Dept. of Population Studies-UGC SAP (Phase-1), *Women, Health and Development.* Tirupati: Sri Venkateswara University.

Registrar General of India (2003). *Final population tables, 2001 Census of India.* New Delhi: Government of India.

Registrar General of India (2011). *Maternal and child mortality and total fertility rates.* New Delhi: Government of India.

Saran, R. (2003, July 28). How we live. *India Today.*

Sinha, A. (2009). Women, media and health information. In S. R. Joshi & K. Prasad (Eds.), *Feminist development communication.* New Delhi: The Women Press.

Somayajulu, U. V. (2004). Behaviour change communication for empowerment of women: experiences from AP Urban Slum Health Care Project. In K. Prasad (Ed.), *Communication and empowerment of women: Strategies and policy insights from India* (Vols. 1 & 2). New Delhi: The Women Press.

UNICEF (2002). *Meena Communication Initiative. http://gkaims.globalknowledge.org.* Accessed 2 Nov 2009.

United Nations (UN) (2010). *State of the world cities 2010/11: Bridging the urban divide.* New York: UN.

Warrior, S. (2003, July). A Positive Network for Women. www.rediff.com/news/2001/dec/01spec. htm. Accessed 9 Jan 2007.

WHO (1991). *Epidemiological, Social and Technical Aspects of Indoor Air Pollution from Biomass fuel.* Geneva: Report of WHO Consultation.

World Bank (2003). *2003 World Development Indicators.* Washington: The World Bank.

Chapter 9
Integrating HIV/FP Programs: Opportunities for Strategic Communication

Susan Adamchak, Jennifer Reierson and Jennifer Liku

Strategic Communication

Communicators were once able to target the "masses" with a single message in a single outlet. Now, the technology-driven, increasingly global, and overcrowded marketplace demands a more strategic approach to communication that was once based on experience and assumptions. A strategic approach is grounded in research and positioned as a cyclical process of research and analysis, development, execution, monitoring, and evaluation. Similarly, such principles are being applied to develop communication aimed at social change initiatives (UNICEF 2005).

Communication (i.e., messages conveyed by various agents such as consumer marketers, corporate communicators, or individual health care providers) was once dominated by a linear, unidirectional approach that was generally top-down or expert-to-novice. While this allowed for message control, it alienated and discounted the abilities and individuality of message receivers or publics. The linear approach lacks an understanding and incorporation of audience capacity, perceptions, needs, and desires into the messaging. Publics, however, can no longer be ignored or treated as a cohesive whole, as evidenced in the permeation of online, digital, and social tools that allow individuals to create, share, and monitor messages with the potential for greater reach than organized media campaigns. Publics utilize such tools as Facebook, Twitter, and YouTube to express their frustrations, as well as perceptions, desires and needs related to organizations, products, and services. This power shift, from organizations or perceived experts to individuals and concerned publics, requires more focused efforts by an organization's key individuals to respond to and engage with publics in meaningful ways.

S. Adamchak (✉)
FHI 360, Durham, NC, USA
e-mail: sadamchak@fhi360.org

J. Reierson
University of Minnesota Duluth, Duluth, USA

J. Liku
FHI 360, Durham, NC, USA

C. C. Okigbo (ed.), *Strategic Urban Health Communication,*
DOI 10.1007/978-1-4614-9335-8_9, © Springer Science+Business Media New York 2014

Strategic communication broadly refers to communication efforts based on a solid planning process, but more specifically can be related to organizational or interpersonal communication efforts. Effective strategic communication, in contrast to the more directive, linear models, can be seen as a two-way dialogic process that both informs publics as well as the originating organization or provider and fosters trust and mutual understanding (Grunig et al. 2002). By recognizing various stakeholders and engaging them in dialogue that allows their perceptions, lifestyle choices, behaviors, passions, and concerns to emerge, a strategic communicator is setting the groundwork for a successful communication plan. With an understanding of various stakeholers, messages and messaging outlets can be targeted effectively.

The need for strategic communication is even more potent when risks, for instance health or behavioral, are of concern. In this case, it is essential that those wishing to convey information to reduce or mitigate risk fully understand the characteristics of the population of concern, in order to convey salient information in a format and manner that triggers recognition and response from the intended target. Schloss (2008) found that theory and research related to strategic communication is not being applied in the health care field related to organizational public relations and marketing efforts as well as practitioner practices. Specifically, communication in the health care setting is reflective of the one-way model, is based on informal research techniques rather than formal, and lacks planning and strategic focus. These findings are alarming given consequences of faulty, insufficient, or ineffective communication practices in health care.

The goal of this chapter is first to develop an understanding of strategic communication, recognize how it might prove beneficial in the health care setting, and finally utilize a case study to demonstrate the potential for developing and initiating strategic communication efforts within a health care context. Strategic communication includes developing strategies and tactics. While these can be specific to a particular case or situation, there is potential in developing and recognizing possibilities on a broad scale related to the health care field. Specifically, a broad understanding will allow strategic communication suggestions to emerge from the case study.

Strategic Communication: Strategies and tactics

The implementation of strategic communication in health care settings carries significant implications. Goals of strategic communication programs aim to seek positive change, while nurturing open, trusting, and stable relationships and reducing conflict (Grunig et al. 2002). Grunig et al. (2002) reinforced the potential positive influence of strategic communication. They proposed:

1. The greater the communication excellence in organizations, the more successful such organizations are at achieving positive change in relationships with key publics.

2. The more strategic the origins and management of programs for key publics, the more positive are the outcomes achieved with publics.
3. The more scanning and evaluations research conducted on key publics, the more demonstrable are the outcomes achieved with publics (p. 389).

Strategic communication planning starts with research that includes understanding a situation and the target audience or publics (Lattimore et al. 2009; Wilson 2001). Once this knowledge is collected, objectives, goals, and subsequently strategies and tactics can be developed. An objective notes what you want to accomplish, specifically, in a measureable way, with a timeframe indicator. Communication strategies and tactics differ in that a strategy focuses on higher-level initiatives that emerge directly from campaign or communication goals and objectives (Lattimore et al. 2007; Watson and Noble 2007). Tactics, then, are particular action steps that help fulfill or realize strategies (Lattimore et al. 2009; Wilson 2001).

Strategic communication is a process rooted in planning and strategies are emergent based on foundational elements of the plan (situation analysis, formal and informational research, audience analysis, etc). However, it is possible, given the health care setting, to infer strategies that may support broad objectives of increasing patient-provider communication effectiveness to result in responsive and responsible patient behaviors as well as improved provider care. Specific time-oriented and measureable outcomes could be applied on a case-by-case basis. Communication strategies, related to these broad objectives, might include: (1) creating platforms that foster patient-provider dialogue and two-way responsive communication and (2) developing educational programs and opportunities for both providers and patients.

Tactics are the action steps that work to fulfill the strategies. A plethora of new communication tools and tactics are available. Many are utilized and implemented by companies and organizations without thought as to how they actually work to fulfill strategies and achieve objectives. Significant time and effort is wasted if tactics are not thoroughly considered and clearly linked to execution of particular strategies within a plan. Additionally, strategic communication must meet the intended audience (in this case, patients) in mediums where they spend time. Research must establish technology use, access, and preference. When and where a targeted public seeks health information, who they trust, how they prefer to receive such information, whether they want or need an opportunity to respond or ask questions immediately, and when they are most attentive and likely to engage in communication related to health and health care are all necessary considerations. Therefore, while the following tactics provide means for distributing messages and fostering communication efforts, they should be implemented only with a clear rationale and understanding of their appropriateness related to specific audiences, goals, objectives, and strategies.

Tactics that will work to realize the strategy of creating forums and platforms for patient-provider dialogue might include the following actions. Develop an interface linked to the health care facility's Internet homepage where patients can ask questions anonymously and receive provider responses in a secure setting. Create a provider blog in which new information and research findings are presented clearly and in lay terms with an opportunity for patient response and other provider input. Set up a Twitter or similar account that allows patients to follow provider, hospital, or clinic news, advice and to respond with their questions or comments. These are illustrative suggestions and by no means an exhaustive list.

The strategy related to developing educational opportunities might be realized in a number of ways. For instance, community fora or meetings related to a particular health care issue of concern to the local population may be held at a community center, place of worship, or school campus. Health professionals may organize and develop support groups that meet virtually (in an online community, which can allow for anonymity) or in-person. Publications and collateral pieces (newsletters, brochure, pamphlets), blogs, social media sites, text and email campaigns can be developed to target specific audiences and health issues. Such initiatives might also be directed at providers. Provider education, whether through online or in-person training sessions, educational emails, or blogs, might also focus on enhancing interpersonal skills and fostering patient dialogue.

The efforts and tactics listed here require focused attention and time commitment on behalf of those implementing them, whether clinic or hospital staff, public relations personnel, providers, or patients. The success of these and similar efforts will depend on consideration of the above in the planning process, making necessary adjustments in workload, designating appropriate resources, and assigning qualified and appropriate personnel to development, implementation, and maintenance.

The remainder of this chapter uses data from a survey of HIV/AIDS services in five countries to demonstrate how strategic communication might be used in order to more effectively integrate health care and risk prevention programs. Opportunities to incorporate dialogic processes that empower, educate, and recognize patients as individuals are identified. Additionally, gaps in provider preparedness reveal a need for strategic communication and supporting resources. Finally, conclusions for strategic communication in health care are developed.

A Case for Strategic Communication: Family Planning and HIV Service Integration

Background

In recent years, there has been a growing international dialogue on the feasibility and desirability of providing integrated FP and HIV services. The reasons for offering joint, complementary services are many. Adding family planning services to counseling and testing may provide an opportunity to reach populations that do not typically visit family planning clinics, such as the sexually active young and unmarried, men, and members of high-risk groups such as sex workers. Adding FP services to care and treatment protocols may facilitate the uptake of contraception by HIV-positive individuals, helping to maintain their health, plan safer pregnancies, and reduce the rate of mother-to-child transmission of HIV. Including HIV services, particularly counseling and testing, in FP services would allow earlier diagnosis and referral to care and treatment.

A study conducted by FHI 360 with support from the US Agency for International Development (USAID) explored early integration efforts in five countries (Ethiopia, Kenya, Rwanda, South Africa, and Uganda) to establish a baseline "snapshot" to inform USAID and national programs in order to improve service integration. Three models of integrated HIV and family planning services were included in the study: family planning in HIV counseling and testing (FP in HCT), family planning in HIV care and treatment services (FP in C&Tx), and HIV services (particularly HCT) into family planning (HCT in FP). This chapter uses some of the findings from one of these models, FP in HCT, to illustrate intervention points in which strategic health communication can be introduced to improve client screening and service delivery.

This research identified weaknesses in provider readiness to integrate services, knowledge, and attitudes in relation to the integration of these services. Moreover, the study showed discrepancies in provider perceptions of services offered and patient perceptions of services received. This gap poses a substantial risk in fully meeting client needs, despite performance protocols that encourage open communication between provider and client, in regard to FP and HIV issues. This chapter addresses the need for improved communication behaviors by identifying and proposing opportunities to incorporate strategic communication (focused on integrated services) into provider behavior. A focus on strategic communication includes techniques to ready the providers and encourage their participation. It also includes suggestions of means to facilitate client advocacy and education as well as influence health-seeking behavior in order to nurture multiple trigger points for dialogue.

Project Findings

Across all countries, provider readiness, knowledge, and attitudes related to integration of FP, HCT, and C&Tx services were shown to be important factors in patient care and experience. A considerable gap was also shown to exist between providers' perception of care provided and patient perceptions of the same care, both across countries and services.

Provider Readiness Commonly accepted indicators of provider readiness include training in new service, supervision, and availability of job aids. Overall, clinical training was not common among HCT providers. Many of the HCT providers interviewed had not been trained to offer FP counseling or services, and they were unfamiliar with integration guidelines. Adequate screening for FP needs seems unlikely, even in the "best" program sites. One program manager in South Africa explained, *"Nurses are proscriptive and they don't counsel, and lay counselors are not trained in family planning."* A Kenyan AIDS official echoed concerns with provider readiness, *"Every VCT (Voluntary Counseling and Testing) site stocks condoms, and after training they are supposed to have pills. But non-clinical officers are not confident to initiate."*

Most HCT providers lacked job aids to assist in delivering integrated services, most profoundly in Ethiopia. While many providers noted the availability of contraceptive samples to use in counseling clients, resources such as flip charts and check lists with FP information were generally scarce. Many providers met weekly with supervisors, but for some, such meetings were not perceived to improve service delivery but rather served to deliver supplies or arrange training. Regular contact with supervisors is an underutilized opportunity to strengthen and support HCT providers' capacity for delivering integrated services.

Provider Knowledge and Attitudes HCT providers require unbiased attitudes and accurate knowledge of various contraceptive methods in order to effectively counsel clients. Lack of training and job aids may exacerbate knowledge gaps and biased attitudes and therefore perpetuate counseling weaknesses related to specific methods such as injectable contraceptives, oral contraceptive pills, and implants. Furthermore, due to high client load, providers may frequently have insufficient time to communicate vital information.

HCT providers overwhelmingly view condoms as the best contraceptive method for HIV-positive women (and give this message to their clients), while also counseling the use of other methods. Far fewer providers identified condoms as the best method for HIV-negative women, seemingly viewing condoms as a way to prevent transmission by infected women rather than as a way to protect HIV-negative women from infection. This is particularly ironic and surprising considering condoms are the method most often associated with HCT services. This situation is further complicated in some contexts by the proliferation of advertisements and public service announcements that promote condoms solely for prevention of HIV and other sexually transmitted infections.

Few providers (with exception of those in South Africa) correctly defined "dual method" contraceptive use: using a condom with another contraceptive method. Similarly, many providers were unable to correctly define the ability of condoms to offer "dual protection" (i.e., protection from pregnancy and sexually transmitted infections). While these findings may be related more to the comprehension of the providers of survey questions rather than their full understanding of dual protection or dual method use, providers need to recognize, appreciate, and clearly convey information on the multiple uses of condoms in the context of HIV/AIDS and family planning.

Opinions regarding whether integration improves services were mixed among providers in these countries. Positive aspects of integration included the convenience of providing information at one site and seeing more HCT clients seek FP services. Those with negative perceptions cited the lack of coordination between HIV and FP services.

Provider Reports of Services Offered Integrated services had already been introduced in the study sites yet results show limited evidence of actual delivery of integrated service. Less than two-thirds of providers reported referring clients for FP in the past week and with the exception of providers in South Africa, less than half reported having discussed contraception with clients on the day of the interview. This is a missed opportunity to share detailed information that could lead to uptake of services.

According to one program manager in Uganda, *"family planning knocks them (counselors) off their track. VCT (voluntary counseling and testing) is highly scripted, and it is an enormous step to look at individual needs."*

Client Reports of Services Received Screening clients for complementary service needs is the foundation of integrated services so multiple health concerns can be addressed in a single visit. In the context of a supportive, comfortable environment, screening questions to determine need for family planning typically follow a basic logic: Are you sexually active? Do you want to become pregnant? Are you currently using contraception? Appropriate contraceptive methods should be discussed as needs are identified.

Client reports, however, reveal that at most 68 % were screened for sexual activity. While providers may assume sexual activity in women seeking HCT services, on the presumption that the majority of those seeking testing are doing so because they may have been exposed to HIV through intercourse, women should still be asked about fertility desires. The data show, however, that screening for fertility desires and contraceptive use is not the norm.

In all but one country, South Africa, discussion of contraceptive methods other than condoms occurred in less than 40 % of client-provider interactions, begging the question of how integration of FP services changes the original counseling model if condom promotion is an integral component of HCT services.

Using client data, the unmet need for FP was estimated by using the proportion sexually active in the 3 months prior to the study, desire for children, and current contraceptive use. Unmet need varied across countries from a high of 46 % in South Africa to a low of 17 % in Ethiopia. Need varies for two reasons. Either very high percentages of women were pregnant (as some were tested during antenatal care visits) and intended the pregnancy (Ethiopia and Rwanda) and thus were not in need, or high percentages were using contraception (Kenya and Uganda).

Integrating family planning into counseling and HIV testing has clear benefits in theory, but presents significant challenges in practice. This case revealed a need for provider education and training (which may require reviewing and revising current methodologies as well as related policies and practices) as well as increased screening and communication efforts at all levels and with all clients. Likewise, clients require educational information and resources to prepare them for interaction with providers. Clients must learn to be proactive in identifying and discussing their needs, concerns, and options in regard to family planning when receiving counseling and HIV testing services. Similar themes were echoed in each of the other two integrated models. Cross-national comparisons reveal numerous risk areas and service gaps but also opportunities for integrating and promoting strategic health communication.

Opportunities for Strategic Health Communication

"We are mopping a leaking house." (MOH official, Kenya)

Given the process of planning related to strategic communication and how specific efforts might be related to either organizational or interpersonal communication, the case and problems presented above reveal multiple opportunities for initiating and developing strategic communication. Each of the areas noted, namely provider readiness, provider knowledge and attitudes, provider reports of services offered, and client reports of services received, illustrate conditions that could and should drive the development of a strategic communication plan. While this chapter is not focused on developing a communications plan, elements needed for the communications planning process are identified below. Strategies can be inferred from the identified needs and tactics specific to the intended and affected audience, i.e., patient, provider, supervisor, etc., are suggested.

Need for Training and Support Functions

The support functions that help increase and sustain quality of care—training, job aids, and supervision—are not adequate to offer the newly integrated services. If an overall goal is to improve care and patient-provider communication, a related strategy might entail developing appropriate training and support resources for providers. In general, providers in care and treatment and in family planning services tend to be clinically trained; these include doctors, clinical officers, nurses, and midwives. In contrast, those offering HCT services mostly include nonmedical counselors, without training in family planning. While training alone is not sufficient to prepare providers to offer integrated services, it is an essential component. Providers must have accurate and up-to-date information that allows them to screen, counsel, refer, and offer services. Sharing findings from various program and research efforts, whether through targeted mobile phone texts, short courses offered in-house, newsletters, or electronic media as computer use becomes more widespread such as emails, blogs, online forums, or intranets, could provide needed evidence on gaps. Providers should be trained to engage patients in a two-way dialogue in order to assess patient needs, concerns, and behaviors that may affect care. Such dialogue can be initiated with simple open-ended or standard direct questions at the onset of an encounter.

These services frequently lack basic job aids to support providers in their work; providers need check lists, flip charts, and sample contraceptives to support service delivery, and there is a need for wider dissemination of these tools. Providing visual or sensory depictions of contraceptive options can effectively convey potentially complex information and may also serve as a reminder to providers. Using such tools at opportune times can prompt provider-patient dialogue and provide insight into patient knowledge, perceptions, and behaviors.

In addition, supervisors do not appear to be helping providers to do their jobs. This is a lost opportunity for job coaching. Supervisors need to help providers to understand the value of integrated services. Supervisory skills need to be addressed as a complement to provider training and support. Again, opportunities for dialogue between supervisor and provider must be nurtured. Whether through quarterly reviews, weekly meetings, daily check-ins, posts, discussion boards, incentive programs, or other locally designed tactics, improved supervisor-provider communication and mentorship is a clear opportunity for improving integration of services. Supervisors must be willing to listen to provider needs and concerns as well and to respond appropriately with resources or suggestions. Similarly, there should be opportunities developed to facilitate client feedback as a means to foster self-reflection by providers.

Need for Provider Education and Awareness

Provider knowledge and attitudes on provision of integrated services need to be improved. Again, this might be envisioned as a strategy within a strategic communication plan: develop and initiate an education program aimed at provider understanding and attitudes of regarding integrated services and contraceptive methods. Providers make a sharp distinction between contraceptive methods that are best for HIV-positive and HIV- women. The majority of HCT providers in all countries but Rwanda said that condoms were the best method for HIV-positive women to use. HCT providers in South Africa indicated that condoms were the best method for HIV-negative women to use. Few providers could correctly define "dual method use" or "dual protection."

Providers are apparently unaware of recently updated World Health Organization (WHO) medical eligibility criteria regarding contraceptive use by HIV-positive women. Changing the community's perception and clarifying appropriate use is necessary, but it is not an easy task. Training on the current guidelines is needed, and providers must believe and trust the content of the guidelines if they are to use them in counseling clients. Additionally, it is necessary to ensure that those who get the training are in direct contact with clients, not managers who sit in offices. The need to cover these issues in preservice training is critical. Such misunderstandings and knowledge gaps have dangerous implications for delivery of high-quality care. One strategy that may mitigate such gaps is a secure, integrated online community that provides education modules, news updates, a question and answer area, discussion boards, and resources that link offices and providers. Participation might be mandatory or voluntary depending on the location and availability of necessary technology.

If condom use is to be a cornerstone of risk reduction, frank debate needs to take place to develop strategies to destigmatize condom use (and especially the age-old notion that condoms are stop gap measures and best for short-term relationships) among HIV-negative women. Such debate might be encouraged through various

tactics that provide places and opportunities for such debate (i.e., community meetings, group education sessions, informal social groups, and in areas with computer
access, forums, blogs, and virtual social communities). Provider knowledge and
skills can be improved by introducing systematic in-service training to ensure that:
(1) providers are knowledgeable about and ready to accept WHO medical eligibility criteria for various contraceptive methods and (2) they promote condoms both
to reduce transmission from infected individuals and to protect those not infected.

Need for a Two-Way Model of Care: Screening and Patient Self-Advocacy

Many clients are not being systematically screened for unmet need for family planning. Screening efforts need to be increased in order to improve the provision of
family planning counseling and methods. This problem might be addressed by introducing a strategy that develops a screening process that fosters two-way dialogic
communication exchanges. To determine need for family planning services, providers must ask clients about their sexual activity, their fertility desires, and their
contraceptive use history. Even taking into consideration that some clients may not
have to be asked all three questions to determine need, our results show that the
percentages asked any of these questions are not high. Not only should clients be
asked these questions, but they should also be provided an opportunity to express
concerns or desires related to their care such as contraceptive method and services
desired. Preencounter preparation (video viewing, self-completed worksheet, relevant brochures and pamphlets) might empower patients to ask questions and understand availability of services.

Client and provider reports of service provision often varied. Though sites were
selected because they were supposed to have integrated services, only in South
Africa did more than half the HTC providers report that they spoke with a client
about FP on the day of the interview, and no more than two-thirds in all countries
reported having referred a client for FP during the prior week. Also, while providers
say that they make contraceptives available to clients, few clients in HCT received
a method. Very few clients reported having received a referral to go elsewhere for a
method. Thus, the reports of clients are at variance with those of providers.

This discrepancy highlights an opportunity for patient empowerment and self-
advocacy. Preencounter literature, provided in a format most appropriate for a specific location (i.e., brochure, electronically, via phone, text), and supplied in advance of the day of visit or at check-in, can educate patients about care opportunities
(i.e., integrated services) and contraception options. These communication efforts
might empower patients and provide the confidence and knowledge to ask relevant
questions and to seek care solutions most appropriate to their situation.

Strategic health communication in this type of setting (FP in HCT), based on education and awareness of both provider and patient, should foster productive and appropriate two-way dialogue, prompted by patient or provider. Essentially, the power
dynamic between provider and patient might shift with improved patient education

and willingness to take a more active role in their care. In this way, integration of services might emerge more organically and effectively, albeit prompted by strategic communication.

Conclusions and Recommendations

Specific to the case, the bottom line is that much remains to be done to offer fully integrated FP-HIV services, and to develop effective, scalable models. As yet, we have little evidence to indicate that one model offers strong advantages over another. In fact, it is quite likely that the mode of service delivery should be tailored to the specific situation in which each clinic functions, implying that there might be need to overhaul current systems and to offer more than a minimum package of care in some facilities.

Administrators of family planning and HIV programs must take into account the human and financial resources available to them, and make rational decisions based on local data. The characteristics of their clients and local availability of complementary health services should drive the particular components included in integrated services.

Principles of strategic communication support the need to understand a specific audience or public and then tailor programs or communication efforts that will effectively target and engage the public. While this may appear to be a daunting task for an already overwhelmed system, basic research efforts and increased use of mobile phone and computer technology can go a long way in collecting and interpreting pertinent data. Most important is the need to focus on creating opportunities for dialogue and information flow between provider and patient. Such opportunities can be nurtured with minimal effort and hopefully significantly improve care and integration of services.

Given the significance of strategic communication in the health care setting, organizations providing care might do best to step back and invest the time, energy, and effort into developing an inclusive strategic communication plan that: (1) starts with organizational goals, (2) engages in research to identify current problems (as evidenced above), environmental influences, and audience and public characteristics, (3) involves management, public relations personnel, providers, patients, and any other relevant groups in determining content and communication strategies, (4) defines clear objectives, (5) develops strategies based on objectives, (6) identifies tactics that will fulfill the strategies and are specific to targeted publics, and (7) engages in ongoing and formative evaluation in order to adjust efforts as needed to achieve desired impact. In this way, positive change in key relationships (patient-provider, provider-supervisor, organizational management-provider supervisors) that fosters positive, demonstrable outcomes can be effectively nurtured and realized. Communication efforts in urban health must move toward a more strategic approach if improvement of care, patient-provider relationships, and integration of services is the goal. Without strategic planning that facilitates implementation of a two-way symmetrical and dialogic process, severe health consequences for populations in need will persist.

References

Grunig, L. A., Grunig, J. E., & Dozier, D. M. (2002). *Excellent public relations and effective organizations: A study of communication management in three countries*. Mahwah: Lawrence Erlbaum Associates.

Lattimore, D., Baskin, O., Heiman, S. T., & Toth, E. L. (2009). *Public relations: The profession and the practice* (3rd ed.). New York: McGraw Hill.

Schloss, R. (2008). *Health care public relations and strategic communication: How public relations practitioners make meaning of communication management in a medical center* (pp. 1–35). Presented at the National Communication Association Conference [EBSCO].

UNICEF. (2005). *Strategic communication: For behaviour and social change in South Asia*. Working paper. www.unicef.org/.../Strategic_Communication_for_Behaviour_and_Social_Change.pdf. Accessed 22 July 2007.

Watson, T., & Noble, P. (2007). *Evaluating public relations: A best practice guide to public relations planning, research, and evaluation* (2nd ed.). Great Britain: Kogan Page.

Wilson, L. J. (2001). Extending strategic planning to communication tactics. In R. L. Heath(Ed.), *The handbook of public relations*, (pp. 215–222). Thousand Oaks: Sage.

Chapter 10
Communicating for Action: Tackling Health Inequity in Urban Areas

Amit Prasad, Francisco Armada, Yumi Kimura, Yagaantsetseg Radnaabazar and Khongorzul Byambajav

Urban Health Is Threatened by Inequities

In 2008, the world's urban population outnumbered the rural population for the first time. At the start of the twentieth century only two out of ten people lived in urban areas. By 2050, it is expected that 67% of the world's population will reside in urban areas. Virtually all population growth in the next 30 years will be in urban areas (UN-HABITAT 2010; UNDESA 2011). Urbanization trends vary across the world. Some cities and regions are experiencing rapid population growth, whereas other cities and regions are in decline. However, the world's urban population in the less developed regions is projected to increase from 1.9 billion people living in cities in 2000 to 3.9 billion in 2030 (Brockerhoff 2000). According to projections by the United Nations, 83 % of the world's urban population will reside in developing and middle-income countries by 2050 (Fig. 10.1).

Urbanization is not inherently bad for health. Urban populations are more likely to have access to social and health services, literacy rates are higher, and life expectancy is longer. However, evidence shows that even though, on average, people in urban areas may be better off than people in rural areas, these averages often mask wide disparities between more and less disadvantaged populations (WHO 1993; Smith et al. 2005; Bitran et al. 2005; Fotso 2007). A well-known example is

A. Prasad (✉) · F. Armada
World Health Organization, Kobe, Japan
e-mail: prasada@who.int

Y. Kimura
Center for Southeast Asian Studies,
Kyoto University, Kyoto, Japan

Y. Radnaabazar
Social Development Department,
City Governor's Office, Ulaanbaatar, Mongolia

K. Byambajav
Information, Monitoring and Evaluation Division,
Ministry of Health, Ulaanbaatar, Mongolia

C. C. Okigbo (ed.), *Strategic Urban Health Communication,*   115
DOI 10.1007/978-1-4614-9335-8_10, © Springer Science+Business Media New York 2014

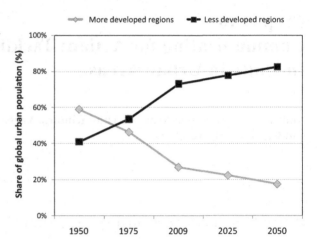

Fig. 10.1 Share of global urban population by developmental levels, projections till 2050. (Source: World Urbanization Prospects, the 2009 Revision (United Nations Population Division))

Glasgow, UK, where male life expectancy in Calton ward was 54 years in 2006 in contrast to 82 years in Lenzie, a nearby ward in the same city (Hanlon et al. 2006).

Why should inequities in urban health and living standards matter? Most obviously, the consequences of poverty and ill-health, including mental health, are contagious in a city setting. They are detrimental to all city dwellers. Urban poverty and squalor are strongly linked to social unrest, mental disorders, crime, violence, and outbreaks of disease associated with crowding and lack of hygiene. These threats can easily spread beyond a single neighborhood or district to endanger all citizens and taint a city's reputation. In addition, health inequities are a powerful social accountant. They are a reliable way to measure how well a city is meeting the needs of its residents. Poor health, including mental health, is one of the most visible and measurable expressions of urban harm. Health inequities can also be a rallying point for public demands for change that compel political leaders to take action (WHO 2010; Montgomery 2008).

Regardless of the evidence, only a few countries and cities have examined their intercity or intracity health inequalities, and even fewer do so regularly. Information that shows the gaps between cities or within the same city is crucial to triggering appropriate local actions to promote health equity. Furthermore, the evidence should be comprehensive enough to provide hints on key health determinants and, at the same time, concise enough to facilitate policy-making and prioritization of interventions. How such evidence is collected and then analyzed and communicated to policy-makers and the public is vital to proper action on inequalities. In this chapter, we present an alternative to do so, and illustrate it using an example from the city of Ulaanbaatar, Mongolia.

Table 10.1 Selected list of tools available for addressing urban health

No.	Tool	Responsible agency	Year	Key target audience
1	Big Cities Health Inventory (BCHI)	US National Association of County and City Officials (NACCHO)	1997	Media, policy-makers, public
2	Equity Gauge	Global Equity Gauge Alliance (GEGA)	1999	Decision-makers, civil society, disadvantaged groups
3	Euro Urban Health Information System (URHIS)	University of Manchester, UK	2005	Policy-makers
4	Health Inequities Intervention Tool	London Health Observatory, UK	2007	Primary care trusts, policy-makers, health practitioners
5	Urban Audit	European Union	1997	Policy-makers
6	Urban HEART (Health Equity Assessment and Response Tool)	World Health Organization (WHO)	2008	Mayors, local and national governments, communities
7	Urban Info	UN-HABITAT	2003	Policy-makers

Tools to Assist Policy-Makers Reduce Urban Health Inequity

Although urban health is evidently influenced by a dynamic interaction between global, national, and subnational policies, city governments can play an important role in increasing their citizens' quality of life (Goldstein 2000; Marmot et al. 2008; Baum et al. 2010; Borrell and Artazcoc 2008). Therefore, it is important that local governments and communities are adequately informed about the inequities in their cities and their main determinants, in order to facilitate effective interventions. Useful options for such a challenge are evidence-based tools to identify these health inequities systematically and link them with proper interventions.

Government, nongovernment, and international organizations have all made efforts with regard to assisting local policy-makers tackle health and health equity. Some key initiatives, identified through a review of peer-reviewed and gray literature, are presented in Table 10.1. These tools are primarily focused on guiding local policy-makers through a set of indicators to assess the health and/or health equity situation. The exceptions are the Equity Gauge and Urban HEART, which also provide guidance on the process to identify the most appropriate interventions to promote health equity. All seven tools are focused on informing policy-makers with three tools stating an interest in reaching out to the community, civil society, or the public. Only one tool specified the media as a target audience; three have a European focus; one is specific to the USA, and three have a global focus.

Each tool is designed to achieve its own objectives. While a detailed description of each tool is beyond the scope of this chapter, a brief introduction is provided here:

1. *Big Cities Health Inventory* (BCHI) provides city-to-city comparisons of leading measures of health, presenting a broad overview of the health of the 54 largest metropolitan areas in the USA. It attempts to increase knowledge of the issues faced by large cities and stimulate dialogue leading to healthier city populations (Big cities health inventory, http://www.naccho.org/; Benbow et al. 1998).

2. *Equity Gauge* is a health development project that uses an active approach to monitoring and addressing inequity in health and health care (Brockerhoff 2000). It moves from monitoring of equity indicators to a set of concrete actions designed to effect real and sustained change in reducing health inequity (GEGA 2003; McCoy et al. 2003; Scott et al. 2008; Barten et al. 2007a).

3. *Euro Urban Health Information System* (URHIS) The European Union Public Health Programme work plan 2005 identified the development of an urban health indicator system as an essential part of a comprehensive and integrated EU health information and knowledge system (Tugwell 2006; URHIS, http://www.urhis.eu/).

4. *Health Inequalities Intervention Tool* was developed by the London Health Observatory (LHO) as an integral part of a network of 12 public health observatories across the United Kingdom and Ireland (London Health Observatory, http://www.lho.org.uk/). It is primarily designed to support Primary Care Trusts with their local delivery planning and commissioning.

5. *Urban Audit* provides European statistics for 357 cities across 27 European countries (Urban Audit, http://www.urbanaudit.org/index.aspx). It contains more than 250 statistical indicators presenting information on matters such as demography, society, economy, environment, transport, the information society, and leisure.

6. *Urban Health Equity Assessment and Response Tool (Urban HEART)* is a user-friendly guide for policy-makers at local and national levels to address health inequities in cities (Urban HEART, http://www.who.or.jp/urbanheart/index.html). It combines guidance on the collection of indicators, presentation of data to policy-makers, and identification of best practices for taking action on health inequities.

7. *Urban Info* has been developed as an initiative of the Global Urban Observatory (GUO) of UN-HABITAT (Urban Info, http://www.devinfo.info/urbaninfo/). GUO supports a number of country and city projects designed to strengthen local and national capacity for monitoring urban development and local government performance.

A Global Strategy to Tackle Health Inequities

The work of the World Health Organization (WHO) Commission on Social Determinants of Health (CSDH) has contributed to increasing global awareness for health equity (WHO 2008a; Sheiham 2009; Barten et al. 2007). In its final report, the Commission points out that addressing these huge and remediable differences in health between and within countries is a matter of social justice, and an ethical imperative. It proposes three principles of action to do so:

1. *Improve daily living conditions* by improving the circumstances in which children are born, putting major emphasis on early childhood development and education, improving living and working conditions and creating social protection policy supportive of all.
2. *Tackle inequitable distribution of power, money, and resources*, which requires strengthened governance including legitimacy, space, and support for civil society, an accountable private sector, and for people across society to agree on the public interest and reinvest in the value of collective action.
3. *Measure and understand the problem and assess the impact of action,* requiring that local, national, and international agencies set up health equity surveillance systems for routine monitoring of health inequity and the social determinants of health, and evaluate the health equity impact of policy and action.

Notably, the Commission recognized the importance of the urban setting as a determinant of health. One of the nine Knowledge Networks of the Commission was dedicated to the issue—the Knowledge Network on Urban Settings (KNUS) (WHO 2008b). Based on evidence and information synthesized by experts worldwide, KNUS and the CSDH laid out principles for addressing urban health inequities. These include:

- Establishing local participatory governance mechanisms that enable communities and local government to partner in building healthier and safer cities;
- Managing urban development including greater availability of affordable quality housing, water and sanitation, electricity, paved streets, etc.;
- Designing urban areas to promote physical activity, encourage healthy eating, reduce violence and crime, etc.;
- Considering the health equity impact of agriculture, industry, transport, fuel, and buildings;
- Strengthening public sector leadership by national governments in collaboration with multilateral agencies in the provision of health services and goods.

Further, the Commission recognizes that values alone are insufficient. Evidence is required on what is likely to work in practice to improve health and reduce health inequities. Evidence should be collected not only on the immediate causes of disease but also on the "causes of the causes." Those causes are defined as the fundamental national and global structures of social hierarchy and the socially determined conditions these create in which people grow, live, work, and age. In this respect, the Commission calls on multilateral agencies including the World Health Organization to:

- Use a common global framework of indicators to monitor development progress;
- Adopt a stewardship role including strengthening the technical capacity of Member States and developing mechanisms for intersectoral action for health;
- Monitor progress on health equity; support the establishment of global and national health equity surveillance systems; convene global meetings.

From a review of 121 case studies, KNUS developed a framework of indicators for assessing urban health inequities and responses. In addition to health outcomes, which include summary health measures, communicable and noncommunicable diseases, mental health, and violence and injuries, the framework includes four policy domains:

1. *Physical environment and infrastructure*: relates to environmental and physical hazards associated with *living conditions*, such as access to safe water and sanitation services, and exposure to indoor air pollution; as well as environmental conditions in the *neighborhood, community, and workplace*, such as exposure to road traffic and job-related hazards.
2. *Social and human development*: includes determinants and interactions that influence aspects of human development and issues of social exclusion, such as barriers to access education and health services, nutrition and food security, and other social services. Also included are the obstacles to better health-seeking behavior and improved personal lifestyle and health practices associated with low health literacy.
3. *Economics*: includes various measures of economic status and barriers to economic opportunities faced by the population in general or by specific population groups. This domain includes indicators measuring lack of access to credit and capital, poor job opportunities, low potential for generating income, and other stumbling blocks to moving out of poverty.
4. *Governance*: includes aspects related to people's rights and political exclusion such as those associated with the legal status of the urban poor, property and ownership rights, participation in decision-making processes, and priorities in the allocation of resources to improve health and its determinants.

A Tool to Tackle to Urban Health Inequities: Urban HEART

The Urban Health Equity Assessment and Response Tool (Urban HEART) aids decision-making to address health inequities in cities. It is based on the principles elicited by the WHO Commission on Social Determinants of Health, and World Health Report 2008 on Primary Health Care. The tool was developed by international experts in collaboration with city officials and communities from ten countries—Brazil, Islamic Republic of Iran, Indonesia, Kenya, Malaysia, Mexico, Mongolia, the Philippines, Sri Lanka and Vietnam—where the tool was piloted.

Urban HEART is a user-friendly guide for policy-makers at local and national levels to address health inequities in cities (Urban HEART http://www.who.or.jp/urbanheart/index.html). It consists of two key components:

• *Assessment*: this section analyses (A) health outcomes, and (B) health determinants. Health determinants are grouped into four policy domains:

a. Physical environment and infrastructure;
b. Social and human development;
c. Economics;
d. Governance.

* *Response*: this section identifies interventions and strategies for action from a list of best practice interventions. While interventions would be modified to address the specifics of the local context, the tool provides the basis to prioritize appropriate interventions.

The target audience includes:

* Mayors and local governments;
* Central government ministries including health, education, transport, etc.;
* Community groups and civil society organizations, e.g., Healthy Cities.

Further, given that health and health equity problems should often be tackled by the health sector working in coordination with other sectors, Urban HEART relies strongly on a multisectoral approach. Empowering the community to use evidence to advocate for key health and health equity issues, and engaging them productively in selecting interventions is central to the application of the tool.

Example: Applying Urban HEART in Ulaanbaatar

Ulaanbaatar, Mongolia, was selected as one of the sites for testing the feasibility of applying Urban HEART to systematically address urban health inequities. The overall level of urbanization in Mongolia is around 57 %. Ulaanbaatar is a city of 1.1 million people, and is the political, economic, and cultural center of Mongolia. Its population growth rate is 2.5 % per annum, near the East Asian norm, but has previously been much higher. In contrast, the annual population growth rate of provincial towns, known as aimag centers, is negative (− 1.6 %).

Approximately 70 % of recent population growth in Ulaanbaatar has been the result of immigration. Essentially, urban population growth exceeds that of employment. Average incomes are not higher in Ulaanbaatar than for the country as a whole, an unusual situation, which is probably a product of the imbalance between population growth and employment creation.

Summary of the Process

For the purpose of applying Urban HEART in Ulaanbaatar, the tool was translated into Mongolian and validated during the meetings of a technical working group to carry out health equity assessment and develop response strategy. The technical working group for Urban HEART was established by City Governor's resolution

201 of 2009 The technical working group consisted of representatives from institutions including the Ministry of Health, WHO Country office in Mongolia, Ulaanbaatar City Governor's office, City Department of Health office, City Statistical Office, City Labor Office, City Social Care office. Specific terms of reference were developed for the participation of various stakeholders in the process (Urban HEART Team 2009).

The objectives of applying Urban HEART are:

- To identify health equity issues among the population of Ulaanbaatar city
- To develop interventions based on the assessment findings

Based on Urban HEART, the following domains were included in the assessment:

- Physical environment and infrastructure
- Social and human development
- Economics
- Governance

The data, as of 2008, were collected from nine districts of Ulaanbaatar city. The indicators in the assessment tool were adjusted to a country context, and a total of 42 indicators were used for the assessment. Data collection and analysis took place from June to August which was followed by identification of response strategy and interventions between the period of September to October, 2009.

In Fig. 10.2, we can see the performance of the nine districts of Ulaanbaatar (columns) across 12 selected indicators for illustration (of the 42 collected). Three colors were used to denote the relative performance of a district for a particular indicator. The color coding for the performance of districts used here to illustrate the Ulaanbaatar exercise is:

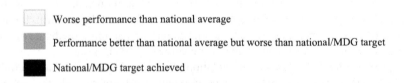

Worse performance than national average

Performance better than national average but worse than national/MDG target

National/MDG target achieved

The results of Urban HEART highlighted key priority areas to address in the city including improved access to health services, safe drinking water, and greater employment opportunities for residents of the city, among other issues (Fig. 10.2). For example, for the "employment contribution rate" (employment rate) indicator under the economics domain, six of the nine districts have a worse performance than the national average, while only two districts are performing better than an intended target.

From the exercise, it was also clear that the city as a whole was performing well on providing a variety of health and education services to the population. For example, access to skilled birth attendance had reached the intended target in all the nine districts.

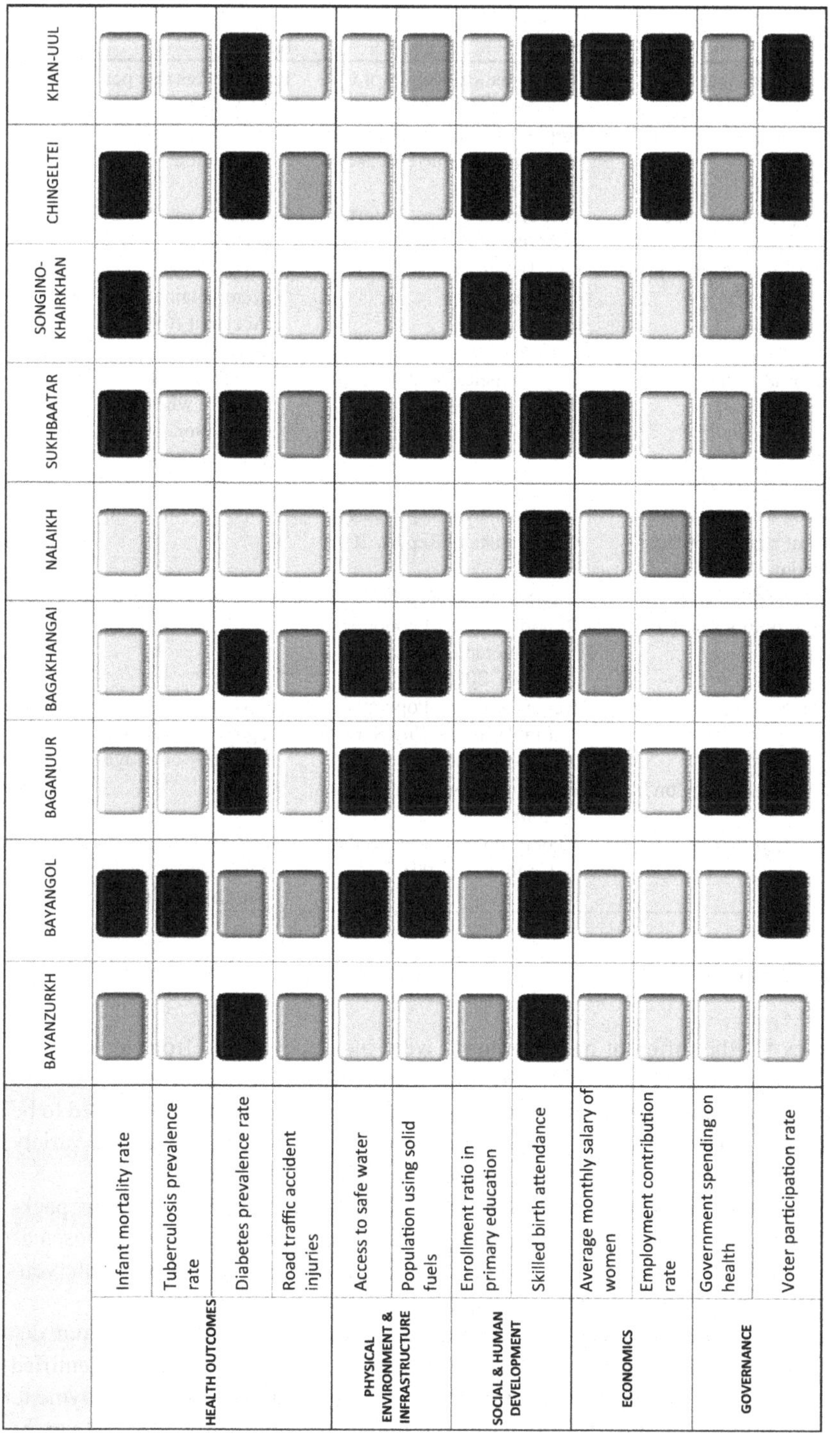

Fig. 10.2 Urban health equity matrix for Ulaanbaatar, selected indicators, 2008

Table 10.2 Notes on indicators in Fig. 10.2 (Urban Health Equity Matrix)

Indicator	Source	Notes
Infant mortality rate	The Statistical Report of City Health, 2008	Expressed as rate per 1,000 live births
Tuberculosis prevalence rate	Report of National Centre for Communicable Diseases, 2008	Expressed as rate per 10,000 population
Diabetes prevalence rate	City Health Office Report, 2008	Expressed as rate per 10,000 population
Road traffic accident injuries	City Health Office Report, 2008	Road traffic injury statistics were obtained from the Accident Abnormality National Research Center
Access to safe water	City Statistical Report, 2008	This indicator takes into account whether or not the population is constantly supplied by a safe water source
Population using solid fuels	City Statistical Report, 2008	
Enrolment ratio in primary education	City Statistical Report, 2008	
Skilled birth attendance	City Statistical Report, 2008	
Average monthly salary of women	Report of City's Economic Character, City Statistics Office, 2008	
Employment rate	Report of City's Population Employment, City Statistics Office, 2008	Refers to the ratio of working age population who are gainfully employed
Government spending on health	Financial Report of districts, 2008	
Voter participation rate	Report of City's Election Committee, 2008	The voter participation rate with respect to elections to the Great Hural (Parliament)

Data Sources

Statistics for the different neighborhoods were mostly available from local or national publications (Table 10.2). However, as evident from the sources of data in Table 10.2, a number of different government departments or agencies needed to be contacted for data sharing. This is one practical reason for engaging a wide variety of stakeholders from the beginning of the Urban HEART exercise.

With the use of selection criteria in Urban HEART, one of the five strategy packages, "Incorporate health more in urban planning and development" was chosen as a response strategy for addressing health equity in Ulaanbaatar. Priority interventions were also identified under response strategy package A.

Interventions were selected so as to address inequities in each of the four domains described in Urban HEART. Furthermore, targets for 2010 were identified by the Urban HEART team. For example, to tackle the issue of low employment, the team proposed to provide professional training and jobs to at least 6,500 youths from low-income households by the end of 2010. The identified interventions were

Table 10.3 Priority measures reflected in the social and economic development direction, 2010, for Ulaanbaatar (approved by the Civil Representatives Hural (Parliament) on 23 December 2009, based on Urban HEART results)

No.	Intervention	2010 target	Financial source	Responsible institution
1	The water supply system in 4 ger districts will be operationalized and not less than 1,000 households and offices will be connected into centralized networking	210,000 residents in ger districts will be provided with drinking water from a centralized water supply system and an ability to connect drinking water pipes into their gers on their own expense	The World Bank	"Improving Public Utilities" Project
2	Promote entities that produce and sell processed fuel or energy with environmentally friendly technologies	Project proposal will be developed in cooperation with JICA and other international organizations	City Budget 2010, JICA	City Air Quality Department
3	Effective service of medical aid for remote Districts and Khoroos (subdistricts) will be delivered linking with emergency medical care and inquiry system	A new station of Emergency Medical Care Center in Bayanzurkh District will be established	State Budget, 2010	City Health Department
4	Medical aid and care conditions for vulnerable and high-risk groups to be further planned and organized	Improve quality and range of medical care services for vulnerable and high-risk groups, including for patients with tuberculosis in District hospitals	State Budget, 2010	City Health Department
5	Operationalize the "General Plan of Land Management of the Capital City"	Provide 4,000 households in a new residential zone with safe living conditions	City Budget, 2010	City Land Department
6	Professional training and employment to be provided to at least 6,500 youths (16–35 years) from lower-income households	At least 6,525 youths from lower income households to be provided training for developing professional skills	State Budget 2010	City Labour Department
7	Distribute food coupons to identified vulnerable populations	Will distribute coupon for purchasing food worth 15,000 tugriks to 80,000 low-income citizens every month	State Budget 2010	City Social Security Service Department

then approved by a session of the Great Hural (Parliament) on December 23, 2009, and included in the Ulaanbaatar Social and Economic Development Direction 2010. The list of interventions approved for further action based on the Urban HEART results for 42 indicators in Ulaanbaatar are shown in Table 10.3.

This is, therefore, one example of how local governments and nongovernment institutions can collaboratively apply a tool to collect relevant evidence and develop appropriate interventions and targets to resolve health inequities in their cities. Engaging a wide group of stakeholders and strategically communicating the results to policy-makers proved key in obtaining the support for further action.

Conclusions: Key Elements for Strategic Communication to Tackle Health Inequities in Urban Settings

Strategic communication of health inequities is vital to triggering sustainable action to tackle them. The process of translating evidence into action requires, first of all, effective communication to policy-makers and communities of both the inequities and their determinants. Tools with this objective can thus be very helpful if they contain elements that can effectively communicate the complex problems of urban areas to policy-makers and communities, as seen in Ulaanbaatar.

Strategic communication in urban health must clearly link the problem with the intervention. Health inequalities should be presented in such way that the existing differences between different categories of the population are highlighted, making such differences traceable to their social determinants. Communication must be context specific, with technically and politically feasible solutions that can be subsequently related to the identified inequalities. The communication is only strategic if the framing and understanding of the problems can be linked, or followed, by feasible interventions. This is the crucial element of Urban HEART in comparison with the other approaches studied. A more detailed analysis of those elements follows, including a final reference to the importance of the policy commitment for this approach to strategic communication.

First, to portray differences in health and living conditions among different groups of the population, the selection of the *unit of analysis* is a key factor, whether it is geographical (such as neighborhood) or a population category (such as gender or social class). The process of strategic communication should stress the use of data disaggregated by socioeconomic group within a city, as well as by different geographical areas or neighborhoods. Comparisons between small areas are useful to understand the inequalities and their determinants, although sometimes existing administrative divisions do not correspond to real living conditions and can mask inequalities.

Indeed, the selection of the variables to be analyzed involves several challenges for effective and sustainable strategic communication. Available existing information systems often do not have the required information disaggregated by neighborhood or the desired unit of analysis, making it necessary to use proxy variables or even to carry out surveys to collect the needed information. However, the sustainability of interventions often depends on using existing information systems as much as possible. It can become a dilemma between effective communication at a single time and sustainable, but imprecise, data. The experience with Urban

HEART seems to favor the option of using—improving and adapting where possible—existing sources of information as the most strategic alternative.

The use of a previously agreed value could be useful to portray existing differences; Urban HEART shows how the different units of analysis behave in relation to the agreed standard and organizes them into three groups. The standard can be the mean of the total area under scrutiny, or a national or regional average; the use of goals such as the MDGs or national goals has also proven useful. In the example from Ulaanbaatar, officials were able to use national and international goals where appropriate to benchmark performance on various indicators.

Having a simple and consolidated way to communicate differences does facilitate understanding of existing health inequalities and the urgency for action. One of the strengths of Urban HEART is a summary chart that shows the differences for all the analyzed variables simultaneously using a simple three-color classification (see a monochromatic version in Fig. 10.2).

Second, strategic communication requires a recognition that *social structures in urban areas are the main determinant of health inequity*. The final report of the CSDH clearly states this, revisiting a time-honored finding of public health (WHO 2008a). Moreover, overwhelming evidence suggests that health services alone are insufficient to improve health (Broyles et al. 2000; Annett 2009; Choy and Duke 2000; Webb et al. 2001). Hence, communication of health inequalities to policymakers must adopt a framework that recognizes the crucial role of the social determinants, and takes into account the risk factors and interactions of multiple sectors in the urban environment as they impact on communicable and noncommunicable diseases as well as violence and injuries. Several of the tools analyzed, accomplish this objective by complementing the description of the differences in health outcomes with analysis of social, economical, and political variables that can explain, or suggest, their structural determinants.

Once again, the selection and availability of information is a challenge that needs to be overcome based on the context. For instance, a political indicator such as voter participation rate can be very useful to explain health differences, but not in all contexts. Nevertheless, omitting the governance dimension can jeopardize deeper understanding of the roots of health inequalities and blur the process of selecting the proper intervention.

Third, the evidence collected should be linked clearly to actionable interventions and policies. The use of data disaggregated by socioeconomic group, by geographical area or neighborhood, inclusion of information on social determinants, and easily understandable presentations facilitates the development of guidance on multisectoral action and community participation as key strategies. In addition, guidance on the process of moving from the assessment of the health inequalities to the selection of interventions and policies could be a useful path for effective strategic communication, although prescriptive, one-size-fits-all approaches should be avoided.

Urban HEART uses a two-pronged strategy, presenting the policy cycle as an orientation on how to transit from the assessment to the response, and providing a set of evidence-based interventions organized into five different strategies: (1) incorporate health in urban planning and development; (2) emphasize and strengthen the role of urban primary health care; (3) strengthen the health equity focus in urban settings; (4) put health equity higher on the agenda of local governments; (5) pursue a national agenda. By providing sources and examples of interventions, it also facilitates the selection of proper actions and, therefore, real strategic communication. For instance, WHO has prepared a compilation of evidence that support interventions to address healthy nutrition and promote physical activity (Ni Mhurchu et al. 2010; Spahn et al. 2010; Michie et al. 2009), which are included in Urban HEART.

Fourth, tools to assess health equity in urban settings could be an effective aide to strategic communication, as long as the tool follows the characteristics explained. In addition to that, such tools should be simple and user-friendly. A wide variety of stakeholders including local and national government officials, civil society and other independent agencies should be able to apply it for decision-making and impact assessment purposes. Moreover, implementation should be operationally feasible and sustainable. This is facilitated, for instance, when the evidence can be gathered from routinely available data within existing institutional mechanisms.

Finally, for strategic communication to effectively contribute to tackling health inequity, an instrument needs to promote sustainability of action and therefore to go beyond providing a set of principles and recommendations. Therefore, *political commitment* is required as a crucial ingredient of successfully addressing health inequities rooted in unfair distribution of resources among populations. For instance, one city that piloted Urban HEART has made the application of the tool compulsory by ordinance. This expresses the political commitment of a city to establishing a permanent mechanism to disentangle and respond to its health inequities.

References

Annett, H. (2009). Leadership in public health: A view from a large English PCT co-terminous with a local authority. *Journal of Public Health (Oxf)*, *31*, 205–207.

Barten, F., Mitlin, D., Mulholland, C., et al. (2007, May). Integrated approaches to address the social determinants of health for reducing health inequity. *Journal of Urban Health*, *84*(Suppl 1), i164–173.

Baum, F., Newman, L., Biedrzycki, K., & Patterson, J. (2010, Jun). Can a regional government's social inclusion initiative contribute to the quest for health equity? *Health Promotion International*.

Benbow, N., Wang, Y., & Whitman, S. (1998, Dec). The big cities health inventory, 1997. *Journal of Community Health*, *23*(6), 471–489.

Bitran, R., Giedion, U., Valenzuela, R., & Monkkonen, P. (2005). Keeping health in an urban environment: Public health challenges for the urban poor. In M. Fay (Ed.), *The urban poor in Latin America* (pp. 179–195). Washington DC: The World Bank.

Borrell, C., & Artazcoz, L. (2008). Policies to reduce health inequalities. *Gaceta Sanitaria*, *22*, 465–473.

Brockerhoff, M. (2000). An urbanizing world. *Population Bulletin*, *55*(3), 3–4. (Source: UNDESA. *World Urbanization Prospects: The 1999 Revision*. United Nations, New York, 2001.)

Broyles, R. W., Narine, L., Brandt, E. N., Jr., & Biard-Holmes D. (2000). Health risks, ability to pay, and the use of primary care: Is the distribution of service effective and equitable? *Preventive Medicine, 30*, 453–462.

Choy, R., & Duke, T. (2000). The role of non-government organizations in supporting and integrating interventions to improve child health. *Papua New Guinea Medical Journal, 43*, 76–81.

Fotso, J. C. (2007). Urban-rural differentials in child malnutrition: Trends and socioeconomic correlates in Sub-Saharan Africa. *Health and Place, 13*, 205–223.

GEGA (2003). The Equity Gauge, concepts, principles and guidelines, 2003. http://www.gega.org.za/. Accessed Oct. 19, 2013.

Goldstein, G. (2000). Healthy cities: Overview of a WHO international program. *Reviews on Environment Health, 15*, 207–214.

Hanlon, P., Walsh, D., & Whyte B. (2006). *Let Glasgow flourish.* Glasgow: Glasgow centre for population health.

Marmot, M., Friel, S., Bell, R., Houweling, T. A., & Taylor S. (2008). Closing the gap in a generation: Health equity through action on the social determinants of health. *The Lancet, 372*, 1661–1669.

McCoy, D., Bambas, L., Acurio, D., et al. (2003, Sep). Global equity gauge alliance: Reflections on early experiences. *Journal of Health Population Nutrition, 21*(3), 273–287.

Michie, S., Abraham, C., Whittington, C., McAteer, J., & Gupta, S. (2009). Effective techniques in healthy eating and physical activity interventions: A meta-regression. *Health Psychology, 28*, 690–701.

Montgomery, M. R. (2008). The urban transformation of the developing world. *Science, 319*(5864), 761–764.

Ni Mhurchu, C., Aston, L. M., Jebb, S. A. (2010). Effects of worksite health promotion interventions on employee diets: A systematic review. *BMC Public Health, 10*, 62.

Scott, V., Stern, R., Sanders, D., et al. (2008). Research to action to address inequities: The experience of the Cape Town equity gauge. *International Journal for Equity in Health, 7*, 6.

Sheiham, A. (2009). Closing the gap in a generation: Health equity through action on the social determinants of health. A report of the WHO Commission on Social Determinants of Health (CSDH) 2008. *Community Dental Health, 26*, 2–3.

Smith, L. C., Ruel, M. T., & Ndiaye, A. (2005). Why is child malnutrition lower in urban than in rural areas? Evidence from 36 developing countries. *World Development, 33*(8), 1285–1305.

Spahn, J. M., Reeves, R. S., Keim K. S., et al. (2010). State of the evidence regarding behavior change theories and strategies in nutrition counseling to facilitate health and food behavior change. *Journal of the American Dietetic Association, 110*, 879–891.

Tugwell, P., O'Connor, A., Andersson, N., et al. (2006). Reduction of inequalities in health: Assessing evidence-based tools. *International Journal of Equity in Health, 5*, 11.

UNDESA (2011). United Nations, Department of Economic and Social Affairs, Population Division. World Urbanization Prospects: The 2011 Revision. United Nations, New York, http://esa.un.org/unup [last updated April 26, 2012]. Accessed Oct. 20, 2013.

UN-HABITAT (2010). *The state of the world's cities, 2010–2011.* Nairobi: UN–HABITAT.

Urban HEART Team (2009). Report of Ulaanbaatar Urban HEART Team. City of Ulaanbaatar & Ministry of Health, Mongolia 2009.

Webb, K., Hawe, P., & Noort, M. (2001). Collaborative intersectoral approaches to nutrition in a community on the urban fringe. *Health Education & Behaviour, 28*, 306–319.

WHO (1993). UN Expert Group Meeting on Population Distribution and Migration, UN Department of Economic and Social Affairs. *Health and Urbanization in Developing Countries.* World Health Organization, Santa Cruz, Bolivia, 1993.

WHO (2008a). *Closing the gap in a generation: Health equity through action on the social determinants of health.* Final Report of the Commission on Social Determinants of Health. Geneva, World Health Organization, 2008.

WHO (2008b). *Knowledge network on urban settings. Our cities, our health, our future: Acting on social determinants of health equity in urban settings.* Report to the WHO Commission on Social Determinants of Health. Geneva, World Health Organization, 2008.

WHO (2010). *Why urban health matters.* World Health Day 2010 Technical Paper. World Health Organization 2010, Geneva, Switzerland.

Chapter 11
Beyond Thinking and Planning Strategically to Improve Urban Residents' Health

Cornelius B. Pratt

> *Cities are growing larger and larger, and their populations of the poor are growing larger even faster. The consequences for health are immense.*
>
> -Margaret Chan (2010, p. 18),
> *Director-General of the World Health Organization*

> *[Sub-Saharan Africa] is the only region in the world where the absolute number and proportion of undernourished children have increased in the last decade.*
>
> -Chopra and Darnton-Hill (2006, p. 544)

In a speech celebrating "World Health Day 2010: Urban Health Matters," Margaret Chan, director-general of the World Health Organization, noted the hazards of environmental degradation, of unhealthful lifestyles, and of congested urban communities. For one thing, they exacerbate urban poverty and malnutrition (e.g., Chopra and Darnton-Hill 2006; Haddad et al. 1999). For another, they place additional responsibilities on health specialists and nongovernmental organizations, which must now double their efforts, largely because of dwindling international donor support in a global economy with a tepid outlook, to stay abreast of a public-health challenge with expanding and deepening social consequences. The minuscule resources and the inadequate urban planning to address burgeoning urban residents' health challenges result in urban challenges that are as multifactorial as their solutions are myriad. Chan (2010) observed that "urban growth has outpaced the ability of governments to build essential infrastructures and enact and enforce the legislation needed to make life in cities safe, rewarding, and healthy" (p. 6). And Fotso (2006)

C. B. Pratt (✉)
Temple University, Philadelphia, USA
e-mail: cbpratt@temple.edu

Temple University, Japan Campus,
Tokyo, Japan

C. C. Okigbo (ed.), *Strategic Urban Health Communication,*
DOI 10.1007/978-1-4614-9335-8_11, © Springer Science+Business Media New York 2014

found that, regardless of the urban–rural divide, African children from the poorest households have a significantly higher risk for malnutrition than their counterparts in privileged households; however, because socioeconomic inequalities are higher in cities than in rural areas, child malnutrition tends to be significantly higher in urban areas. Such outcomes further threaten the accomplishment of Millennium Development Goals-related projects, such as reducing child mortality, hunger and malnutrition and increasing primary education enrollment (United Nations 2008). Therefore, partnerships between organizations such as the World Food Program and the Millennium Villages project can be used to end hunger and malnutrition across Africa, particularly in its urban communities.

From a health-communication standpoint, however, this chapter argues that while strategic action underpins most health-communication campaigns in under-served urban communities, even as they espouse participatory communication and community empowerment, such action, at bottom, contradicts the collective norms and values of such communities, which tend to be enamored with public health campaigns that empower them to respond to their health challenges. Paradoxically, such action undermines the very notion of community empowerment as currently indicated in development programs.

A strategy for accomplishing Africa's social and economic development is to ensure community empowerment. The clamor for empowerment among Africans in general is rooted in their penchant for consensus as "crucial in decision making. In African terms, reaching a decision through consensus has the advantage of taking into account all reasons for concern or disagreement. This custom of consultation, even though there is a great degree of hierarchy, is a key African value… " (Amoako-Agyei 2009, p. 336).

Based on the preceding background, then, the purpose of this chapter is threefold. First, it presents an overview of the dominant health-communication theories commonly used in health delivery in sub-Saharan Africa, noting that, while they encourage public participation, they still fall short of engendering a much-needed symmetry, which encourages negotiation that influences the care patients receive and the decision-making processes between the public (as recipients of health services) and organizations (as health-care providers). Second, it discusses an alternative to the dominant theoretical approaches to health delivery in sub-Saharan Africa, thereby providing a field guide to applying that alternative theoretical framework as a complement to extant health practices. Third, it presents four propositions that have heuristic significance to theory expansion for establishing a research agenda on and for improving health-delivery services in Africa's urban communities, particularly those in which child malnutrition tends to be exacerbated by the spotty availability of clinical facilities. In accomplishing the foregoing purposes, then, this chapter expands our conversation on the intersection between health-communication theories and emerging perspectives on communicative action for effective delivery of health services in urban areas, particularly those in sub-Saharan Africa, where endogenous cultural practices determine for the most part health-communication effectiveness.

Dominant Health-Communication Theories

Field practices indicate that the development and implementation of a variety of health programs in sub-Saharan Africa have been informed by a coalescence of five theories: health belief model (HBM), community mobilization model (CMM), participatory models, social cognitive theory, and diffusion theory. The health belief model focuses on the individual as a unit of analysis. Issues raised in this form of investigation are on individuals' perceptions of their susceptibility to a health issue and on how efficacious they think they are in responding effectively to such challenges.

In the African context, individualism is so de-emphasized that it is unavailing. It is the community, that is, the collectivity, that counts, hence the African expression *ubuntu* (Amoako-Agyei 2009), which means group significance, collective good, and community effort are the primary foci of society's interest. CMM moves the focus of health campaigns beyond the individual, viewing campaigns as a "social-action process in which individuals and groups act to gain mastery over their lives in the context of changing their social and political environment" (Wallerstein and Bernstein 1994, p. 142). Through CMM "community groups are helped to identify common problems, mobilize resources, and develop and implement strategies to reach collective goals" (U.S. Department of Health and Human Services 2005, p. 23).

The participatory model stresses the importance of (a) participating at all levels (international, national, local, and individual); (b) collaborating throughout all levels of participation; and (c) listening to what others say, respecting counterparts' attitudes, and having mutual trust (Servaes et al. 1996; Servaes 2004).

The social cognitive theory posits that health-behavior change is contingent on three major factors: self-efficacy, program goals, and outcome expectations.

And diffusion theory recognizes five stages of the innovation-decision process that can lead to either adopting or rejecting an innovation (Rogers 1995).

All the preceding theories have one key commonality: a focus on the individual or the community whose interests are the drivers (or enabling forces) in health campaigns. Empowerment, for example, occurs at two levels: at the individual level (à la HBM), by which patients develop their health-related competencies, such as knowledge of resources; and at the community level (à la CMM), by which additional networks, resources, and opportunities are developed. Confidence in an individual's or in a group's ability to take action and exude confidence in such action is contingent on reciprocal determinism where there is a bidirectional change resulting from interaction between people or communities and their environments. But such action is better enabled in interactions grounded more in symmetry than in asymmetry.

Because communication between health-care providers and patients is largely structured and asymmetrical (e.g., Brown et al. 2003), it calls into question the true value of the continuing application of the tenets of health-communication theories to health campaigns. This chapter holds that much still needs to be done to enhance the outcomes of provider–patient interactions, or, in the case of child malnutrition, the interaction between the health agency and urban parents of, or caregivers to, malnourished children or children at risk for malnutrition. One approach that has been offered in urban South Africa is negotiation through communication, by which patients bargained for much-needed care while being active players in the health-care system and maintaining their dignity and self-worth (Schneider et al. 2010).

A Theoretical Complement to Dominant Theoretical Perspectives

This chapter draws upon key components of the theory of communicative action (Habermas 1984, 1987) as a complement to the application of dominant theories of health communication on the ground. That perspective is grounded in symmetrical, egalitarian—not hierarchical—relationships between health-care providers and their patients. Such relationships will be accomplished through responsibility-sharing—that is, reasoned dialogue and negotiation, both of which are critical to patient care. Habermas's (1984, 1987) theory of communicative action (TCA), which has been applied to health-care settings (e.g., Brown 2008) will emphasize patient or patient's caregiver participation, dialogue, consensus, cooperation, and negotiation, all geared toward understandings that are rationally negotiated by all parties in the care of the patient. Such outcomes are outside the bailiwick of those current practices that are grounded in extant health-communication theories.

One of the health scourges in Africa's urban communities is malnutrition. In some African countries, such as Kenya, higher urban than rural child mortality results from, among other things, extreme poverty, low nutritional status, and family disintegration (Garenne 2010).

The application of a Habermasian analysis to reducing child malnutrition is one in which parents or caregivers engage in reasoning, "not merely for reasoning in general, but for reasons in a form of argumentation" (Habermas 1984, p. 249) geared toward facilitating their cooperative, rationalistic efforts and shared understanding of the menacing outcome of such malnutrition and the importance of its prevention. Its key feature, therefore, is that it engages participants in "the argumentative redemption of validity claims" (Habermas) in every stage of the process, including the argumentative rationalization of the very essence of a child-malnutrition-reduction program. It enables health-care providers to conduct specifically effective, tailored interventions that resonate with specific audiences (that is, the urban poor at risk for child malnutrition). It would aim to engage the lifeworld of patient populations—that is, moving beyond the medical realm per se and integrating parents' or caregivers' taken-for-granted convictions into a negotiation process for preventing child malnutrition. The rationale for this theoretical proposal is borne out by the characteristics of TCA (e.g., emphasis on the pragmatics of language, a linguistic expression) as a medium for transmitting culture and building consensus on criticizable validity claims) and by its relevance to the sensitivity of health management in an urban environment.

Current health campaigns, hewn to theoretical guidelines, are essentially strategic actions. The argument here is that the antithetical properties of strategic action justify the significance of communicative action as a complement to the dominant health-communication theories that provide much of the framework for Africa's health campaigns. This implies that health-care providers are at liberty to engage in practices that are contingent on either of those two forms of actions. Nutrition field agents can act either strategically or communicatively. Strategic action, which can be either open (read: symmetrical) or concealed, focuses on, say, program effectiveness. Concealed strategic action has two forms. The first is unconscious deception, by which communication is systematically distorted; and conscious deception, which is full-scale manipulation. The second is communicative action, framed by mutual understanding and acceptability of public accountability and commitments. It is action oriented toward reaching an understanding and a consensus, both possible outcomes consistent with African discursive norms. This is the crux of this chapter, namely, that campaigns for urban health not only engage in symmetrical communication but also in one that fosters (a) expert patients who have better access to knowledge, make necessary changes in lifestyle and repeated visits to health services, and adhere to drug regimens; (b) creative agents as patients who operate within the constraints of the health-care environment; (c) informed, involved patients who have a positive effect and a noncontentious approach to communication; and (d) better opportunities for participation by patients in, and negotiation of, the health care they receive (Schneider et al. 2010).

It must be pointedly acknowledged here that "Habermas does not reject the instrumental conception of rationality and replace it with an alternative, 'communicative' conception.... his claim is simply that instrumental models do not provide a sufficient basis for a *general* theory of rational action" (Heath 2001, p. 13). Habermas (1984) writes: "A communicatively achieved agreement has a rational basis; it cannot be imposed by either party, whether instrumentally through intervention in the situation directly or strategically through influencing the decision of opponents" (p. 287).

Consequently, Habermas describes a symmetry condition in which there is unconstrained dialogue to which all speakers have access, and in which they have the prevailing force of better judgment. It is devoid of domination or sheer influence and bereft of all coercive distortion. Ideal speech is defined in relation to a number of symmetry conditions which, if obtained, can be used to identify speech approximating ideal conditions: (a) there must be a symmetrical distribution of opportunities to contribute to discussions, i.e., all can speak; (b) there must be opportunities for participants to raise any and all subjects they wish to see addressed, i.e., nothing is "off the table"; and (c) there must be an inviting environment to discuss every topic fully and to the satisfaction of those who raised the topic (Habermas 1990). All of those conditions are consistent with argumentation, negotiation, and consensus that are fundamental to the cultural underpinning of decision making in

Africa. Health-care providers, therefore, seek through speech acts an orientation toward understanding, consensus and agreement, rather than toward fulfilling their own specific agendas or personal goals. Such a theoretical perspective emphasizes planning through widespread participation by the community, dialogue, consensus, cooperation, and negotiation, not necessarily through strategic action.

Habermas identifies as a speech act that which is being engaged by both senders and receivers of linguistic acts geared toward understandings that are rationally negotiated by all parties. But there are limits to such negotiations. While, say, parties to a speech act can understand the conditions under which a message recipient can understand, accept and endorse the speech act and be persuaded by its claims (e.g., "Keeping your child healthy by having a sanitary environment," or "Ensuring up-to-date vaccination records means having healthy children"), neither the recipient nor the sender can know the conditions of the acceptability of the speech act relative to the actual attitudes and beliefs of the individual other.

TCA has both strategic and communicative relevance to community or national development initiatives. As noted in a preceding paragraph, TCA has been applied to a variety of investigations in disparate disciplines such as community development, social movements, politics, education, theology, organizational processes, and the performing arts. Its key theoretical elements—e.g., ideal speech situation and the cultural tradition—can lead health-care providers to manage effectively childhood malnutrition and its consequences by encouraging parents and caregivers to (a) question or introduce any counterproposals (the ideal speech in symmetry conditions); (b) discuss malnutrition issues within the contexts of a community's life world (the cultural tradition); (c) ensure that message themes are subject to validity challenges ("scope for freedom"), even as communicative action is oriented toward reaching an understanding, yet not requiring an agreement, but welcoming an agreement to disagree; and (d) analyze cultural change and cultural plurality. If undertaken in proper settings, the likelihood of attitude and behavior change occasioned by effective campaigns (instrumental action) will be more likely. Because of the cultural sensitivity that childhood malnutrition issues particularly engender in sub-Saharan Africa, for example, it is important that field workers and interventionists apply Habermas's notion of the ideal speech situation to analyze at multiple scales the interactions between them and parents and caregivers, the targets of campaigns. Such communicative interactions are relevant to nutrition management for at least four reasons.

First, the participation inherent in communicative interactions can be an additional opportunity to increase the chances for the messages to be accepted politically by the government and socially by the community, even as it offers a forum to parents and their children to collaborate in the process of crafting campaign messages generally perceived as culturally and endogenously sensitive.

Second, the interactions can be used as a means to improve nutrition-management objectives, goals, and protocols through presuppositions of argumentation and negotiation, for which Africans have a growing penchant (e.g., Schneider et al. 2010; Scholtz et al. 2008).

Third, the interactions can provide opportunities for participants to ground communicative action within a lifeworld; that will help them reach a reasoned consensus centered in a local agency. Current practices tend to undermine such rationalization.

Fourth, the interactions are a basis for evaluating patient involvement; that will ensure that communicative action is inherently measurable and campaign outcomes scientifically determined. Did parents of malnourished children, for example, report that they had ample opportunities to raise issues in dialogues or negotiations? Such evaluations of communicative action can be combined with overall campaign evaluations to determine audience exposure to mass media plans (who were exposed to the campaigns and at what frequency and what do they now know?); and outcomes (did the communicative experience engender reason and persuasion, leading in the long run to the desired behavior change?).

Granted, certain realities in Africa, for example, the minuscule presence of liberal democracies, do not bode well for an application of TCA. Quite apart from the continent's massive economic struggles, it has been estimated that "In sub-Saharan Africa, the number of malnourished children is projected to grow from 33 million in 1997 to 49 million in 2020, representing 10 million more malnourished children than in the baseline" (Rosegrant and Meijer 2002, p. 3439S).

It bears noting here that a communicative model of action is not synonymous with mere speaking; it is not mere argumentation. And it is also important to note that conversations must be held in the dominant local language—the linguistic medium—enabled by participants' performative attitude and skills in "language mixing." That means code-switching and borrowing justified by the disparate languages and dialects over even small geographic areas and by the geographic mobility occasioned in an age of growing cosmopolitanism—even in Africa's rural areas. This calls for the participation of initiating actors versed in using different languages in the same conversation to coordinate action.

Illustrating Communicative Action—As a Field Guide

Urban health specialists will find the application of communicative action to their campaigns a welcome departure from the orthodoxy and constraints that tend to bedevil the application of dominant health-communication theories to the field. I now provide an illustration, under symmetry conditions, of an ideal speech situation between a provider (Speaker) and a parent (Hearer A) and caregivers (Hearers B and C):

1. *Speaker*, implying a validity claim to a propositional truth: *Our children's nutritional health is a major cause of their other debilitating conditions, including performance in school later in life.*

Hearer A: Yes, in my division, I see hordes and hordes of children who hardly look energetic to me.

Hearer B: No, it's not the children; it is the entire community's welfare that is at stake here. (Whenever a consensus cannot be reached, the alternative is to act strategically.)

Hearer C: Undecided (or abstain)—for the time being.

2. *Speaker*, implying a validity claim to a normative rightness: *Measures must be taken to bring childhood malnutrition under control.*

Hearer A: Yes, doing nothing could worsen our already worsening health situation.

Hearer B: No, nothing seems pressing for our children as such.

Hearer C: Undecided (or abstain)—for the time being.

3. *Speaker*, implying a validity claim to the subjective truthfulness and sincerity of a speaker's symbolic expression: *I believe our children's nutritional health is among the world's lowest, placing the future of our entire population at risk for more severe economic challenges in the years ahead.*

Hearer A: Yes, I see the signs all over town.

Hearer B: No, that sounds like propaganda. Our own rate seems within the norm for our nation, resulting in no national policies on it. Shared wealth is the best antidote to childhood malnutrition.

Hearer C: Undecided (or abstain)—for the time being.

These initial exchanges can occur in dyads that encourage the treatment of each communicative action as unique to a setting. There is ample room to disagree and to abstain, without the subject being publicly shamed in a focus-group session and, thereby, being stigmatized. And because of the homophily that exists between the cultures of the speaker and the hearers, the chances for a truly open communication geared toward reaching an agreement or consensus and mutually, symmetrically influencing attitudes and beliefs through arguments are significantly enhanced. Because these initial dyads must quickly morph into full public exchanges, the challenge here is to avoid the constraint of social influence as a pressure point for behavior change—a hallmark of strategic action.

Assessing Outcomes of Health Campaigns

Habermas is not silent on assessing program outcomes. He proffers strategic action as a measure of success and operational effectiveness. Because of the strategic features of such assessment, e.g., influence, control, and manipulation, it need not be framed to generate validity claims. Strategic action, as a complement to communicative action, is *not* the preferred method for attaining an understanding of the health issues at stake and for reaching a consensus on them.

Four Propositions for Health-Communication Research

Rosegrant and Meijer (2002) observed that "significant reduction in child malnutrition is possible, but it will require *renewed* (emphasis added) efforts from national governments, international donors and research institutions and civil society" (p. 3440S). It is in response to that exhortation that this chapter concludes with a nutrition-campaign objective and four accompanying propositions (P's) that could guide future investigations into child malnutrition in Africa.

Nutrition-campaign objective: To assess the effects of enhanced health-care providers' communication strategies on parents and caregivers charged with the nutritional health of children at risk for malnutrition.

P_1: Health-care providers in intervention groups will be more likely than those in comparison groups to use argumentation and negotiation to communicate child malnutrition-related information to parents and caregivers.

P_2: Argumentation and negotiation communication strategies will each be a positive predictor of parents' and caregivers' delivery of appropriate nutrition to reduce child malnutrition.

P_3: Health-care providers who use argumentation and negotiation to convey child malnutrition information to patients and caregivers will be more likely than those in comparison groups to report significant reductions in malnutrition.

P_4: Among parents of and caregivers to children at risk for malnutrition, perceptions of benefits from argumentation and negotiation aimed at reducing child malnutrition will be positively associated with health-care providers' use of argumentation and negotiation to convey child malnutrition information to the parents of and caregivers to malnourished children or those at risk for malnutrition.

Conclusion

Sub-Saharan African nations attribute their urban health challenges to eviscerating national population policies, burgeoning urban migration, dwindling public-health services, and taxing political and economic environments. But as the two epigraphs at the beginning of this chapter indicate, urban health is as much a bane of sub-Saharan Africa as is the singular issue of child malnutrition. To the degree that Africa is in the throes of a higher incidence of child malnutrition, this chapter outlines at the outset some of the theoretical perspectives that frame much of health interventions in Africa, identifies their missing component, and then argues that health specialists (e.g., nongovernmental organizations and multilateral donors) strive to ensure that parents and caregivers, as participants in a development process (read: preventing child malnutrition), become more responsible than is traditionally the case for the nutritional health of their charges. The application of TCA will acknowledge and de-emphasize strategic action, along with its emphasis on both open and concealed actions, which guide current health campaigns, and will emphasize communicative action, which can be particularly beneficial to child malnutrition-management efforts for at least three reasons.

First, parents of and caregivers to children at risk for malnutrition can engage in a communicative action as partners in "interactions in which *all* participants harmonize their individual plans of action with one another and thus pursue their illocutionary aims *without reservation...*" (Habermas 1984, p. 294). This permits an unfettered, unconstrained communication among all parties.

Second, parents and caregivers are parties to making cogent arguments that could lead to negotiated compromises and agreements on whether a strict nutrition-management program is necessary in the first place; to establishing a process that approves messages and themes used in a health campaign; and to raising "validity claims... to truth, rightness, appropriateness or comprehensibility (or "well-formedness)" (Habermas 1984, p. 39). The alignment of ideal speech acts with symmetry conditions serves as an enabler of understanding and consensus building.

Finally, parents of and caregivers to children are also parties to open, free, and unconstrained conversations that frame symmetrically each participant's worldviews, yet ensuring their consistency with their lifeworld. Ford et al. (2005) described this approach as community integrated management of childhood illnesses, in which "community engagements," "guided conversations," or dialogue occur at many levels: "inside households, between household members and other community members, among community members and local health workers and service providers—since this is the environment in which children grow and develop" (p. 385). And all parties in interactive situations are amenable to integrating the cultural tradition into the messages. Because current health-communication programs tend to give all of those considerations short shrift, even as they consciously and dutifully apply the tenets of health-communication theories to the field and express the strengths of full participation, future health campaigns or programs that benefit from lessons learned from investigating the four propositions outlined in this chapter will have a better chance to respond more effectively to the challenges of Africa's urban residents' health.

In light of the preceding analysis, then, it must be acknowledged here that not all strategic action should be avoided, even within the context of applying current health-communication theories to ground activities. Granted, its open form tends to be significantly more symmetrical and more audience-centered than its concealed form. Thus, to the degree that influence is the goal of strategic action in a concealed form, communicative action is accentuated in that it engenders symmetry conditions amenable to having parents and caregivers negotiate to engage in action geared toward reaching both an understanding and a consensus among all parties working toward alleviating the nutritional risks or preventing malnutrition in Africa's teeming children population. The current dominant health-communication theories have proved feasible in helping enhance the nutritional status of Africa's children. This chapter, however, concludes that such theories need to be reframed on the ground in a manner that palpably complements the African inclination to negotiate and argue in decision making, particularly in those situations in which a child's nutritional health is the beachhead for its physical and educational development, its social adaptation, and its overall well-being.

References

Amoako-Agyei, E. (2009). Cross-cultural management and organizational behavior in Africa. *Thunderbird International Business Review, 51*(4), 329–339.

Brown, P. R. (2008). Trusting in The New NHS: Instrumental versus communicative action. *Sociology of Health & Illness, 30*(3), 349–363.

Brown, J. B., Stewart, M., & Ryan, B. L. (2003). Outcomes of patient-provider interaction. In T. L. Thompson, A. Dorsey, K. I. Miller & R. Parrott (Eds.), *Handbook of health communication* (pp. 141–161). Mahwah: Lawrence Erlbaum.

Chan, M. (2010). Urban health threatened by inequities. Retrieved from http://www.who.int/dg/speeches/2010/urban_health_20100407/en/index.html

Chopra, M., & Darnton-Hill, I. (2006). Responding to the crisis in sub-Saharan Africa: The role of nutrition. *Public Health Nutrition, 9*(5), 544–550.

Ford, N., Williams, A., Renshaw, M., & Nkum, J. (2005). Communication strategy for Implementing community IMCI. *Journal of Health Communication: International Perspectives, 10*(5), 379–401. doi:10.1080/10810730591009817.

Fotso, J.-C. (2006). Child health inequities in developing countries: Differences across urban and rural areas. *International Journal for Equity in Health, 5*(9). doi:10.1186/1475-9276-5-9.

Garenne, M. (2010). Urbanization and child health in resource poor settings with special reference to under-five mortality in Africa. *Archives of Diseases in Childhood, 95*(6), 464–468. doi:10.1136/adc.2009.172585.

Habermas, J. (1984). *The theory of communicative action: Reason and the rationalization of society (Vol. 1) (trans: T. McCarthy).* Boston: Beacon. (Original work published.

Habermas, J. (1987). *The theory of communicative action: Lifeworld and system: A critique of functionalist reason (Vol. 2) (trans: T. McCarthy).* Boston: Beacon. (Original work published.

Habermas, J. (1990). *Moral consciousness and communicative action.* Cambridge: MIT Press.

Haddad, L., Ruel, M. T., & Garrett, J. L. (1999). Are urban poverty and undernutrition growing? Some newly assembled evidence. *World Development, 27*(11), 1891–1904.

Heath, J. (2001). *Communicative action and rational choice.* Cambridge: MIT Press.

Rogers, E. M. (1995). *Diffusion of innovations* (4th ed.). New York: Free Press.

Rosegrant, M. W., & Meijer, S. (2002). Appropriate food policies and investments could reduce malnutrition by 43 % in 2020. *The Journal of Nutrition, 132*(11), 3437S–3440S.

Schneider, H., Marcis, F. L., Grard, J., Penn-Kekana, L., Blaauw, D., & Fassin, D. (2010). Negotiating care: Patient tactics at an urban South African hospital. *Journal of Health Services Research & Policy, 15*(3), 137–142. doi:10.1258/jhsrp.2010.008174.

Scholtz, Z., Braund, M., Hodges, M., Koopman, R., & Lubben, F. (2008). South African teachers' ability to argue: The emergence of inclusive argumentation. *International Journal of Educational Development, 28*(1), 21–34.

Servaes, J. (2004). Multiple perspectives on development communication. In C. C. Okigbo & F. Eribo (Eds.). *Development and communication in Africa* (pp. 55–64). Lanham, MD: Rowman & Littlefield.

Servaes, J., Jacobson, T. L., & White, S. A. (Eds.). (1996). *Participatory communication for social change.* New Delhi: Sage.

U.S. Department of Health and Human Services, National Institutes of Health, National Cancer Institute (2005). *Theory at a glance: A guide for health promotion practice* (NIH Publication No. 05-3896 2005)

United Nations Department of Economic and Social Affairs. (2008). *The millennium development goals report 2008.* New York: Author.

Wallerstein, N., & Bernstein, E. (1994). Introduction to community empowerment, participatory education, and health. *Health Education & Behavior, 21*(2), 141–148.

Chapter 12
Health Communication Strategies for Sustainable Development in a Globalized World

Patchanee Malikhao and Jan Servaes

This chapter starts exploring some different but interconnected discourses: health, health communication, development, sustainability, and globalization. It elaborates on the rights to well-being as a development goal. In order to achieve this goal, the authors present strategies in a comprehensive health communication planning to attain and sustain health awareness, attitude, and behavior change. Globalization, urbanization and sustainable development are intrinsically intertwined in this discussion, as the 2010 World Health Day theme—Urbanization and Health—reflected the rising number of people living in cities around the world. In 2007, the world's urban population surpassed 50 % for the first time in history, and this proportion is growing—by 2050, it is estimated to exceed 70 %.

Interconnected Discourses: Health, Health Communication, Development, Sustainability, and Globalization

Health Discourse

Let's start with *"health."* In the past, health was thought of as related to biomedical conditions; being healthy meant being free from diseases. However, a social constructivist would argue that for an individual the state of being healthy is being conditioned by the political and socioeconomical environment within which that individual lives. People who live in a lower socioeconomical status tend to have higher mortality and morbidity rates (Schneider 2006). No wonder that people who live in

P. Malikhao (✉)
Fecund Com Consultancy,
Bangkok, Thailand
e-mail: pmalikhao@gmail.com

J. Servaes
Dept. of Media & Communication, City University of Hong Kong,
Kowloon, Hong Kong

C. C. Okigbo (ed.), *Strategic Urban Health Communication*,
DOI 10.1007/978-1-4614-9335-8_12, © Springer Science+Business Media New York 2014

the so-called Third World have higher mortality and morbidity than those who live in the so-called First World. At the same time people in the Third World who live in the urban centers of growth and development would live longer than those living in the rural peripheries, who tend to lack quality health care services, access to health information, good nutrition, safe water supply, hygienic sanitation, safe shelter and community, meaningful employment, and safety from violence and coercion. Being healthy is thus the state of being well physically, spiritually, environmentally, and psychologically (Sharf and Vanderford 2003, p. 13).

Now a new question arises. If a person has a chronic disease but manages it well, lives in a suitable environment, and feels good about him/herself, do we consider that person healthy? The World Health Organization stated clearly that yes, that person is considered healthy (WHO 2003). Being in a state of good health or wellness is the result of "well-being" and that can be achieved through participation between the individuals and their communities in sustainable social, political, environmental and cultural processes which got rid of poverty, promoted quality of life, and assured human rights (The Broker 2009). Therefore, the socioeconomic status of a person is very important as it determines the quality of healthcare providers and services; the education of the person to take care of him/herself; or the ability to pay for healthcare insurance and good medication in order to stay healthy. Health can be interpreted as "personal" and/or as a "commodity"; or a "common good." Why is that? Because what we think as personal in one culture may not be personal at all in another cultural context. For instance, in the United States, the Republicans perceive health care as a commodity. This means that they believe in the ability of the individual to pay for the quality of his or her health care services. However, the US health care system may not be viewed as adequate in the European Union, because the Europeans believe that health care should be accessible and affordable for rich and poor people alike. Thus, for the Europeans, health care is perceived as a common good. When Americans believe that they have choices for their health care policies they may in fact be governed by only two big conglomerates. So, health care choices are merely an illusion. After all it is a made-believe system for which the ultimate goal is profit-driven, to make money.

Health Communication Discourse

The discourse on health discussed above leads to the discourse on "health communication." Health communication stems from the communication discipline. Theories in mass communication and interpersonal communication are used in conventional health communication. This discourse is framed within the modernization paradigm of development. Health communication research based on this school is aiming mostly at the microlevel. A participatory-based discourse, on the other hand, is framed within the multiplicity paradigm of development. Health communication research based on this school of thought will be a combination of micro and macro levels of health communication (for more details, see Servaes 1999, 2008).

The Conventional Health Communication Approach—Social Marketing: Using Mass Media and/or Interpersonal Communication

Some health communicators equate health communication as health promotion by ways of a social marketing strategy; i.e., using the mass media to sell health awareness, health efficacy, and health behavior to the public. Examples are "click it or ticket" to warn drivers that if they do not wear seatbelts they will be fined; or "get talking, get tested" to tell people to use counseling services and get tested for their HIV status. Some health communicators equate health communication as health education by ways of teaching, training, and counseling. Some health communicators borrow the theory of diffusion of innovation to introduce "health messages" to opinion leaders and to the individuals by means of interpersonal communication (Rogers 1983, 2003). They believe that the use of mass media alone is not powerful enough to change the recalcitrant mass awareness, attitude, and behavior. The combination of interpersonal and mass communication is used to get things done the way the public health authority wants, such as allowing interpersonal communication to advise new mothers about breastfeeding or single-shot immunizations. In a more complex scenario, the mass media are used, together with interpersonal communication, to promote more complex health solutions, such as using videos and radio, together with a public health officer, to advise the people how to mix a drink for oral rehydration therapy. Also more complex vaccinations, such as the vaccination against polio, use the mass media together with the visit of a public health officer to raise awareness that the vaccination needs to be taken twice.

From the US Office of Disease Prevention and Health Promotion "Healthy People 2010" (2010, pp. 11–3) report, *health communication* is defined as

> …the study and use of communication strategies to inform and influence individual and community decisions that enhance health. It links the domains of communication and health and is increasingly recognized as a necessary element of efforts to improve personal and public health.

In Servaes and Malikhao (2010) we argued that the health communication policy of the US office of Disease Prevention and Health Promotion focuses on the word dissemination of health messages via education, the mass media as well as community health services and environment in a top-down fashion (Office of Disease Prevention and Health Promotion 2010, pp. 11–3).

The policy still conforms to the conventional model which views the communication process mainly as a "message" going from a "sender" (public health offices/centers) to a "receiver" (the public). It can be summarized in Laswell's classic formula, *"Who says What through Which channel to Whom with What effect?"* The diffusion model (Rogers 1983, 2003) explains diffusion and adoption of innovations in a more systematic and comprehensive way. But the main thrust remains on the introduction of innovations from outside (*top-down*). The innovation-decision process consists of a sequence of five stages: knowledge, persuasion, decision, implementation, and confirmation. Similar stage theories of behavior change have been proposed for health behavior communication, and attitude change (for overviews, see Sallis et al. 2008; Piotrow et al. 1997; Thompson et al. 2003). Although the stage aspect of these models is intuitively appealing and useful for planning interventions, behavior change is more complex with respect to time than such models are capable of representing. Authors of stage theories warn that an individual does not necessarily move through each stage in the exact order as specified and that it is possible for individuals to "loop" or fall back into an earlier stage after reaching a stage further along in the process, depending on social structure, environmental and political constraints, and cultural support or resistance.

And it is in the process of *interpersonal communication* (through opinion leaders, gatekeepers and/or change agents) that the concerns of the people are identified, issues debated and decisions to adopt or not to adopt are reached through interactive processes. It is through such interactive processes that public pressure and demand are developed to influence policymakers. Therefore, the general conclusion of this line of thought is that mass communication is less likely than personal influence to have a direct effect on attitude and behavior change.

In other words, these strategies work up to a certain level. However, some questions remain: why do some people still smoke, take drugs, binge drink, or do not use a seat belt even though they learned from the media or from schools or from opinion leaders that these behaviors are risk-taking ones? One analysis to these top-down strategies stresses the underlying assumption that individuals would change their own attitude and eventually behavior without considering the policies and the enabling environment that affect the people physically and mentally (Manoncourt 2000, pp. 6–8).

Conventional Media Advocacy

This leads to another discourse of health communication: *media advocacy*. The idea is to use the mainstream commercial media to induce policy makers to consider changing the media policies for promoting health-related resolutions in a community. The usual pattern for mass media has been predominantly the same: informing the population about projects, illustrating the advantages of these projects, and recommending that they be supported. Generally a number of media are used to achieve a persuasive or informational purpose with a chosen population, the most common examples being found in politics, advertising, fund-raising, and public information for health and safety. This top-down approach to community-based health promotion really lacks the "spirit and involvement" of communities in terms of what the grass roots really needs. Rather, it focuses more on what the public health authority thinks the communities might need.

Social Mobilization for Health Communication

Community-Served Communication Advocacy

Newer perspectives claim that the conventional media advocacy is still a limited view. They argue that active involvement in the process of the communication itself will accelerate change. Adequate knowledge and desirable attitudes are not necessarily followed by appropriate practices. The gap between knowledge and practice is well recognized. Behavior change and acceptance of new practices become easy and possible when there is material and human support from the community. Also other factors play a significant role in bringing about desirable behavior conducive to change. New practices become difficult to sustain when there is social disapproval. Therefore, the *support of society* is an important factor in making choices for action. So it is important when planning advocacy strategies to target those individuals and groups in society who influence change-related practices (Fraser and Estrepo-Estrada 1998).

In other words, if the media are sufficiently accessible, the public can make its needs known. At the same time, the mass media can play a strong advocacy role in creating public awareness and bringing about action for change; and they can also target decision-makers as well as interest groups, who in turn press for suitable policies. On the other hand, at the same time, the decision-makers too need this information to reach a (socially acceptable) decision. Therefore, the point of departure must be the "*community*" or the "public." It means that the viewpoint of the local groups of the public is considered before the resources for health projects are allocated and distributed, and that suggestions for changes in the policy are taken into consideration. However, experience has shown that no single approach in itself can suffice to ensure successful advocacy for health-supportive public policies. *Advocacy is most effective when, besides mass media, individuals and groups, and all sectors of society are engaged in this process.* However, this newer perspective of media advocacy has also been criticized for not always being successful as long as elitist democracy is still being practiced and participatory democracy tends to be romanticized (Gibson 2010, pp. 52–55).

Participatory-Based Communication Advocacy

Hence, there came along another strategy: social mobilization in health communication by using participatory and advocacy participatory approaches or a *bottom-up approach*. For social mobilization, there are two types of policy: participatory and participatory-based advocacy communication. The first policy is bottom-up but the latter is a mixture of both top-down and bottom-up communication. Media used for both types must promote group identity: video, film, community radio, community TV, or a community website (either accessed from a personal computer or from a community telecenter). *Participatory communication* can be distinguished in two discourses: the Freirian approach which emphasizes dialogic communication, and the UNESCO approach which is more pragmatic and strategic. It emphasizes the participation in media production and management. The participatory communication approach is also called a contextual rights-based approach. It is more focused on listening and cooperation rather than on telling people what to do. Not only getting the support of the public as well as the policy maker is important, but one should also build alliances for social support and empowering individuals with knowledge, values and skills. However, this perspective has been criticized as well: it really depends upon the culture of a community to empower the people and mobilize the health issue resolutions across the board.

Globalization, Urbanization, and Sustainable Development

In order to plan for health communication effectively, we cannot ignore three more concepts: globalization, urbanization, and sustainable development.

Globalization

Globalization depicts how people from different states, nations, or territories are becoming more interconnected and interdependent on one another. Manifestations of globalization are in different areas: economic, political, cultural, technological, social, and ideological (Lie and Servaes 2008). Globalization involves development, progress, and disparity. For some, it may be the future of opportunities and wealth accumulations but for others it may cause unequal access to information, opportunities and wealth and that leads to economic disadvantages, exploitation, distraught and unhappiness, and sickness. It cannot be denied that communication technology in the dominance of capitalism, influenced by neo-liberal ideologies, is the propelling factor of globalization so that there exists worldwide exchanges in labor, trade, technology, production, and capitals.

According to Lee (2005), globalization encompasses three dimensions of global change: spatial, temporal, and cognitive. Globalized interactions make us perceive an extension of our space perception—that is the spatial dimension. We also perceive and experience the compression of time for global interactions—that is the temporal dimension. Lastly, by exchanging ideas, values, ideologies, policies, or knowledge via the global interactions, we form our own postmodern identities and worldviews—that is the cognitive dimension. This leads to *social change* and its health consequences. With the growth of cultural globalization, which is mostly westernization, we experience changes of lifestyles: eating, recreating, dating, arts, sports, games, clothing; sexuality and media consumption. With more sedentary lifestyles, chaotic life, and fast food consumption, we witness the rise of chronic non-communicable diseases such as obesity, type 2 diabetes, cardiovascular disease, cancer, and mental illnesses. Spatial globalization brings more problems of migration and that enhances the outbreaks of communicable diseases in the twenty-first century such as HIV/AIDS, SARS, and H1N1 pandemics. These communicable and noncommunicable diseases display the negative side of globalization.

Urbanization

Urbanization is by no means a symbolic representation of globalization. Nearly half the world's population now lives in urban settlements. Cities offer the lure of better employment, education, health care, and culture; and they contribute disproportionately to national economies. However, rapid and often unplanned urban growth is often associated with poverty, environmental degradation, and population demands that outstrip service capacity. These conditions place human health at risk. Low- and middle-income countries are the most affected by demographic changes, bearing 80 % of the world's burden of disease and the highest attrition rates of doctors and nurses to other parts of the world. Inarguably, these trends influence the accessibility, quality, and cost of long-term health care in urban and rural communities, alike.

The distinction between urban and rural is not merely a distinction based on the nature of settlements, it is a distinction rooted in the economic structure and social relations of production and reproduction, and in the processes of social and political consciousness and its articulation. Therefore, urbanization is often taken as a proxy for the level of development in general.

Data that are available indicate a range of urban health hazards and associated health risks: substandard housing, crowding, air pollution, insufficient or contaminated drinking water, inadequate sanitation and solid waste disposal services, vector-borne diseases, industrial waste, increased motor vehicle traffic, stress associated with poverty and unemployment, among others. Local and national governments and multilateral organizations are all grappling with the challenges of urbanization. Urban health risks and concerns involve many different sectors, including health, environment, housing, energy, transportation, urban planning, and others (Moore et al. 2003).

Globalization and urbanization make us think of development in the global-local perspective. The term global village is a cliché because disparities have always existed. There are always differentiations in the level of development internationally or within a nation. Take the US as a good example. The United States is the only developed nation that has no national health insurance that guarantees rights to healthcare access for all (Morone 2008, p. 1). In 2005, more than 45 million Americans still had no health insurance at all (Leichter 2008, p. 173). In the United States there remains a big gap in development level according to ethnic groups. White Americans, who are the majority, enjoy the wealth and privileges of better education and employments more than the Hispanics or the African-Americans.

White Americans live longer and suffer less from diseases than the other ethnic groups (Allen and Easley 2006, pp. 48–50). One explanation of this is that the other ethnic groups have no inheritance or accumulation of assets, because the African-Americans started from being slaves in agricultural regions in the South of the United States and the Hispanics arrived as cheap migrant workers. Poverty affects health and life courses in terms of disease prevention, nutrition, recreation, safety and security in workplace, etc. This leads us to think of development in a global perspective—the modernization paradigm, the dependency paradigm, and the multiplicity paradigm (see more details in Servaes 1999, 2008)—and raises the question of sustainability.

Sustainable Development

Sustainable development is also a discourse. One meaning is from a "Western" perspective represented by the Brundtland Commission, and the other is an "Eastern" Buddhist perspective as represented by the Thai philosopher and monk Phra Dhammapidhok (Payutto 1998).

For the Western perspective, the World Commission on Environment and Development (WCED), also known as the Brundtland Commission, defined sustainable development in 1987 as "*development which meets the needs of the present without compromising the ability of future generations to meet their own needs*" (Elliott 1994, p. 4). The WCED emphasizes core issues and conditions such as population and development, food security, species and ecosystems, energy, industry, and the urban challenge. All of these issues have an impact on environmental health, food-borne diseases, mental health, injuries, and accidents as major concerns for public health.

Phra Dhammapidhok (Payutto 1998), a famous Buddhist monk and philosopher, points out that sustainable development in a Western perspective lacks the human development dimension. He states that the Western ideology emphasizes "competition." Therefore the concept of "compromising" is used in the above WCED definition. Compromising means lessen the needs of all parties. If the other parties do not want to compromise, you have to compromise your own needs and that will lead to frustration. Development will not be sustained if people are not happy. From a Buddhist perspective, *sustainability concerns ecology, economy, and evolvability*. The concept "evolvability" means the potential of human beings to develop themselves into less selfish persons. The main core of sustainable development is to encourage and convince human beings to live in harmony with their environment, not to control or destroy it. If humans have been socialized correctly, they will express the correct attitude toward nature and the environment and act accordingly (Servaes and Malikhao 2004). This perspective ensures the last dimension of health: *spirituality*.

Development and Health Strategies

Development paradigms dictate the health communication strategies: modernization versus multiplicity.

Modernization Versus Multiplicity

Those who use the modernization paradigm as their operational framework would emphasize more quantitative and measurable indicators, such as gross national product and mortality, morbidity, birth rate, and prevalence and occurrence of communicable diseases. They would aim at the standards of the so-called developed world as the ultimate goal of development. Their health communication strategies tend to rely on *the health belief model, transtheoretical model, or the theory of reasoned action and planned behavior*. UNAIDS (1999, pp. 18–19) defines each theory as follows:

> The Health Belief Model (HBM) was developed in the 1950s to predict individual response to, and use of, screening and other preventive health services.
> The Theory of Reasoned Action attempts to explain individual behavior by examining attitudes, beliefs, behavioral intentions, and observed, expressed acts.
> Social Learning and Cognitive Theories are based on the assumption that individual behavior is the result of interaction among cognition, behavior, environment, and physiology.
> The AIDS Risk Reduction Model is based on the belief that one has to label a behavior as risky before a change can be effected. Once the behavior is considered risky, a commitment is made to reduce the behavior before action to perform the behavior is expected. Fear or anxiety and social norms are considered factors that influence moving from one stage to the next.
> Stage of Change is based on the conception that individual behavior change goes through a process involving a series of five interrelated stages.
> Hierarchy of effects models focus on individual behavior change in a linear fashion, which begins with exposure to information and assumes that knowledge, attitude, trial, and adoption of the desired behavior will necessarily follow.
> Diffusion of Innovation focuses on the communication process through which new ideas or products become known and used in a target population.

These theories have a similar pattern in common: assuming linearity and consequences of knowledge, attitude and behavior/practice (KAP) of an individual. If the individual does not change his or her KAP, a new tailored message will be sent either via a social marketing campaign; training or education; or a diffusion of innovation scheme.

Those who use the multiplicity paradigm as their operational framework would use more sociocultural indicators to combine with the measurable indicators. For instance, they may use the gross national happiness as an indicator together with the GDP. They may consider the cost of healthcare administration per capita together with the prevalence and incidence of diseases. They would consider to improve poor neighborhoods in a more integrated way, making sure they have grocery stores, recreation areas, nurseries, preschools, a hospital within reach, primary health care

units, parks, and transportation, rather than only investing in new tailored messages to change individual's health behavior. In other words, they would consider
a holistic framework on health communication by advocating for a participatory
communication process to empower the people in the community. They would not
evaluate the change of the individual KAP only, but they would assess the change
at the community level as well.

Health Communication Strategies for Sustainable Development

Servaes (2007a, b, 2008) and Servaes and Liu (2007) propose five levels of communication strategies for development and social change:

a. *Behavior change communication* (BCC) (mainly interpersonal communication),
b. *Mass communication* (MC) (community media, mass media, and ICTs),
c. *Advocacy communication* (AC) (interpersonal and/or mass communication),
d. *Participatory communication* (PC) (interpersonal communication and community media), and
e. *Communication for structural and sustainable social change* (CSSC) (interpersonal communication, participatory communication, and mass communication).

Servaes and Malikhao (2010) advocated the participatory-based advocacy which
combines participatory and advocacy communication, or advocacy and communication for structural and sustainable social change. They state that advocacy is most
effective when individuals, groups and all sectors of society are involved, through
three interrelated strategies for action: (a) *Advocacy* generating political commitment for supportive policies and heightening public interest and demand for health
issues; (b) *Social support* developing alliances and social support systems that le-
gitimize and encourage development-related actions as a social norm; and (c) *Empowerment* equipping individuals and groups with the knowledge, values and skills
that encourage effective action for change" (Servaes and Malikhao 2010, pp. 43).

There are a wide variety of advocacy strategies. In any strategy three basic dimensions of action can be distinguished: (a) the organization of activities; (b) the
substance of activities, and (c) the "climate" of human relations in which activities
take place. *At all these dimensions media and public pressure do play a major role.*

Divergent theories in each of these three dimensions of action need to be re-
viewed in an attempt to uncover the source of behavior in different types of strategies. Special attention should be given to the impact of attitudes and behavioral sciences on (a) organization theory, (b) knowledge utilization, and (c) policy analysis.

The *choice of advocacy strategies* will vary with the nature of the issue and
the expectation of the people or the stakeholders. It depends on the pattern of involvement of particular policy stakeholders—that is, individuals or groups, which
have a stake in policies because they affect and are affected by governmental decisions. Policy stakeholders often respond in markedly different ways to the same

information about a policy environment. A policy environment, which is the specific context in which events surrounding a policy issue occur, influences and is in turn influenced by policy stakeholders and public policies. Hence, policy systems contain processes which are dialectical in nature, meaning that objective and subjective dimensions of the policy-making process are inseparable in practice. Policy systems are subjective human products created by the conscious choices of policy stakeholders; policy systems are an objective reality manifested in observable actions and their consequences; policy stakeholders are products of policy systems. Policy analysts no less than other policy actors, are both creators and products of policy systems.

Challenges for the Future

Several challenges remain ahead for the health communication community, including practitioners, academics, and policy makers. Below we briefly discuss what we feel are the most relevant ones.

Wide Ranging Challenges

Arguably, the conceptualization of health as development has brought additional challenges to policy makers and practitioners. This has led practitioners to also face important challenges in reference to working (a) across sectors, (b) within regions, or (c) with a focus on larger societal issues (Sallis et al. 2008).

a. *Across sectors*: More complex health issues have forced health practitioners to address a number of issues that cut across different sectors, including agriculture, education, social, and cultural issues.
b. *Within a region*: Natural disasters and emergencies have demonstrated the need to design and implement region-wide strategies, which require strong communication components. How have health communication practitioners responded to this reality? The Tsunami showed lack of cooperation both in the immediate emergency and the subsequent responses. On the contrary, the international response to the potential avian flu pandemic suggests increasing coordination and cooperation to implement regional plans and strategies. Also, several international initiatives have provided strategic guidance for global and regional responses to health challenges, e.g., infant feeding, HIV/AIDS, child health. However, the communication component within these regional and global strategies is often limited to dissemination efforts and lacks specificity on specific communication strategies. That is why the UN-agencies have agreed to what they call a "One Country" approach to development issues with one agency (most often UNDP) in charge of the coordination and supervision of the implementation of projects in the same region or country (see Servaes 2007a, b, or UNESCO 2007).

c. *More societal issues related to the meta-development process*: Lifestyle issues and urban planning issues are two key entry points to public health in the modern world. In these cases, communication cuts across a number of issues that have society-wide implications. The example of the transformation of China's capital, Beijing, during the Olympics and its implications for health is a case in point.

Monitoring, Evaluation, and Indicators

There has been an increased emphasis on moving from a uniform focus on results to an increased *focus on process*. While monitoring and evaluation approaches focused on health outcomes and impact communication indicators should remain essential to health communication interventions, a focus on process will provide deeper understanding of the nuances and particularities of development and health, especially those that remain embedded in cultural practices. Similarly, a focus on context and communities as units of analysis has emerged as critical to understand the effectiveness of interventions in health promotion and communication. Proponents of the limitations of evidence-based public health for health promotion and health policy point out the difficulties health promotion specialists and health policy makers face when relying primarily on evidence-based approaches. For instance, while evidence-based data emerge from experimental designs, a particular approach always operates in a particular context. Understanding this context becomes essential, hence the need for a focus on *process*.

Unfortunately, the politics and economics of public health and public health communication leave very little room and resources for longitudinal approaches, particularly under the realization that health changes take time. To counter for that requires for example to engage with universities that can provide a space for developing longitudinal *and* external monitoring and evaluation. The discussion on monitoring and evaluation also has brought increasing attention to issues of indicators in health communication. Perhaps, the most significant change over time is the increased attention given to *process indicators* and to the role *qualitative approaches* could play in this context.

Human Resources and Capacity Building Efforts

Over the past decade, many developing countries have moved toward increasing decentralization of their health systems; thus, availability of human resources at national, regional, and local levels has emerged as a central element to ensure effective health interventions, including health communication. Building and strengthening local capacities must be a core element of health policy and health promotion efforts. The theme of the 2006 World Health Day highlighted this issue as it chose *human resources* as the year's theme. The international donor and technical cooperation community also seems to recognize this as an important issue, as new declarations and position papers have brought *capacity building* and development to the forefront of their agendas. In the case of health communication, capacity needs to be developed both in service and preservice settings as well as across disciplines in public health.

Developing Health Communication Competencies

The discussion on human resources also highlights the importance of paying special attention to the development of the *right competencies* needed to develop effective health communication interventions. This is true both for practitioners originally trained as communicators, who generally speaking come to the field with little understanding of issues such as social mobilization, social and behavioral theories, and sustainable change, and for practitioners trained in public health and other areas, who come to the field with little understanding of communication issues. Training institutions, particularly universities, should play a central role in this effort. There have been some efforts made in the past, which have aimed at identifying and operationalizing key competencies for development and health communication (DANIDA 2005; Storey et al. 2005). These contributions might be brought more intensely before academic institutions in efforts to create training programs that could lead into the creation of a critical mass of practitioners with the fundamental competencies in health communication.

Funding Issues

A realistic approach indicates that the above challenges could only be met if sufficient funding is available to undertake the necessary initiatives and programs. While the international public health community has allocated significant resources to a variety of areas in public health—vaccine development, eradication of infectious diseases, control of epidemics, emergency responses, etc.—resources allocated to further develop the health communication field are rather limited. Increased funding for ongoing programs that contribute to tackling pressing public health issues should be coupled with increased funding for efforts aimed at assessing the value added by health communication to public health efforts, exploring new methodologies to monitor and evaluate interventions, and strengthening long-term efforts for human resource development. Without a firm commitment in this area, little progress can be made in the long run to expand the role of health communication in solving the public health challenges of the twenty-first century.

The Importance of Research

Following Carol Weiss (1977a, b), it is widely recognized that, although research may not have direct influence on specific policies, the production of research may exert a powerful indirect influence through introducing new terms and shaping the policy discourse. Overall, one can explore how research can influence policy-makers horizons, policy development, declared public policy regimes, funding patters, and policy implementation or practice (Lindquist 2003).

Cultural Competence in Health Communication

We would like to emphasize that a form of cultural relativism or more cultural sensitivity in health communication is a way to scrub off one's own ethnocentricity, prejudice and stereotyping for a better and hopefully healthier world.

Conclusion

Health communication is not limited to communication between patients and healthcare providers only, it is also about the communication between or among an observable unit (individual/group of people of virtual group/community/organization/nation) to achieve health awareness, attitude and behavior, either through the mass media, or the new media, or through human communication. In order to achieve competent and effective health communication, one needs to look at health and disparities in the world system from the perspective of sustainable development. In order to master the complexity of health communication strategies in today's world, one needs to be interdisciplinary trained in Communication for Development, Intercultural communication, Public health, and Social Science. Cultural competencies are needed for health communicators, health care providers, and public health personnel to enhance compassion, tolerance and peace, and to fully comprehend and handle the future challenges of health communication.

References

Allen, C. A., & Easley, C. E. (2006). Racial and ethnic minorities. In B. S. Levy & V. W. Sidel (Eds.), *Social injustice and public health* (pp. 46–68). Oxford: Oxford University Press.
DANIDA (2005). *Monitoring and indicators for communication for development*. Copenhagen: DANIDA.
Elliot, J. (1994). *An introduction to sustainable development* (pp. 4–5). London: Routledge.
Fraser, C., & Restrepo-Estrada, S. (1998). Communicating for development. *Human change for survival*. London: I.B. Tauris.
Gibson, T. A. (2010, March). The limits of media advocacy. *Communication, Culture and Critique*, 3(1), 44–65.
Lee, K. (2005). Introduction to global health. In K. Lee & J. Collin (Eds.), *Global ghange and health* (pp. 3–12). Berkshire: Open University Press.

Leichter, H. M. (2008). State Governments: E Pluribus Multa. In J. A. Morone, T. J. Litman, & L. S. Robins (Eds.), *Health politics and policy* (4th ed., pp. 173–195). New York: Delmar Cengage Learning.

Lie, R., & Servaes, J. (2000). Globalization: Consumption and identit. In G. Wang, J. Servaes, & A. Goonasekera (Eds.), *The new communications landscape. Demystifying media globalization.* London: Routledge.

Lindquist, E. A. (2003). *Discerning policy influence: Framework for a strategic evaluation of IDRC-supported research.* Canada: International Development Research Centre (IDRC).

Manoncourt, E. (2000). Why do people behave as they do? Theories and framework. In N. McKee, E. Manoncourt, C. S. Yoon, & R. Carnegie (Eds.), *Involving people evolving behaviour* (pp. 1–42). New York: UNICEF.

Moore, M., Gould, P., Keary, B. S. (2003). Global urbanization and impact on health. *International Journal of Hygiene and Environmental Health, 206,* 269–278.

Morone, J. A. (2008). Introduction. Health politics and policy. In J. A. Morone, T. J. Litman, & L. S. Robins (Eds.), *Health politics and policy* (4th ed., pp. 1–22). New York: Delmar Cengage Learning.

Office of Disease Prevention and Health Promotion (2010). Healthy People 2010, Centers for Disease Control and Prevention. http://www.cdc.org. Accessed 25 Feb 2010.

Payutto, P. (1998). *Sustainable development.* Bangkok: Buddhadham Foundation.

Piotrow, P., Kincaid, D., Rimon, J., & Rinehart, W. (1997). *Health communication: Lessons from family planning and reproductive health.* Westport: Praeger.

Rogers, E. M. (1983). *Diffusion of innovations.* (3rd ed.). New York: The Free Press.

Rogers, E. M. (2003). *Diffusion of innovations* (5th ed). New York: The Free Press.

Sallis, J., Owen, N., & Fisher, E. (2008). Ecological models of health behavior. In Glanz, K., Rimer, B., & Vishwanath, K. (Eds.), *Health behavior and health education: Theory, research and practice* (4th ed., p. 465). San Francisco: Jossey-Bass.

Schneider, M-J. (2006). *Introduction to public health.* Boston: Jones and Bartlett.

Servaes, J. (1999). *Communication for development. One World, Multiple Cultures.* Creskill: Hampton.

Servaes, J. (Ed.) (2007a). Communication for development. Making a difference—A WCCD background study, in *World Congress on Communication for Development: Lessons, Challenges and the Way Forward,* World Bank, Washington DC, 209–292 (ISBN 0-8213-7137-4).

Servaes, J. (2007b) Harnessing the UN System into a common approach on communication for development. *The International Communication Gazette Sage, 69*(6), 483–507. http://gaz.sagepub.com.

Servaes, J. (Ed.) (2008). *Communication for development and social change.* Los Angeles: Sage. (ISBN 9780761936091).

Servaes, J., & Liu S. (Eds.) (2007). *Moving targets. Mapping the paths between communication, technology and social change in communities* (p. 275). Penang: . (ISBN 978-983-9054-50-7).

Servaes, J., & Malikhao, P. (2004). *Communication and sustainable development.* Rome: FAO.

Servaes, J., & Malikhao, P. (2010). Advocacy strategies for health communication. *Public Relations Review, Elsevier, 36,* 42–49.

Sharf, B. F., & Vanderford, M. L. (2003). Illness narratives and the social construction of health. In T. L. Thompson, A. Dorsey, K. I. Miller, & R. Parrot (Eds.), *Hand book of health communication* (pp. 9–34). New York: Lawrence Erbaum.

Storey, J., Figueroa M., Kincaid, D. (2005). *Health competence communication: A systems approach to sustainable preventive health.* Technical report. Baltimore: John Hopkins Bloomberg School of Public Health.

The Broker (February, (2009). The Broker Special Report: Health for All. https://www.thebrokeronline.eu. Accessed 1 Mar 2010.

Thompson, T., Dorsey, A., Miller, K., & Parrott, R. (Eds.) (2003). *Handbook of Health Communication.* Mahwah: Lawrence Erlbaum.

UNAIDS (1999). *Reducing Girls' Vulnerability to HIV/AIDS: The Thai Approach* (case study). Geneva: UNAIDS.

UNESCO (2007). *Harnessing communication to achieve the millennium development goals*. Paris: UNESCO.

Weiss, C. (Ed.) (1977a). *Using social research in public policy making*. Lexington: Lexington Books.

Weiss, C. (1977b). Research for policy's sake: The enlightenment function of social research. *Policy analysis* (Vol. 3, no. 4.), 531–545.

WHO (2003). *Global Health-Sector Strategy for HIV/AIDS 2003–2007*. Geneva: World Health Organization.

Chapter 13
Urbanization and Strategic Health Communication in India

Margaret U. D'Silva, Vinita Agarwal, Steve Sohn and Vijay Sharma

The world's population continues to grow, primarily in developing countries, despite increasing awareness of the negative consequences of this tremendous population increase. Snowden (2008) states, "Population has soared above all in the poorest and most vulnerable regions of the world with the global urban population growing at four times the rate of the rural" (p. 16). As a result, urbanization is becoming a global social challenge.

The pace of urbanization has increased in recent decades. It took two centuries to create the urban industrial societies in developed countries; it is taking just a few decades to bring rapid urbanization to developing countries (UNFPA 2007). The United Nations (UN) declared in 2008 that half of the world's population lives in urban areas (Haub 2009); the UN predicts that in the next decade almost all urbanization will take place in developing countries. For example, in 1975, the urban population was estimated to be 813 million in less developed countries compared to 704 million in more developed countries. Yet 30 years later, in 2005, the urban population grew to 2,266 million in less developed countries versus only 344 million in more developed countries (UN Habitat 2006). This rapid urbanization occurred in the most dramatic way in less developed Asian nations. In 1975, four Asian cities were ranked as one of the top ten megacities in the world: Tokyo and Osaka in Japan, and Shanghai and Beijing in China. In 2013, the first seven of the top 10 megacities are in Asia: Tokyo, Japan; Jakarta, Indonesia; Seoul, South Korea; Delhi, India; Shanghai, China; Manila, Philippines; and Karachi, Pakistan. (Cox 2013).

Although urbanization in developing countries is making a significant contribution to those nations' economies, it is also producing serious public health problems

M. U. D'Silva (✉) · S. Sohn
University of Louisville, 310 Strickler Hall,
40292 Louisville, KY, USA
e-mail: Margaret.dsilva@louisville.edu

V. Agarwal
Salisbury University, Salisbury, USA

V. Sharma
New Delhi, India

C. C. Okigbo (ed.), *Strategic Urban Health Communication*,
DOI 10.1007/978-1-4614-9335-8_13, © Springer Science+Business Media New York 2014

among the urban poor. These problems arise due to overcrowded living conditions and lack of proper housing and sanitation. For instance, in the Indian megacity of Delhi, an estimated population of over 22 million lives within a land area of 750 square miles with a density of 30,400 as compared to Tokyo with its population of over 37 million living on a land area of 3,300 square miles and a density of 11,300 (Cox 2013). Additionally, the continued migration of people to the already crowded urban areas compounds the problem. This chapter provides an overview of global urbanization and examines the potential of theory-based strategic health communication in addressing urban public health issues in India.

Global Urbanization

Urbanization occurs for two major reasons: (1) increase in the population and (2) migration of people to urban areas for employment opportunities and for improved living conditions. In fact, the World Health Organization (2013) reports that approximately one billion of the three billion people who live in urban settings live in slums. People migrate to urban areas as economies develop; they come for better jobs and more income.

Despite the economic growth and the innovation that occur in cities, problems abound in the urbanized parts of the developing world. The growth is chaotic and the cities are not prepared for it. The rapid increase in population creates a strain in areas such as sanitation, water, and power (UNFPA 2007). Unplanned urbanization results in "escalating poverty, widening social inequality, the birth of megacities and the spawning of teeming peri-urban slums without sanitary, educational and other infrastructure." (Snowden 2008, p. 20). Child mortality in the slums of cities in Nairobi, where approximately 60 % of the city's population lives, is 2.5 times greater than in other areas of the city (World Health Organization 2013). This massive population growth in urban areas puts an enormous burden on the resources of the region and of the nation. For instance, the intensive use of resources in these urban areas results in environmental challenges including waste disposal, noise, air, and water pollution, soil erosion, and deforestation among others (Jakarta Post 2009).

Overcrowding in urban areas, particularly in slums, also makes the population vulnerable to infectious diseases. Indeed, the city is the microcosm of the nation; its citizens are biologically connected: no individual is immune to infection. In such an environment, epidemic diseases easily occur and reoccur and that happens because of the continuous movement of large numbers of products and people from place to place. Migration is a key factor affecting "the balance between microbes and man" (Snowden 2008, p. 16).

Urbanization in the Indian Context

India is no exception to urbanization's travails and triumphs. Its three large cities, Mumbai, Delhi, and Calcutta (Kolkata), with their enormous populations, present both the economic rewards and unique challenges of urbanization. Delhi has an estimated population of over 20 million, Mumbai over 17 million, and Kolkata over 15 million (Cox 2013). In India, urban is defined as, "specified towns with governments and places with 5,000 or more and at least three-fourths of the male labor force not in agriculture" (Haub 2009, p. 1). Other factors not specified in the definition include population density and specific urban characteristics (Haub 2009). While less than a third of India's population lives in urban areas, these population-dense spaces create more than two-thirds of the nation's gross domestic product (GDP) and generate 90 % of government revenues (World Bank 2009). Gender equality is also a driving force behind economic prosperity. Women are a vital part of India's growing work force. For instance, those states with greater gender equality are "also the fastest growing and have greater anti-poverty effectiveness of growth" (Besley et al. 2004, p. 3). However, the increased migration of people to the megacities spawns gargantuan slums where the migrant laborers create homes for themselves. In Mumbai, slum dwellers who were one in six in 1971, are now the majority. When a plane descends in the Mumbai airport, the sprawling Dharavi slum with blue roof tops is clearly visible from the air. Slums in Mumbai, unlike those in other cities, are located close to places of work. Mumbai is also home to Bollywood, which includes India's wealthiest movie moghuls and stars. This lively business center has a thriving business community, a sizeable middle class, and slum dwellers.

India's slum population, which was 41 million in 2001, is estimated to become 69 million in 2017 while the urban population is expected to rise to 500 million (World Bank 2009). The Millennium Development Goals Report 2009 (MDG 2009) notes that in 2005 about 35 % of the urban population was living in slums. Slums can be described as neighborhoods that are "lacking in at least one of four basic amenities: clean water, improved sanitation, durable housing, and adequate living space" (MDG 2009, p. 47). The harsh living conditions in the slums highlight the urgent need to focus attention on the health needs of the urban poor. While the poor living in slums might have a harder time than the poor living elsewhere in the city, this is not applicable for all cities and, in some cases, there is no noticeable difference. The greater gap, however, is between the urban poor and the nonpoor. The disparity is in both living and health conditions. Programs that assist those in the slums would be a definite benefit, but focusing only on slum dwellers would not help the pressing needs of the large number of poor not dwelling in the slums (Gupta et al. 2009).

Urban Health Disparities

While there are huge health disparities between the urban poor and the urban rich, there are also enormous differences in the population between cities and among different groups of the population in the same city. The urban poor are overwhelmingly impacted by new public health challenges in communicable, maternal, perinatal, and nutritional conditions (Blas and Kurup 2010). For example, the under-five mortality rate was substantially higher for the urban poor in the state of Madhya Pradesh (132) than for urban areas of Madhya Pradesh as a whole (83). Among the urban poor in India, only 25 % of pregnant mothers receive complete antenatal care (ANC), which includes at least three ANC visits, iron, and folic acid tablets for at

162 M. U. D'Silva et al.

least 3 months, and at least two tetanus toxoid injections. Among the urban poor, about "three-quarters of babies are delivered at home" (Gupta et al. 2009, p. 10).

The health status of migrant populations in urban contexts is also affected by social issues like child marriage and its attendant problems of negative maternal-child health outcomes. Research shows that girls in rural areas are more likely to marry a year and a half earlier than those in urban areas (Westoff 2003) and that those who marry early are more likely to be associated with early childbirth. Additionally, one-third of women in developing countries give birth before they reached 20 years of age (Save the Children 2004). The maternal health consequences of early marriage include higher rates of maternal mortality (CDC 2002), obstetric fistula (Murray and Lopez 1998), and increased risk of contracting HIV/AIDS (Clark 2004). In every urban area, poor women and men as compared to nonpoor women and men are more likely to be "abnormally thin, and undernourished. At least four in ten women are anemic in both slum and non-slum areas in every city" (Gupta et al. 2009, p. 44). Despite India's impressive economic growth, it has more maternal deaths (56,000 per year) than any other country in the world (Save the Children 2013).

Given these challenging health circumstances, it is imperative that any meaningful and effective health communication strategy considers these uniquely urban circumstances.

Strategic Health Communication

Broadly understood, strategic health communication frameworks examine evidence of key communication problems to bring about planned and targeted behavioral change in specific audiences. From their roots in early models of community organization and social change (for example, the knowledge gap hypothesis, Mosteller and Moynihan 1972; Tichenor et al. 1970) to more tailored community-based interventions (Rimer et al. 2001), the foci of these frameworks range from communicating vision, shared sense making, soliciting feedback, establishing legitimacy, to communicating goal achievements (Lewis 2000). Increasing evidence supports the need for communication interventions to be strategic and evidence-based, to adopt culturally sensitive communication practices and to incorporate multiple stakeholders such as active community participants in designing the communication strategy (Kreps and Sparks 2008).

The strategic health communication perspective can be employed to further define two major and closely related target groups: publics and stakeholders. A public is defined as a group of people who relate to the issue or organization, who demonstrate varying degrees of activity or passivity, and who might or might not interact with others concerning their relationship (Aldoory 2001; Hallahan 1999). Stakeholders, on the other hand, are those publics who have an active stake or interest in the issue or the organization. Strategic communication can be understood as a purposeful and deliberative communicative activity with a goal of interpreting the source (e.g., an organization's) vision, values, mission, or message to key publics (see also Steyn 2007). However, strategic communication is not merely a linear, one-way, controlled process. To be meaningfully successful, it should privilege multiple perspectives of those affected, and productively integrate alternatives that are culturally sensitive to the contexts of the stakeholders and publics within which they will be enacted.

Therefore, a strategic health communication framework approach examines planned programmatic behavior change from three perspectives: (a) the source/ goal, (b) the key stakeholders, and (c) the target publics. In other words, strategic health communication can be defined as an informational or persuasive activity involving relationship-building between both stakeholders and publics that encompasses "intentional communication undertaken by an [organization or group] with a purpose and a plan, in which alternatives are considered and decisions are justified" in order to bring about a desired health-related planned behavioral change (Smith 2009, p. 4). Thus although strategic health communication is goal-oriented, as a public relations function it productively integrates programmatic elements of health communication intervention design, channel, and message selection with the involvement of all key stakeholder groups and affected publics.

Public relations theory can usefully inform the conception, design, and implementation of strategic health communication interventions to address public health issues in India (see also Toth 2006). Thus, within the strategic health communication perspective, we now provide an overview of two key theoretical frameworks: (a) the stakeholder theoretical perspective, and (b) the situational theory of publics that can be used to involve publics and stakeholders in the process of planned change implementation.

Stakeholder Theoretical Perspective

In essence, stakeholder analyses help researchers identify project stakeholders, conduct needs assessments, and find ways in which their interests affect the program's implementation. Research is an important part of the public relations practitioner's goal in this endeavor (Macleod and Michaelson 2007). Some of the ways in which stakeholder analyses examine the intersection of stakeholders and program implementers are by incorporating research that: (a) identifies ways of harnessing the support of target publics in favor of the intervention, (b) effectively addresses the risks posed by stakeholders who oppose the intervention, and (c) identifies the specific role that a particular stakeholder can play to achieve the intervention's objectives. In this manner, stakeholder analyses provide a useful framework for implementing planned communication activities involving stakeholders and publics, and thus make an important contribution to strategic health communication.

Therefore, stakeholder theory examines the role of communicative processes in managing relationship-building strategies with stakeholders in the community implementation of health initiatives. Because stakeholder theory integrates processes to meaningfully negotiate the voices of implementers, target publics, and stakeholders within a community-based context, it has been applied in the implementation of public health programs like HIV/AIDS interventions in India. This is particularly useful because stakeholder analyses combine relationship-building with the community during the information gathering stage and contributes to the partnership of stakeholders, affected publics, and the community opinion leaders in program implementation.

For example, for HIV/AIDS interventions targeted toward migrant populations, the primary stakeholders and the target publics include: (a) the migrant workers who interact with high-risk sexual networks, (b) the spouses and sexual partners of migrants, and (c) the migrants living with or who are affected by HIV and AIDS. Multifaceted strategies have been employed to increase involvement of stakeholders and target publics. These strategies include: (a) targeting the prioritized workplaces and areas around them such as canteens and roadside cafés (*dhabas*), as well as residential areas (slums, temporary shelters); (b) targeting influential stakeholders such as owners of village square informal wrestling game (*kabbadi*) shops, tea stalls, and cigarette shops; (c) targeting private medical practitioners providing services within the migrant neighborhoods, or areas where sex worker operations are concentrated: cinema halls, and union offices such as *rickshaw* (a hand-driven bike with an open seat at the back for passengers) pullers unions, auto drivers associations, and traders associations in informal vegetable markets (*sabzi mandis*). In some cases, programs have been designed to obtain the support of law enforcement so that they would not be an obstacle to HIV prevention and treatment (UNAIDS 2012a, b).

In involving important stakeholders within the programmatic planned change, the stakeholder theory allows researchers and practitioners to give all participants a voice in achieving program goals.

Situational Theory of Publics

While the focus of stakeholder analyses is on communicating program goals to the key stakeholders in order to obtain their involvement, the situational theory of publics foregrounds an analysis of the key publics and thus makes an important contribution to the strategic health communication perspective in implementing community-based health behavior change initiatives. By emphasizing effective message design in interventions keeping public segmentation in mind, this public relations theory has been successfully utilized in persuasive communication (Parrott 2004; Pfau and Wan 2006). Essentially, this perspective envisages the public as an entity having something in common: members of the public could be affected by the same problem or issue, or adopt a similar behavior toward the problem (Grunig and Hunt 1984). The situational theory of publics predicts communication behavior according to three factors: (a) problem recognition, (b) constraint recognition, and (c) level of involvement (Grunig and Hunt 1984). These factors affect the extent to which individuals engage in either passive forms of information processing or more active forms of information seeking behaviors. In the case of information processing, publics do not seek information, but they will pay attention to it, which distinguishes processing from mere exposure to a message (Slater et al. 1992). Information seeking, on the other hand, is the active and deliberate search by the individual for information on a particular issue.

The first factor in the theory, problem recognition, is that people do not really think about problematic situations unless they perceive that something needs to be done to improve the situation. Indeed problem recognition aids the likelihood of communication because once people recognize something as a problem, they are more likely to engage in information seeking and information processing. The second factor, constraint recognition, is defined as the extent to which individuals see their behaviors as limited by obstacles or barriers beyond their control. That is, perceived high constraints will tend to lead to reduced communication. The third factor in the theory, involvement, is a key concept for many theories and has been used in studies pertaining to health communication campaigns, persuasion, and public relations (Chaffee and Roser 1986; Grunig and Hunt 1984). Involvement is defined as the extent to which an issue is perceived as being personally relevant for the individual (Grunig and Hunt 1984). Clearly, if the particular issue or message is perceived as being of high relevance to the person, that person will be more likely to attend to and comprehend it. It stands to reason, therefore, that people with high involvement elaborate upon issues more deeply (Petty and Cacioppo 1996) and attain greater knowledge levels (Engelberg et al. 1995). In addition, highly involved publics will be more likely to seek information and communicate actively when they perceive an issue to be a problem or perceive that the issue involves them and believe they can do something about it (Grunig 1989). An active public will be involved enough to engage in information seeking from various avenues: the media, interpersonal contacts, and specialized channels, whereas a passive public is more likely to simply process information from mass media (Heath and Douglas 1991). The situational theory, therefore, has significant implications for designing messages in health communication campaigns. The theory is especially relevant for messages that are perceived to be of high relevance to the target audience who are then more likely to recognize the problem as well as seek out information on it.

Strategic Health Communication in Urban Contexts in India

In a developing country like India, strategic health communication provides a useful framework to design and examine the efficacy of strategies concerning the implementation of behavioral health initiatives among at-risk populations. By incorporating stakeholders and segmenting publics, organizations can envision message design as an inclusive, dynamic, and nonlinear process whereby behavior change is organically conceived rather than imposed (Fig. 13.1). For instance, female sex workers in India who are older, married, and practicing sex work for longer duration with a higher clientele are more likely to engage in risky sexual practices (Mahapa-

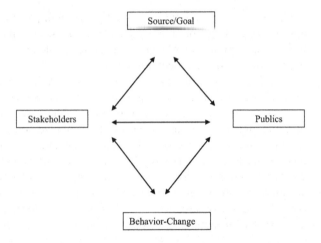

Fig. 13.1 A stakeholder-publics theoretical approach model of strategic health communication

tra et al. 2013). Therefore, the key challenges facing the urban marginalized lie in the area of assessing progress on social issues that have been traditionally intransigent to planned programmatic change. Some challenges include providing access to adolescent girls' education, awareness initiatives in sexual and reproductive health, property and inheritance rights, and gender-based violence, among others. Social issues including violence against women are also associated with increased vulnerability to HIV. For example, married women in India who had experienced physical and sexual violence from intimate partners were three times more likely to be HIV-positive than those who had experienced no violence (UNAIDS 2012b). Data from the International Labor Organization (ILO) also show that gender wage gaps have risen in parts of the world, such as India and China that are most affected by globalization and labor market shifts (ILO 2007).

Studies by several organizations such as the International Center for Research on Women (ICRW 2006) have found strategic health approaches can contribute in increasing implementation effectiveness, monitoring, and evaluation, especially in the realm of women's public health issues in urban contexts. In particular, the framework of strategic health communication provides a useful focus to critique public health initiatives through the lens of public relations theory by foregrounding the stakeholders and key publics within health communication interventions (see also, Wise 2001). For example, one advantage of employing multistakeholder teams (MSTs) is that they can help in empowering marginalized women and in mobilizing community support for the planned implementations. Some of the ways MSTs can help are through influencing community members to participate in resolving tensions between members and staff. In this case, MSTs help achieve project goals by serving as a liaison between "key populations and groups within the community, such as 'gate keepers' for the key populations, influential representatives within the community, members of associations such as youth clubs, health watch committees and women's groups" (ICRW 2006, p. 14). Such bridging across networks of influence is especially important for women in urban contexts particularly migrant women who struggle with the fragmentation of traditional social roles and communities.

For instance, in India and Nepal, HIV-positive women who use drugs work with local organizations as peer advocates promoting access to HIV prevention services as well as to sensitize police from violence toward sex workers using drugs (UN-AIDS 2012a, b). The Avahan HIV/AIDS prevention program in India supported by the Bill and Melinda Gates Foundation contributes to the efforts of the National AIDS Control Program III (NACP III) government policy by seeking feedback from multiple stakeholders including key informants, staff of implementing partners, policy and decision-makers to suggest strategic channels for communication (Tran et al. 2013). The following section further discusses the applicability of strategic health communication interventions in the HIV/AIDS domain in India.

Strategic Health Communication in HIV/AIDS Interventions

The rapid mobilization of women in the migrant workforce has caused many public health issues, the more urgent perhaps being the growing HIV/AIDS epidemic. This target public of migrant women workers is particularly vulnerable. Research suggests that female sex workers in noncommercial, nonregular relationships report greater likelihood of being HIV positive, having syphilis, using condoms inconsistently with occasional clients, and having forced sex, as opposed to those in regular partnerships (Somanath et al. 2013). Although in urban areas HIV/AIDS is largely concentrated in traditional at-risk populations such as sex workers, injecting drug users, truck drivers, and men who have sex with men (MSM), surveillance data suggest that increasingly the epidemic is moving into the larger population. This trend is a cause of increasing alarm because of its potential to influence traditional and larger, hitherto unaffected, populations. The lack of education for women, the difficulty women face in obtaining medications and resources, and the stigma associated with the epidemic are responsible for the particular vulnerability of migrant women. The shift in those affected by the epidemic suggests that awareness and campaigns for the empowerment of women and adolescent girls might be the best strategies for combating its spread.

For example, in the early stages of the HIV/AIDS epidemic, governments and donor agencies devoted most resources to technical interventions (TIs) with at-risk groups, such as sex workers, truckers, and migrant laborers. However, such targeted action often stigmatized People Living with HIV/AIDS (PLWH/A) and were considered counterproductive because they ultimately reinforced the denial of risk among the general population. To counter stigmatization, strategic communication initiatives using a planned combination of well-targeted mix of mass media and interpersonal channels, together with both social and community mobilization were utilized to increase public discourse and acceptance of the threat of HIV/AIDS. When incorporated productively, strategic health communication can help: (a) break the silence about HIV/AIDS in identifying the salient dimensions of stigma within the population (D'Silva et al. 2008) and the demographic and psychosocial correlates of these dimensions (Creel at al. 2008), and thus (b) move the discussion about HIV/AIDS from the personal-private to the public-policy sphere. Today, it is believed that this is the only feasible approach to HIV/AIDS prevention programs for large countries like India.

Some innovative behavioral change efforts have recently been initiated by both the Indian government and nongovernmental organizations (NGO) sector. A few Indian states, like Tamil Nadu, and several NGOs including FXB India Suraksha, have utilized *Nai's* (a Hindi word for barbers) as local opinion leaders in a novel way to break the silence about HIV/AIDS. Traditionally Indian barbers have a key social status and play a central role as community healers, confidants, advisors, and matchmakers. A popular saying "To get the king's ear, tell his barber" symbolizes this sentiment in popular culture well. Equally important, in rural areas, the barber's wife is often a *Dai*, a traditional community health worker, functioning as the community midwife and birth attendant. In fact, barbers have the ear of all their clients, and barber shops are considered as a place in the neighborhood where clients can often speak openly and freely about intimate issues with the barber, including those topics that are otherwise taboo in the society. Involving this key group of local community leaders in an innovative program, Tamil Nadu has enrolled more than 5,000 barbers who, while cutting the hair of clients, also discuss issues related to safe sex, HIV/AIDS, and condoms. In fact, FXB India Suraksha still has a successful barber intervention program in many northern states. Barbers, in this instance, function as effective communicators transmitting appropriate messages in a comfortable, informal context.

Future Landscape of Strategic Health Communication in HIV/AIDS

Despite some successful interventions in India, communication scholars and community activists still face several challenges in the successful dissemination of HIV/AIDS programs. Public relations scholars and practitioners have the potential to make a vital contribution to the success of these interventions. This is especially critical in developing contexts such as India where the high-risk publics, stakeholders, and their sociocultural contexts are in a process of continuous change due to rapid urbanization. For example, increasing male migration provides the context for those who are infected with HIV to spread the epidemic from high-risk populations in high prevalence areas to populations in low prevalence areas (Saggurty et al. 2011). Thus changing economic imperatives coupled with changing demographic trends in migration are deeply linked with public health concerns such as the HIV/AIDS epidemic. Migrant males' unprotected and high-risk sexual behaviors in their destination areas, in India, have been found to pose a risk of transmission from high-risk population groups to migrants, and in turn to their married and sexual partners in the places of origin (Saggurty et al. 2011). Thus these trends have to be taken into account through research incorporating all stakeholder and public voices to effect meaningful behavioral change.

Further, the limited diversity of target-specific content and a lack of resources are tough issues that could be remedied by thoughtful planning and increased support from international and national agencies. One of the biggest obstacles, however, is the policies and actions of governments that hamper any work by HIV prevention activists. As in several places around the world, India stigmatizes prostitution. Although prostitution is legal, brothels and any form of organized prostitution are illegal. The law is often used to harass prostitutes (Debabrata 1998). Sex workers cannot legally solicit customers in public and are subjected to moral policing. For example, Goa's state government demolished Baina's red-light district and tried to move prostitutes into other work. NGOs working in the area found it quite impossible to reach the sex workers with prevention messages (Shahmanesh and Wayal 2004). A reexamination of the laws related to prostitution and human trafficking is needed. However, there is cause for optimism in the recent policy change abolishing the Indian law criminalizing homosexuality. Homosexual males are an at-risk population in the AIDS epidemic, and fear of being imprisoned has kept them from obtaining help in preventing the disease or treating it. A policy change like this one helps immensely in changing the future landscape of HIV/AIDS. Social media use has also seen a striking increase in the developing world and social media tools have a great potential to increase awareness, mobilize social action, and provide access for PLWHA (UNAIDS 2013). Its use in Africa, for example, has increased a whopping 2357 % between 2000 and 2010 and about 42 % of the total internet population worldwide is in Asia (UNAIDS 2013).

Conclusion

As the world's population grows, so does the rate of urbanization. Especially among developing nations, urbanization has become a rapid yet unplanned process. This process typically produced several daunting problems in urban public health, such as HIV/AIDS and malnutrition. India is not an exception. In examining online websites of international nongovernmental organizations (INGOs), Agarwal et al. (2013, p. 21) note that "political, socio-cultural, and economic conditions are imbued in the micro-practices of power and identity that define the communicative relationship building tactics" in cross-cultural stakeholder management thus encouraging INGOs working in HIV/AIDS to be constantly self-reflexive about the unintended implications of their actions. Ultimately, the urban health problems experienced in India are not unique to the country but rather shared by other developing nations. Therefore, this chapter used particular cases in India as examples of those common urban public health problems. Given the imperatives of designing implementations for advocacy geared toward spread of awareness and knowledge for behavior change, the strategic health communication framework provides a useful theoretical perspective for meaningful stakeholder management. It enables researchers, program implementers, and grassroots social workers to both assess the efficacy of health communication campaigns with respect to reach of programs and to conceive new initiatives.

The effectiveness of strategic health communication frameworks will depend on the campaign sensitivity and success in integrating the unique local and cultural elements of the campaign target publics. Indeed providing region- and target-specific content is a major communication challenge even within a single country further emphasizing the need for strategic health communication interventions. Due to the absence of effective vaccines or medications preventing/treating HIV/AIDS, the prevention depends largely on behavioral change through strategic health communication. Through illustrating the utility of two public relations theories in the HIV/AIDS context in India, this chapter emphasizes that to be effective in raising awareness, educating the target population and ultimately changing their behaviors, strategic health communication must be conducted within the particular cultural context of the stakeholders and target publics.

The deep-rooted nature of HIV/AIDS-related stigma in India was attested by the content analysis of newspaper articles in Indian media which primarily depicted ostracization due to HIV/AIDs as the dark belly of the Indian sociocultural landscape (D'Silva et al. 2011). Therefore, even though the cases in India provide valuable lessons, important challenges remain. How will these theory-based strategic urban health communication interventions work in different parts of the world? How will the factors in the theories be influenced by the uniqueness of different local or national cultures? The answers to those questions shall be obtained through continuous and sustained efforts made by both academics and practitioners.

Urbanization is an unavoidable step in the modernization process. This chapter contributes to the efforts of urban public health practitioners by providing an understanding of urbanization and its associated public health problems within the framework of two key public relations theories along with a consideration of their practical implications. Only through education, both researchers and practitioners can gain better understandings of the problems and solutions so eventually those living in marginalized urban areas will receive the benefit of urbanization without those negatives associated with urban public health.

References

Agarwal, V., D'Silva, M. U., & Leichty, G. B. (2013). Disease, representation, and public relations. In R. Ahmed & B. Bates (Ed.), *Health communication in media contexts: Research and applications*.

Aldoory, L. (2001). Making health communications meaningful for women: Factors that influence involvement. *Journal of Public Relations Research, 13*, 163–185.

Besley, T., Burgess, R., & Esteve-Volart, B. (2004). *Operationalizing pro-poor growth: India case study*. Washington, DC: World Bank.

Blas, E., & Kurup, A. S. (2010). Equity, social determinants and public health programmes. World Health Organization. http://whqlibdoc.who.int/publications/2010/9789241563970_eng.pdf. Accessed 27 May 2013.

Centers for Disease Control and Prevention (CDC). (2002). *Vital Statistics Report*. Atlanta: CDC.

Chaffee, S. H., & Roser, C. (1986). Involvement and the consistency of knowledge, attitudes, and behaviors. *Communication Research, 13*, 373–399.

Clark, S. (2004). Early marriage and HIV risk in sub-Saharan Africa. *Studies in Family Planning, 35*, 149–160.

Cox, W. (2013). Annual update on world urbanization: 2013. Newgeography.com. http://www.new-geography.com/content/003608-annual-update-world-urbanization-2013. Accessed May 9, 2013.

Creel, A., Rimal, R., Bose, K., Mkandawire, G., Folda, L., & Brown, J. (2008, May). *Strategic health communication and HIV/AIDS stigma reduction: A field experience from Malawi.* Paper presented at the meeting of the International Communication Association, Montreal, Quebec, Canada.

Debabrata, R. (1998). When police act as pimps: Glimpses into child prostitution in India. *Manushi, 105*, 27–31.

D'Silva, M. U., Futrell, A., Alladi, J., & Gohain, Z. (2008). Communicating HIV/AIDS awareness through folk theater and art: Case studies from India. In M. U. D'Silva, J. L. Hart, & K. L Walker (Eds.), *HIV/AIDS prevention and health communication* (pp. 78–91). Tyne: Cambridge Scholars.

D'Silva, M. U., Leichty, G., & Agarwal, V. (2011). Cultural representations of HIV/AIDS in Indian print media. *Intercultural Communication Studies, XX*, 75–88.

Engelberg, M., Flora, J. A., & Nass, C. L. (1995). AIDS knowledge: Effects of channel involvement and interpersonal communication. *Health Communication, 7*, 73–91.

Grunig, J. E. (1989). Sierra Club study shows who become activists. *Public Relations Review, 15*, 3–24.

Grunig, J. E., & Hunt, T. (1984). *Managing public relations.* New York: Rinehart & Winston.

Gupta, K., Arnold, F., & Lhungdim, H. (2009). *Health and living conditions in eight Indian cities.* National Family Health Survey (NFHS-3), India, 2005–06. Mumbai: International Institute for Population Sciences.

Hallahan, K. (1999). *Communicating with inactive publics: The moderating roles of motivation, ability and opportunity.* Paper presented at the annual meeting of the Public Relations Society of America Educators Academy, College Park, MD.

Haub, C. (2009). What is a city? What is Urbanization? http://www.prb.org/Articles/2009/urbanization.aspx. Accessed 27 Oct 2009.

Heath, R. L., & Douglas, W. (1991). Effects of involvement on reactions to sources of messages and to message clusters. In L. A. Grunig & J. E. Grunig (Eds.), *Public relations research annual* (Vol. 3, pp. 179–193). Hillsdale: Lawrence Erlbaum.

International Center for Research on Women (ICRW) (2006). *HIV & AIDS—Stigma and violence reduction intervention manual: Change is possible!!.* Washington, DC: CRWRW.

International Labor Organization (ILO) (2007). *Globalization, industrial revolutions in India and China and Labor markets in advanced countries: Implications for national and international economic policy.* Working Paper No. 81. Geneva, Switzerland.

Jakarta Post (2009). Population, urbanization and environment. http://www.thejakartapost.com/news/2009/07/31/population-urbanization-andenvironment.html. Accessed 26 Oct 2009.

Kreps, G., & Sparks, L. (2008). Meeting the health literacy needs of immigrant populations. *Patient Education and Counseling, 71*, 328–332.

Lewis, L. K. (2000). Communicating change: Four cases of quality programs. *The Journal of Business Communication, 37*, 128–155.

MacLeod, S., & Michaelson, D. (2007). The application of "best practices" in public relations measurement and evaluation systems. *Public Relations Journal, 1*, 1–14.

Mahapatra, B., Lowndes, C. M., Mohanty, S. K., Gurav, K., Ramesh, B. M., Moses, S., Washington, R., Alary, M. (2013). Factors associated with risky sexual practices among female sex workers in Karnataka, India. *PLoS One, 18*, 4: e62167. doi:10.1371/journal.pone.0062167.

Millennium Development Goals Report (2009). *End poverty 2015: Make it happen.* New York: United Nations.

Mosteller, F., & Moynihan, D. P. (1972). *On equity of educational opportunity.* New York: Random House.

Murray, C., & Lopez, A. (1998). *Health dimensions of sex and reproduction.* Geneva: World Health Organization.

Parrott, R. (2004). Emphasizing "communication" in health communication. *Journal of Communication, 54*, 751–787.

Petty, R. E., & Cacioppo, J. P. (1996). *Attitudes and persuasion: Classic and contemporary approaches*. Boulder: Westview.

Pfau, M., & Wan, H. H. (2006). Persuasion: An intrinsic function of public relations. In C. H. Botan & V. H. Hazelton (Eds.), *Public relations theory II* (pp. 101–136). Mahwah: Lawrence Erlbaum.

Rimer, B. K., Glanz, K., & Rasband, G. (2001). Searching for evidence about health education and health behavior interventions. *Health Education and Behavior, 28*, 231–248.

Saggurty, N., Mahapatra, B., Swain, S. N., & Jain, A. K. (2011). Male migration and risky sexual behavior in rural India: Is the place of origin critical for HIV prevention programs? *BMC Public Health, 29, 11*(Suppl. 6), S6. doi:10.1186/1471 2458-11-S6-S6.

Save the Children (2004). State of the world's mothers 2004. Westport: Save the Children.

Save the Children (2013). *Surviving the first day. State of the world's mothers 2013*. http://www.savethechildren.org/site/c.8rKLIXMGIpI4E/b.8585863/k.9F31/State_of_the_Worlds_Mothers.htm. Accessed May 9, 2013.

Shahmanesh, M., & Wayal, S. (2004, October 9). Targeting commercial sex-workers in Goa, India: Time for a strategic rethink. *The Lancet, 364*, 1298.

Slater, M. D., Chipman, H., Auld, G., Keefe, T., & Kendall, P. (1992). Information processing and situational theory: A cognitive response. *Journal of Public Relations Research, 4*, 189–203.

Smith, R. D. (2009). *Strategic planning for public relations*. New York: Routledge.

Snowden, F. M. (2008). Emerging and reemerging diseases: A historical perspective. *Immunological Reviews, 225*(1), 9–26.

Somanath, R. P., Mishra, R. M., Saggurti, N., & Parimi, P. (2013). The association between non-commercial partnerships and risk of HIV among female sex workers: Evidences from a cross-sectional behavioral and biological survey in Southern India. *AIDS Research and Treatment*: 108630. doi:10.1155/2013/108630. Epub 2013 Mar 4.

Steyn, B. (2007). Contribution of public relations to organizational strategy formulation. In E. L. Toth (Ed.), *The future of excellence in public relations and communication management* (pp. 137–172). Mahwah: Lawrence Erlbaum.

Tichenor, P. J., Donohue, G. A., & Olien, C. N. (1970). Mass media flow and differential growth in knowledge. *Public Opinion Quarterly, 34*, 159–170.

Toth, E. L. (2006). On the challenge of practice informed by theory. *Journal of Communication Management, 10*, 110–111.

Tran, N. T., Bennett, S. C., Bishnu, R., & Singh, S. (2013). Analyzing the sources and nature of influence: How the Avahan program used evidence to influence HIV/AIDS prevention policy in India. *Implementation Science, 8*, 44. doi:10.1186/1748-5908-8-44.

UNAIDS (2012a). Global report: UNAIDS Report on the global AIDS epidemic. http://www.unaids.org/en/media/unaids/contentassets/documents/epidemiology/2012/gr2012/20121120_UNAIDS_Global_Report_2012_with_annexes_en.pdf. Accessed 27 May 2013.

UNAIDS (2012b). Women out loud: How women living with HIV will help the world end AIDS. http://www.unaids.org/en/media/unaids/contentassets/documents/unaidspublication/2012/20121211_Women_Out_Loud_en.pdf. Accessed 27 May 2013.

UNAIDS (2013). Social media and UNAIDS. http://www.unaids.org/en/resources/presscentre/socialmedia/. Accessed 27 May 2013.

United Nations Population Fund (UNPFA) (2007). State of World Population 2007. http://www.unfpa.org/swp/2007/english/chapter_1/urbanization.html. Accessed 24 Oct 2009.

UN Habitat (2006). World urban forum III: An international un-habitat event on urban sustainability. http://www.unhabitat.org/cdrom/docs/WUF1.pdf. Accessed 31 Mar 2010.

Westoff, C. F. (2003). *Trends in marriage and early childbearing in developing countries*. DHS Comparative Reports No. 5. Calverton: Macro International Inc.

Wise, K. (2001). Opportunities for public relations research in public health. *Public Relations Review, 27*, 475–487.

World Bank (2009). Urbanization in India. http://web.worldbank.org/wbsite/external/countries/southasiaext. Accessed 26 Oct 2009.

World Health Organization (2013). Social determinants of health. http://www.who.int/social_determinants/publications/urbanization/factfile/en/. Accessed 27 May 2013.

Chapter 14
Urban Health Communication Strategy of Pro-Poor Growth for Sustained Improvement in Health in South Asia

Rukhsana Ahmed, Momtaz Uddin Ahmed and Zahirul Hasan Khan

Introduction

Issues of health concerns and pro-poor growth are pervasively interlinked. Any strategic communication framework for urban health must include poverty reduction objectives and mainstream both in the overall urban health communication strategy to inform and influence organizational, community, and individual decisions for promoting and protecting the health of the population. There is evidence to suggest that better health is a key determinant of human and economic development and poverty reduction (WHO 2002). The primary objective of this chapter is to argue the case for pro-poor growth as the broad-based urban health communication strategy for sustained improvement in health in order to achieve an optimal combination of higher growth, sustained poverty reduction, and socially inclusive development (i.e., reduction of inequalities) in the face of critical challenges posed by globalization in the countries of South Asia.

More than 3.5 billion of the world's people live in urban areas (UN DESA 2010), and around 1 billion urban dwellers live in urban slums located mainly in developing countries (WHO 2010). Rapid migration driven by complex economic and social pressures leads to unplanned urban growth driven by narrow economic interests and pose a threat to the health and well-being of people (WHO 2010). As the world is becoming increasingly urbanized, urban poverty is also on the rise leading to economic and social inequalities between cities and among social groups (WHO 2010). The forces of economic globalization—free flow of ideas, people, goods, services, and capital across borders—has left the poor in large cities in the

R. Ahmed (✉)
Department of Communication, University of Ottawa,
K1N 6N5, Ottawa, ON, Canada
e-mail: rahmed@uottawa.ca

M. U. Ahmed
Department of Economics, Dhaka University, Dhaka, Bangladesh

Z. H. Khan
Natural Resources, Canada

C. C. Okigbo (ed.), *Strategic Urban Health Communication*,
DOI 10.1007/978-1-4614-9335-8_14, © Springer Science+Business Media New York 2014

developing countries suffer disproportionately from inequitable access to natural resources, unequal division labor, environmental degradation and associated poor health consequences, increased poverty, food insecurity, and increasing health risks from infectious diseases (McMichael 2002). Since the urban poor "demonstrate[s] the world's most obvious health disparities" (WHO 2010, p. 7), poverty reduction becomes a primary concern in urban health issues.

Although in the recent years, a spate of empirical studies has demonstrated close links between economic growth and poverty reduction, neither the link between growth and poverty has been uniform everywhere nor the benefits of growth and poverty reduction have reached all regions and groups within and between countries (Manning 2007; Ravallion 2004). For instance, despite impressive average rates of growth of GDP and per capita GDP (Debopriya et al. 2007) achieved by most countries of South Asia in the last two decades, the region remains the poorest in the world, accommodating an estimated 437 million extremely poor people living below US$ 1 a day. Further, reductions in poverty are not always accompanied by achievement of other Millennium Development Goals (MDGs), which range from reducing hunger, maternal and child mortality, disease, gender inequality, environmental degradation, to providing adequate shelter, and developing global partnership for development. For example, the five East Asian countries (i.e., China, Indonesia, Malaysia, Thailand, and Vietnam) that had achieved the US$ 1-a-day target by 2003 were not on track to meet the environmental goals and those related to water and sanitation (Humphrey 2006). Significant proportion of the poor in several Latin American countries is also noted to have failed to take advantage of the expanding opportunities arising from high growth. Some countries also failed to share the benefits of growth due to being excessively prone to natural disasters or to disruptions caused by political and ethnic conflicts (i.e., Nepal, Sri Lanka, and Cambodia). All these point to fragility of growth, vulnerability of people's livelihoods and the difficult challenges of translating growth into sustained human development.

In the backdrop of rather limited success achieved by the "growth-first" paradigm tried so far to ensure poverty focused, inclusive and equitable development, this chapter proposes policy revisions and institutional reforms required to attach pro-poor growth as the broad-based urban health communication strategy in the face of many difficult challenges arising from globalization at both external and domestic fronts for achieving sustained improvement in health, rapid growth, and sustained poverty reduction in the countries of the South Asian region. In doing so, this chapter offers lessons for other world regions, namely Africa and Latin America, that are also experiencing the fastest rate of urban growth (WHO 2010) and where wealth and health inequalities are most pronounced among and within cities (Harpham 2009; UN-HABITAT 2008).

The major issues covered in the analytical framework include: conceptualization of the concept of urban health and the pro-poor growth thesis; review of current growth-poverty-health nexus, focusing on the results obtained and limitations faced; and policy revisions and institutional reforms suggested in the changed global and domestic contexts; and future pathways to accelerate urban health communication strategy of pro-poor growth for sustained improvement in health.

Urban Health and Pro-Poor Growth: The Concepts and Challenges

The Concept of Urban Health

Recent years have witnessed a focus on health as an important determinant of economic growth (Lopez-Casasnovas et al. 2005). However, we also observe health disparity, a series of events evidenced by a difference in the environment, access to, utilization of, and quality of care, health status, or a particular health outcome that should be carefully examined (Carter-Pokras and Baquet 2002). In this age of globalization, such inequality and inequity in health are likely to be more pronounced in urban areas as "half of humanity now lives in cities, and within two decades, nearly 60 per cent of the world's people will be urban dwellers" (UN-HABITAT 2008, p. iv). Mercado et al. (2007) bring timely attention to the rising urban poverty in developing countries, which "as driven by globalization and rapid uncontrolled urbanization, also needs to be recognized as a social, political, and cultural process that has profound impacts on public health" (p. 7). In cities of the developing world with one out of every three people living in a slum, poverty is becoming increasingly urban with perilous implications for the urban poor who lacks the access to adequate health, water, sanitation, shelter, and thus faces the greatest threat to the burdens of ill health—injuries, communicable diseases, and noncommunicable diseases (UN-HABITAT 2008; WHO 2010). These global demographic trends underscore an urgent need to consider how the characteristics of the social and physical urban environment shape the population health in cities. Such consideration becomes more prominent especially in the face of potential health implications, such as poor nutrition, infectious diseases, respiratory diseases, mental illness, homicide, injuries, and death, of the most evident urban poverty characteristics, respectively, such as reliance on the cash economy, overcrowded living conditions, environmental hazard, social fragmentation, crime and violence, traffic accidents, and natural disasters (Harpham 2009).

Throughout the South Asian region, rapid and unplanned urbanization is on the rise. As seen in Table 14.1, in Maldives, the urban population consisted of 27.5 % of the total population in 2000, 29.6 % in 2005, and is expected to be 34.8 % in 2015. In Pakistan, the urban population consisted of 33.2 % of the total population in 2000, 34.9 % in 2005, and is expected to be 39.6 % in 2015. Although one of the world's fastest growing regions in terms of population and urban growth, South Asia still remains the most impoverished region in the world (Mahbubul Haq Human Development Centre 2006). The urban situation in South Asia is complicated by deep poverty and income inequality bearing direct and complex consequences for the health and well-being of the urban population (Harpham 2009). Because of inadequate water and sanitation provisions, high levels of overcrowding, and poor access to quality primary healthcare services, urban poor in South Asia are more vulnerable to diseases such as, diarrheal diseases, perinatal, heart disease, and respiratory system infections (Harpham 2009).

Recognizing today's cities as the apparatus for economic growth, Mercado et al. (2007) pose two very important questions. The first question asks as to how to

Table 14.1 Percentage of urban population to total population in the South Asian countries. (Source: World Bank 2009)

Countries	Urban population as a % of total population in 2000	Urban population as a % of total population in 2005	Urban population as a % of total population in 2015
Bangladesh	23.2	25.1	29.9
Bhutan	9.6	11.1	14.8
India	27.7	28.7	32.0
Maldives	27.5	29.6	34.8
Nepal	13.4	15.8	20.9
Pakistan	33.2	34.9	39.6
Sri Lanka	15.7	15.1	15.7

connect underprivileged people in cites to the financial and human resources policies and programs in order to help them take control of their health and lives. The second question asks as to how to mobilize the resources for effective facilitation of such a process for the urban poor. This chapter, however, argues that neither health nor economic growth alone is sufficient to achieve sustained reduction of poverty, sustained improvement in health, and equitable development and thus advocates for a consensus for accelerating pro-poor growth as the broad-based urban health communication strategy in developing countries.

The Concept of Pro-Poor Growth

Although pro-poor growth has by now received wider currency as a strategy for poverty reduction and social development, opinions still diverge as to what it is and how it works. Broadly interpreted, two different approaches to the meaning of "pro-poor growth" can be noted in the current literature. One, growth is said to be pro-poor when it is inequality-reducing (Kakwani and Pernia 2000), a situation where the incomes of the poor rises faster relative to that of the nonpoor. Two, growth is considered pro-poor when it helps accelerating the rate of growth of incomes of the poor and hence the rate of poverty reduction (Ravallion 2004).

Both definitions focus essentially on poverty reduction and a rise in the living standards of the poor through taking advantage of the opportunities which are generated by growth (Manning 2007). Thus, growth in this chapter is considered as "pro-poor" when the pace and pattern of growth enhances the ability of the poor women, men, young, and adult to participate in, contribute to, and benefit from growth and achieve better health for socially inclusive development.

Challenges to Sustained Improvement in Health and Sustained Growth in South Asia

Increasing imbalances and rising inequality characterizing the growth process in the South Asian region tend to suggest that sustained improvement in health, future growth, and poverty reduction are threatened by a wide range of factors. These include severe or chronic poverty in the lagging regions, increase in urban poverty particularly among slum dwellers and migrants, environmental degradation, infrastructural deficiencies, institutional weaknesses, and governance inefficiencies (Farrington and Robinson 2006). Furthermore, Chaudhury and Devarajan (2006) note systemic failure in the delivery of essential human development services—health, education, water, sanitation, and electricity, especially to the poor in the lagging regions.

These multiple challenges toward improvement in health and sustaining economic growth and also making those progressively more equitable and inclusive are further intensified by the challenges of globalization at national, regional, and subregional levels. Besides differential impacts on various regions and economic sectors, globalization also leads to short-term fluctuations in trade and investment regimes and distribution of economic and health benefits and risks of growth among geographic regions. In the following, some of these issues and challenges are elaborated on by briefly highlighting the current state of growth-poverty-health nexus in the countries of the South Asian region.

Brief Review of Current Growth, Poverty, and Health Nexus in South Asia.

There are strong and pervasive links between poverty and health (Harpham 2009; WHO 2002). Any effort at reducing poverty (i.e., material deprivation and multiple social disadvantaged) implies a commitment to improving health of the poor and the socially disadvantaged. For the majority of the poor people, the health-damaging impacts of economic poverty, such as low living standards, lack of education, environmental hazards, and poor working conditions are compounded by conditions of ill health and exacerbate the vicious circle of poverty-ill health-poverty. Globally, ill health also can lead to, aggravate, and perpetuate poverty. Thus, efforts that focus exclusively on economic poverty may have limited success in promoting health and breaking the poverty-ill health impasse.

In the following, the discussion on the socioeconomic status of the South Asian region relates to seven out of eight countries (Afghanistan, Bangladesh, Bhutan, India, Pakistan, Maldives, Nepal, and Sri Lanka) excluding Afghanistan because of lack of data. South Asia accommodates 22.8 % of the global population in a land area of only 3.4 % of the world's total landmass. The seven countries together contained 1,469.8 million people with an average density of 321 persons per sq km. as of 2005 (World Bank 2007). However, population density varies widely among the countries, with the highest being 962 in Bangladesh and only 46 in Bhutan (Ahmad 2007). Besides its large absolute size, the population of the region is also growing significantly at an annual average rate of 1.9 % during 1990–2005. Yet another grim feature is that while South Asia is home to over one-fifth of the world's total population, its share in global income is a mere 7 % as of 2004. Ironically, side by side with better growth performance, the problem of income inequality is worsening in all countries of the region. For example, in Bangladesh, it increased from 0.318 in 2000 to 0.465 in 2005. In this situation, even if income increases its effects on poverty reduction is compromised to a significant extent. The region is thus noted to have remained a divided one between the hopes of the rich and the despair of the poor.

Besides income poverty, there is widespread human poverty in South Asia which is manifested in various forms of human deprivations (see Table 14.2) and denies millions in the region to live a respectable life. Human poverty encompasses various forms of deprivations (other than income), such as, premature death, poor health,

Table 14.2 Human development index and other social deprivation indicators of the SAARC countries. (Source: UNDP 2006)

	Bangla-desh	Bhutan	India	Maldi-ves	Nepal	Pakis-tan	Sri Lanka	Average: developing countries	Ave-rage: South Asia
Human develop-ment index, 2004[a]	0.530	0.538	0.611	0.739	0.524	0.539	0.755	0.679	0.599
Life expectancy at birth (years), 2004	63.3	63.4	63.6	67.0	62.1	64.4	74.3	64.7	63.7
Infant mortality rate (per 1,000 live births), 2004	56	67	62	35	59	80	14	57	62
Undernouris-hed people (% of total population), 2001–2003[b]	30	–	20	11	17	23	22	17	20
Adult literacy rate % (ages 15 and above), 2004	–	–	61.0	96.3	48.6	49.9	90.7	78.9	60.9
Population with sustainable access to impro-ved sanitation (%), 2004	39	70	33	59	35	59	91	49	37
Population with sustainable access to an improved water resource (%), 2004	74	62	86	83	90	91	79	79	85

[a] Low human development index countries: below 0.500; medium human development index countries: 0.500–0.799; and high human development index countries: 0.800 and above
[b] Data refer to the most recent year during the period, for which data are available

illiteracy, poor living conditions, and lack of personal security. As indicated by the data in Table 14.2 on certain aspects of human deprivations, the magnitude of human suffering in South Asia is far greater than revealed by income poverty figures, though all the countries of the region are in the upper range of the medium human development category (with Maldives and Sri Lanka almost reaching the upper-medium category).

Major Aspects of Human Deprivation in South Asia

Among the magnitude of human deprivations in South Asia, short span of life, infant and child mortality, illiteracy, lack of health services, lack of access to safe water, poor living conditions, and environmental degradation, put increasing strains on the health and well-being of the urban population, especially the urban poor.

Short Span of Life Short span of life is considered one of the severe forms of human deprivation as it manifests the risks of premature death. Though life expectancy at birth has improved over the years in South Asia, ranging from 62 years in Nepal to 74 years in Sri Lanka in 2004, the region continues to have one of the lowest life expectancies in the world, second only to Sub-Saharan Africa (UNDP 2006).

Infant and Child Mortality Infant and child mortality, which also represents a severe form of deprivation, is also one of the highest (62 per 1,000 live births in 2004) in the region. South Asia still accounts for one-third of the burden of the global under-five deaths (UNDP 2006).

Adult Literacy More than 400 million adults (aged 15 years and above) in South Asia, representing half of the developing world's illiterate population, are unable to read or write. While 39 % of the adult population is illiterate, a major part of the remaining 61 % considered literate is only functionally literate. However, notable progress in adult literacy has been made in Maldives and Sri Lanka where the current rates are 96 % and 91 %, respectively, which compare favorably with the adult literacy rates in the high-income countries (UNDP 2006).

Undernourished People There is high incidence of undernourishment among both adult and children in South Asia which is due to both poverty and nonavailability or inadequate availability of basic health services to people in general. The primary health care services are both limited and expensive. Except for Sri Lanka and Maldives, the per capita public expenditure on health in the region is also very meager, varying between PPP US$ 48 for Pakistan and PPP US$ 82 for India as of 2003 (UNDP 2006).

Access to Water and Sanitation In respect of sustainable access to an improved source of water, South Asia has made commendable progress. But the region's performance in respect of improved sanitation is worse than that of the average of all developing countries. There are still 867 million people in the region without adequate sanitation facilities and 198 million without access to safe water. These are indications of poor living conditions which are another form of human deprivation resulting from poverty (UNDP 2006).

Environmental Degradation In fact, economic and social development in the South Asian region is being currently threatened by ever increasing environmental degradation and continuing climate change. Deforestation, overuse, and unplanned use of land and other natural resources are creating unabated environmental degradation in all the South Asian countries. Ever increasing air and water pollution in the region is considered a major threat to natural environment and hazardous to human health (Ahmad 2007).

It thus transpires from the above that poverty, inequality, and social exclusion in South Asia are enormous and exhibit signs of continued accentuation, especially because of many challenges brought by globalization and liberal market paradigm. The poor in South Asia are disproportionately made up of women and children, ethnic minorities, casual and migrant workers, the youth, and the unemployed. Moreover, many of the urban poor dwell in slums and/or backward and remote areas characterized by lack of proper housing, water, sanitation, security, access to healthcare services, education, employment and income-earning opportunities, and environmental degradation. As a result, these vulnerable and socially disadvantaged urban poor people face a higher burden of diseases. Therefore, specific subpopulations experience poorer health with limited or no access to health care compared with other populations in South Asia. Although rapid development increases life expectancy, unhealthy lifestyle behaviors contribute to certain disease incidence (i.e., cancer). Appropriate policy changes and desirable institutional realignment are thus required to achieve faster and broader pro-poor growth for sustained improvement in health in South Asian, which are outlined next.

Policy Revisions and Institutional Reforms for Pro-Poor Growth for Sustained Improvement in Health in South Asia

The discussion in the preceding sections brings light to the fact that economic growth alone does not guarantee sustained improvement in health, high rate of poverty reduction and socially inclusive development in view of many difficult challenges facing the countries of South Asia. The total well-being of the urban poor in South Asia needs to be enhanced through pursuing strategic health communication that is planned, participatory, and grounded in research, for promoting balanced and socially inclusive development goals. While health communication alone cannot solve all health problems, and that, there is no "one size fits all" approach to strategic communication because "strategic communication involves a mix of appropriate multiple and synergistic communication approaches to help foster individual and social change" (UNICEF 2005, p. xiv), with other strategies, health communication can cause sustained change in individual health behavior, organizational policy direction, and help overcome systemic barriers to access to healthcare. In South Asia, various communication approaches, such as mass media campaigns, radio programs, posters, street plays, and localized community outreach programs, have been used to promote public health behavior, such as immunization, prevention of diarrheal dehydration and HIV/AIDS (UNICEF 2005). However, the issue of urban health is multidimensional as it is deeply rooted in the complex web of growth, poverty, and health and intrinsically linked to larger developmental goals. As such, an urban health communication strategy calls for a "coordinated and synergistic response of a wide spectrum of inter-sectoral and inter-agency collaboration" (UNICEF 2005, p. 2). Accordingly, pro-poor growth as the broad-based urban health communication strategy is championed for achieving sustained improvement in health, rapid growth, and sustained poverty reduction in the countries of the South Asian region.

Pathways to Accelerate Urban Health Communication Strategy of Pro-Poor Growth for Sustained Improvement in Health

The important policy interventions to enable the poor to participate in growth as both agents and beneficiaries for sustained improvement in health for socially inclusive development may be summarized as follows:

Raising Productivity in Urban and Peri-Urban Agriculture

Manning (2007) notes that, a 10% increase in crop yields may lead to a reduction of between 6 and 10% of the poor people living on less than US$ 1 a day. Studies (AFD et al. 2005) have cited positive results of increase in agricultural productivity through Green Revolution in Asia that benefited the poor farmers in Bangladesh and Uganda. Since urban dwellers in the South Asian region are on the brink of outnumbering their rural counterparts, urban and periurban agriculture (UPA) presents promising potential for reducing poverty and enhancing food security on which health can be built. As the majority of the urban poor in South Asia who migrate from rural areas (that are agriculture dependent) become the poorest workers with low-skills, the policy priority in such countries should be to raise agricultural productivity within and around cities and towns to help drive national economies and make healthy food available and affordable.

Investments in Infrastructure

The infrastructure gap facing the urban poor is huge. Increased resource flows from both public and private sectors to urban infrastructure building process should be ensured along with a reasonable tariff structure being put in place to enable the private investors to invest with confidence of reasonable returns. It is also important that past mistakes and inefficacies related to management and maintenance of infrastructure facilities are avoided so that a reliable and affordable infrastructure system reduces the production and transaction costs of doing business and help poor people to connect with the growth process. Improving their mobility and access to infrastructure such as roads, reliable energy, and modern communication services can help mitigate risks to public health and safety.

Promoting Growth of Non-Farm Income-Generating Activities and Employment Opportunities

Most developing countries are currently unable to create enough jobs in the formal sector to absorb the entire annual increase in the workforce in addition to millions already unemployed. Therefore, it is crucially important to create gainful employment opportunities for the urban informal sector workforces through pursuing labor-intensive manufacturing growth, enhancing skills of the work force, developing export processing zones, and special economic zones. In addition, millions working in the urban informal sector and working in low-paid activities should be supported to engage in more productive and secure jobs to help overcome increasing income disparities that adversely impact the health of the urban poor.

Enhancing Work Opportunities and Social Protection for the Poor

It is crucially important to ensure increased availability and access of the poor to remunerative employment opportunities, whether through higher productivity in agriculture, access to markets or creation of accessible jobs. However, creation of new jobs should be complemented by arrangements and mechanisms to ensure protection of the poor involved in high-risk jobs and also those unable to work. Various social protection schemes and safety-nets measures should be implemented side by side to protect the vulnerable at moments of crisis. Many of the Asian countries have currently invested in the production of social goods and services and adopted innovative measures (e.g., Food-for-Work Program (FFWP), Cash for Education, Vulnerable Group Feeding (VGF) Program in Bangladesh, Thailand's "30 bath health scheme" to provide the poor with affordable access to health care services) for their delivery (World Bank 2006). Besides human development, these programs play important roles in providing security and protection and enhancing productivity of the poor, and hence contribute to tackling health vulnerability of the urban poor.

Redistributing Growth Across Regions to Combat Poverty and Exclusion

Conventional strategies for spurring growth of the lagging regions include public investments in physical infrastructures, assisted industrialization and reduction of transaction costs for enterprise and trade through special incentives and support measures. But elements of such strategies are cautioned for involvement of high costs, limited developmental impacts, and in some cases negative impacts on environment. Thus, raising the quality and efficiency of investments in the backward regions has to be a priority which may include investment in human capital through enhanced provision of health and education, in public utilities, institutions, and in environmental protection. For example, low-income housing development and slum upgrading can improve the health of and social welfare for the urban poor by providing water, sanitation, solid waste management, storm drainage, electricity, roads and footpaths, and secure tenure. Such urban planning is central to building healthy and inclusive cities.

Improving Institutions and Governance

Corrupt and inefficient service delivery mechanism, poor bureaucratic procedures, misallocation of resources and lack of decentralization and devolution of power to the local levels of government are the most serious bottlenecks impeding effective implementation of poverty reduction programs in most of the South Asian countries (Ahmed et al. 2007). It is thus crucially important that the institutional bottlenecks are removed and local-level participation and accountability with the public service delivery system or other interventions to combat poverty are enhanced. The recent trends in the engagement of a wider range of actors, stakeholders, and coalitions, particularly from the NGOs and the civil society may also help in overcoming the institutional and governance weaknesses to a considerable extent and hence establish participatory urban governance for building healthy and safe cities.

Environmental Sustainability and Pro-Poor Growth

The poor in South Asia and the poor people in general are disproportionately dependent on environmental assets and natural resources. They continue to rely on agriculture, livestock, fisheries, and forestry for earning significant shares of their incomes which call for the need to improve productivity and ensure sustainable exploitation of these resources. A major thrust will therefore be to move away from high-input, low-efficiency, high-waste approaches to the low-cost and high-efficiency extraction and use of natural resources and toward their more economic, efficient, and sustainable use, namely to generate green growth for healthier cities.

Donor Assistance and Partnerships

In the resource-poor South Asian countries, the development partners can play decisive roles in supporting their urban poverty alleviation and health improvement efforts in many ways and directions. For instance, the donors can play significant role in building infrastructures, and supporting research and development, and education and health sector improvements. The important note of caution is, however, that the donors should forge close cooperation among themselves while participating and supporting the programs of the national governments in order to reduce costs and avoid duplications in their engagements with the recipient countries.

Conclusions

Persistence of acute poverty, inequality, and deprivation in most countries of South Asia despite registering notable growth in the 1990s tends to suggest that the "business as usual" approach to development (i.e., growth-augmenting and income poverty-reducing growth strategy) is inadequate to ensure optimal combination of improved health, growth, and social cohesion. Even high rates of growth in many countries, especially South Asian countries appear to have bypassed the poor in the backward regions, and the poor ethnic groups and other minorities and thereby fail to achieve socially inclusive development. Furthermore, because of systemic failure in the delivery of essential human development services, health, education, water, sanitation, and electricity, especially to the poor in the lagging regions, poverty and deprivation tend to remain chronic and widespread. Thus, the policy consensus is that sustained improvement in health and faster and sustained poverty reduction require urban health communication strategy of pro-poor growth which is a pace and pattern of growth that enhances the capacity of the poor to participate in, contribute to, and benefit from growth. Such a policy consensus echoes with "the shift in thinking about strategic communication as it relates to the contemporary development paradigm" that is guided by human rights principles such as equality and non discrimination (UNICEF 2005, p. 2).

Effective strategic communication should consider existing policy and legislative environment and be linked to service delivery aspects (UNICEF 2005). In view of that, as a concerted plan, the urban health communication strategy of pro-poor growth in South Asia demands a combination of change in policy and resources. For instance, extreme poverty is closely linked with limited or lack of access to safe drinking water and sanitation. Since in a country like Bangladesh, poor water quality or the effects of natural disasters are further barriers to dealing with extreme poverty and improving access to water and sanitation, policies such as social protection services, namely water supply and sanitation, can play an important role in eradicating extreme poverty (UNHRC 2009). The vision of the urban health communication strategy of pro-poor growth is to enable South Asian governments, policy makers, communities, and households to act, communicate, and lead together so that the countries in the region ultimately have the capacity to achieve sustained improvement in health, rapid growth, and sustained poverty reduction.

This chapter set out to show how to pursue the objectives of achieving sustained improvement in health and accelerated economic growth in the face of critical challenges posed by globalization in the countries of South Asia. Focusing on how a faster, participative, and a broad-based inclusive development can be attained, this chapter attempted to connect the local and global issues, build a consensus on the core areas of policy revisions and institutional reforms aimed at facilitating dialogue at the global, regional, and national levels. In doing so, while this chapter advocates for a consensus for accelerating pro-poor growth as the broad-based urban health communication strategy for achieving sustained improvement in health, rapid growth, and sustained poverty reduction in the countries of the South Asian region, it also hopes to show other resource-limited regions of the world the use of strategic health communication in urban contexts through increasing productivity in the urban areas, creating gainful employment for the urban poor, encouraging investment in human development, especially ensuring access of the urban poor to health care facilities, and promoting environmental sustainability, hence, the case for a virtuous circle (see Fig. 14.1) to augment pro-poor growth for sustained improvement in health. Although, based on the review of recent experiences in the South Asian

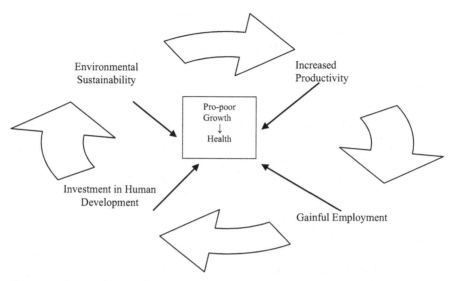

Fig. 14.1 Virtuous circle to augment pro-poor growth for sustained improvement in health

countries, this chapter highlighted some key policy areas and institutional dimensions as important areas of interventions to promote pro-poor growth for sustained improvement in health for socially inclusive development, there is a dearth of systematic, comparative studies of the health problems of the urban poor across the regions of Sub-Saharan Africa, Latin America, and Asia (Harpham 2009). However, some patterns do emerge from "ad hoc studies" (p. 111, emphasis in original) that allows recognition of priority actions for urban health. For example, while the relative distribution of diseases—mental ill health and heart disease in Latin America, HIV/AIDS and diarrhea in Africa, and heart disease and diarrhea in Asia—differs across the regions, "physical environment, social and health services all feature as determinants" of those diseases (p. 114). As such, while the ideal combination will naturally vary depending on the particular regional and country circumstances (i.e., levels of development, poverty, human development, efficiency in governance and institutions) the overall urban health communication strategy of pro-poor growth should aim at addressing the constraints that the poor households face in participating in growth and achieving better health for socially inclusive development.

References

Ahmad, Q. K. (2007). Development in South Asia: A paradigm shift is called for. *Journal of the Asiatic Society of Bangladesh, 52*(2).

Ahmed, M. U., et al. (2007). *Agrarian reform and rural development: Issues concerns and future challenges.* Rural development report, 2007, CIRDAP, Dhaka, Bangladesh.

Agence Francaise de Development (AFD) (2005). Bundesministerium für Wirtschaftliche Zusammenarbeit und Entwicklung, U.K. Department for International Development, The

World Bank. Pro-poor growth in the 1990s—Lessons and insights from 14 countries. A Joint World Bank/DFID Study. Washington, DC. http://siteresources.worldbank.org/INTPGI/Resources/342674-1119450037681/Pro-poor_growth_in_the_1990s.pdf. Accessed 15 May 2008.

Carter-Pokras, O, & Baquet, C. (2002). What is a health disparity? *Public Health Reports, 117,* 426–432.

Chaudhury, N., & Devarajan, S. (2006). Human development and service delivery in Asia. *Development Policy Review, 24*(Supp. 1), s81–97.

Debopriya, B., et al. (2006). *Macroeconomic performance of South Asian economies: A comparative perspective on Bangladesh.* Paper presented to CPD Dialogue on Growth and Equity in South Asia—How has Bangladesh Performed? CIRDAP Auditorium, Dhaka, Bangladesh.

Farrington, J. & Robinson, M. (2006). Introduction: Meeting the challenges to growth and poverty reduction. *Development Policy Review, 24*(Supp. 1), s3–12.

Harpham, T. (2009). Urban health in developing countries: What do we know and where do we go? *Health & Place, 15,* 107–116.

Humphrey, J. (2006). Prospects and challenges for growth and poverty reduction in Asia. *Development Policy Review, 24*(Supp. 1), s29–49.

Kakwani, M., & Pernia, E. M. (2000). What is pro-poor growth? *Asian Development Review, 18*(1), 1–16.

Lopez-Casasnovas, G., et al. (2005). (Eds). Health and economic growth: Findings and policy implications. Cambridge, MA: MIT Press.

Mahbubul Haq Human Development Centre (2006). Human development in South Asia 2006. Oxford University Press.

Manning, R. (2007). Pro-poor growth: Negotiating consensus on a contentious issue. *Development, 50*(2).

McMichael, A. J. (2002). The urban environment and health in a globalizing world: Issues for developing countries. In R. Akhtar (Ed.), *Urban health in the third world* (pp. 423–4). New Delhi: APH Publishing Corporation.

Mercado, S., Havemann, K., Sami, M., & Ueda, Hiroshi. (2007). Urban poverty: An urgent public health issue. *Journal of Urban Health: Bulletin of the New York Academy of the Medicine, 84*(1), 7–15.

Ravallion, M. (2004). *Pro-poor growth: A primer.* World Bank Policy Research Working Paper (Publication No. 324.2). Washington, DC.

UN-HABITAT (2008). *State of the world's cities 2008/2009: Harmonious cities.* USA: Earthscan.

United Nations Children's Fund (UNICEF) (2005). *Strategic communication for behavior and social change in South Asia.* The United Nations Children's Fund Regional Office for South Asia, Kathmandu, Nepal.

United Nations Department of Economic and Social Affairs (UN DESA) (2010). *World urbanization prospects: The 2009 revision.* United Nations Department of Economic and Social Affairs. Population Division. United Nations, New York.

United Nations Development Program (UNDP) (2006). *Human development report 2006.* United Nations, New York.

United Nations Human Rights Council (UNHRC) (2009). Bangladesh: UN experts focus on extreme poverty and water sanitation. United Nations Human Rights Council.

World Health Organization (WHO) (2002). *Health, economic growth, and poverty reduction.* The Report of Working Group 1 of the Commission on Macroeconomics and Health. World Health Organization, Geneva.

World Health Organization (WHO) (2010). Why urban health matters. 1000 Cities 1000 Lives: Urban Health Matters. World Health Day. World Health Organization, Geneva.

World Bank (2006). World development report 2006. Washington, DC: The World Bank.

World Bank (2007). World Development Indicators 2007. Washington, DC: The World Bank.

World Bank (2009). World development report 2009. Washington, DC: The World Bank.

Chapter 15
The Role of Sports in Strategic Health Promotion

Priscilla Wamucii

Introduction

Slum settlements in many parts of the world continue to experience unprecedented growth in population size. An approximated 61.7 % of Sub-Saharan Africa's urban population was projected to be living in slums in 2012 (UN-Habitat 2013, p. 215). This trend will undoubtedly have tremendous effects on health issues that affect people living in slums or informal settlements. Generally, slums are characterized by social and economic factors that range from overcrowding and extreme levels of poverty, to crime and violence. The lack of water, sanitary, and waste disposal services also pose environmental hazards for slum inhabitants. Resultantly, waterborne and respiratory diseases are common and rates of HIV/AIDS prevalence high.

Young people in Kenya, as in other developing countries, have been significantly affected by the growth of slums. This chapter focuses on the Mathare Youth Sports Association (MYSA), an organization located in one of Kenya's largest slums. Specifically, the chapter highlights how the organization has used sports as an entry point as well as a mobilizing platform for addressing health challenges in Mathare. Although many health promotion efforts have used innovative approaches to health such as the use of mass media, interpersonal communication, and entertainment education, few empirical studies have focused on the potential role that sports could play in creating or enhancing understanding of health issues. This chapter attempts to address this gap, by providing a detailed account of the use of sports for health promotion in slum contexts. The next section begins by providing a background of MYSA.

P. Wamucii (✉)
University Canada West, Calgary, Canada
e-mail: pwamucii@yahoo.com

C. C. Okigbo (ed.), *Strategic Urban Health Communication*,
DOI 10.1007/978-1-4614-9335-8_15, © Springer Science+Business Media New York 2014

Background of the Mathare Youth Sports Association

The Mathare Youth Sports Association (MYSA) is located in Nairobi in a slum known as Mathare. Kenya's slums, like those in other parts of the world, grew as a result of urbanization and as large numbers of people migrated into cities looking for employment. Welfare monitoring surveys conducted by the Kenyan government indicate that, although three quarters of the poor live in rural areas, the majority of poor people living in urban areas live in slums and periurban areas (Government of Kenya 2003).

Mathare is located a few miles northeast of Nairobi. The slum was established in 1963 as a settlement for landless people (Hake, cited in Brady and Khan 2002). Since that time, people from all parts of the country have migrated there in the hope of finding land and work. However, these two prospects are difficult to find because of the unemployment problems that face the country as a whole. The living conditions in Mathare are also some of the worst in Nairobi. It is estimated that Mathare holds between half a million to a million people, and that 70 % of the households are single parent families with mothers generally raising children on their own (Hognestad and Tollisen 2004).

In many cases, the slums are referred to as informal settlements, a label that signifies the nonprovision of public and social services, including public health facilities and schools by government (Dodoo et al. 2002). Informal settlements not only typically lack formal connection to municipal services but they are also characterized by extremely large populations. A single sanitation facility, for example, might serve over 500 people (UN-Habitat 2004). In addition, a study conducted in Nairobi informal settlements by the African Population Health Research Council (APHRC 2002) found that only a small percentage of households in slum areas have access to piped water in the form of public water taps or water piped into residences in comparison to 92 % in nonslum areas of Nairobi as a whole. In many parts of Nairobi's slums, residents have no access to running water, electricity, working toilets, or adequate sanitation facilities (Dodoo et al. 2002). The majority of residents are either unemployed or self-employed in the informal sector.

The Mathare Youth Sports Association (MYSA) is a development initiative that works to address the aforementioned issues. MYSA was started in 1987 by Bob Munro, a Canadian expatriate, as a small self-help project to organize young people through sport and clean-up activities. Indeed, the story of MYSA's origin is deeply entrenched in the institution's memory and is often narrated by the youth. Munro, the founder, was approached by young boys who saw him watching them as they played in one of the open spaces in Mathare. The boys requested him to referee one of the games. He said that he would do that on condition that they also did something in return. Munro suggested that they clean-up the football field. The boys agreed to the terms which led to the birth of MYSA. MYSA eventually grew in unexpected ways and was guided by the words exchanged in the initial contact, between Munro and the boys, which were, "*You do something for MYSA, MYSA does something for you.*" The story of MYSA is especially significant because it highlights a shift from development entities that are based on dependency. Bob Munro established a mutual relationship; he provided leather balls as well as his time. The youths put in their fair share, which entailed making a contribution to the communities in which they lived by engaging in clean-ups.

MYSA has now grown into a multifaceted development initiative that focuses on soccer, environmental clean-up activities, HIV/AIDS prevention and awareness, substance abuse, reproductive health, and other community concerns. The above projects are supported by an arts and culture group which utilizes art, drama, music, and puppetry to create awareness on a number of health issues. Other programs include a sports leadership academy; a scholarship project, a youth exchange program and community libraries. The programs of MYSA offer a rich context within which to explore how sports are woven into a web of activities designed to raise awareness and consciousness health and to foster systemic change throughout people's lives. The following section provides an overview of strategic health communication in general.

Strategic Health Communication

Communication scholars and practitioners have been at the forefront of development work, through diffusion of technology, setting agendas for pertinent issues, and increasing community involvement across the borders of countries (Singhal and Rogers 1999). Despite the strategic application of communication technologies, many development programs have failed to achieve their goals (see critiques by Wilkins 2000). Piotrow and Kincaid (2001) attribute the failure of communication approaches to a number of factors that include a lack of strategic design or initiatives that fail to make linkages between health promotion and service delivery programs. At the message development level, there has been an assumption that a once off exposure to messages is sufficient without additional reinforcements. Moreover, communication strategists often present general messages without taking into consideration complexity presented by diversity of the intended audience. Lastly, a number of communication strategies are atheoretical, while others lack an emphasis on research.

In this chapter, the design and implementation processes within MYSA are highlighted. Theoretically, the discussion draws from key principles associated with the social marketing model, which among other things puts emphasis on the selection of an appropriate place, effective promotion of a product, focusing on benefits over costs (price) and promotion. In MYSA's, case the discussion associates place with the sports field, and other places of engagement, for instance, schools and shopping centers. The product concept is linked to health messages on HIV/AIDS prevention, reproductive health, substance abuse, and on issues related to environmental awareness and health. Price is addressed by highlighting potential positive outcomes for MYSA youths as well as the community at large, if they adopted the information provided in the community outreaches through behavioral change. Finally, promotion is evinced in MYSA's strategies that include peer education, drama, music and dance, community clean-ups, and by using uniforms, equipment and vehicles to spread health messages. Caution is taken, though, to guard against the tendency by health strategists who sometimes want to fit implementation processes into the rules of dominant theories or models in social psychology rather than allowing the field experience to shape its own framework (Airhihenbuwa and Obregon 2000). In many ways, the chapter attempts to allow the information provided by MYSA's experience to provide useful pointers for strategic health promotions.

The chapter draws from approaches to health promotions that emphasize participation. In comparison to traditional forms of communication that were hierarchical and primarily message centered, the emergent communication strategies are people-centered. Most contemporary strategic health initiatives also seek to be holistic. Culture, for instance, is seen as central to planning, implementation, and evaluation of health communication and health promotion (Airhihenbuwa and Obregon 2000).

At the heart of strategic communication is a desire to foster dialogue among community members. Dialogue is useful in decentralizing power, which is crucial in health promotion and development in general. As Melkote (2000) argued, "real change is not possible unless we deal squarely with the lack of power among individuals and groups especially at the grassroots" (p. 40). In summary, strategic communication seeks to promote citizen participation in planning, decision-making and ownership of projects. Strategic health communication is also based on common visions, goals and objectives and well-defined ways of evaluating the projects. The next section highlights sports as one of the innovative tools in communication for health.

Sports as a Strategic Tool in Health Promotion

The use of sports has gained popularity over recent years as an appropriate means of creating social change, especially at the grassroots level. The United Nations development agencies, for example, refer to sports as the "universal language," pointing to the ability of sports to be applied to different contexts in the world. In fact, the United Nations declared 2005 as the "International Year of Sports and Physical Education" which highlighted the role of sports in society and the ability of sports to contribute to advancement of the quality of life (United Nations 2005). In a related manner, sports have been promoted as an effective way of achieving the Millennium Development Goals.

A significant share of documentation on sporting organizations and development has focused on the ability of sports to reach out to great masses of people. Kassing et al. (2004), for example, suggested that sports audiences are among the largest in the world. This phenomenon could be explained from a number of perspectives. The first is that sports are considered as having advantages over other cultural forms of expression because they are more readily comprehensible to the mass public (MacClancey 1996). Second, sports serve the function of coproducing communities because they could facilitate the creation of feelings of belongingness and connectedness among participants, and lessen distance between people. Sports often unite wider sections of the population by transcending differences of nationality, sex, age, social positioning, geographical location, and political attitudes (Kassing et al. 2004). The accessibility of sports, therefore, reveals the potential usefulness of soccer as a mechanism for building community and as a vehicle for social change, especially in a context like Kenya where soccer is accessible to and affordable for many people.

More specific cases indicate that sports are increasingly being used in the development of children and youth. Many organizations recognize that sport and play are fundamental to youth development and can be used for teaching youth essential values and life skills, such as teamwork, cooperation, and respect. Extant literature indicates that sports have been used extensively in the health arena, for example, to combat unhealthy, deviant, and antisocial behaviors, such as drunkenness, delinquency, and prostitution. Sports have also been utilized in national and regional campaigns, for example in the "Kick polio out of Africa" campaign that was launched in 1996 by Nelson Mandela and other African leaders which led to a significant reduction of polio-induced paralysis from 205 cases per day to 388 cases for an entire year (Joint Press Release, WHO 2004). Indeed, MYSA was selected as one of the 20 FIFA 2010 projects for Football for Hope, FIFA's 2010 World Cup's official campaign. The main objectives of the campaign were to create 20 centers geared toward the promotion of public health, education, and the development of football within the disadvantaged communities in Africa. MYSA therefore provides an appropriate account for analyzing the use sports for health campaigns. The next section provides descriptive accounts of MYSA's program design and its implementation of projects.

Program Design

MYSA has become a brand name and has now become known not only for sports dexterity but also for its "clean-up" activities. (MYSA member)

MYSA's primary activity is soccer. The organization's approach stands out as an innovation because of its ability to reconstruct sports from a purely entertainment and physical development construct to a platform that addresses pertinent health issues. The organization's strength lies in its ability to mobilize and its capacity to reach youth in large numbers. By 2012, MYSA had a membership of 25,000 young people (MYSA 2013). In addition, MYSA operates in 16 zones in the Mathare area, thereby reaching youths living in different localities. MYSA uses soccer fields in its zones as communication avenues for health promotion.

The organization disseminates various health messages during its matches. The audience is exposed to various performances that include drama, music, and peer counseling during half time. Topical issues such as HIV/AIDs, drug abuse, and crime are presented. The messages focus on creating awareness on these issues and are ultimately intended to lead to behavioral change. MYSA's vehicles and players' uniforms are also utilized as avenues for communication. Health messages such as "Kick Aids out of Africa" are some of the common messages.

MYSA also utilizes its numbers to ensure members' engagement at the community service level by making this exercise mandatory for all members. For each successful clean-up activity approved by the organization, for example, a team wins six points which translates to two wins in the league standing. Success therefore occurs both "on" and "off" the field as MYSA members are generally both players as well as active agents in their community. By combining sports and community activities, MYSA addresses health topics in a number of ways. First, the physical fitness aspect is catered for as youth participate in soccer. Second, MYSA youth attend various workshops on HIV/AIDS, reproductive health and substance abuse, and are trained as peer counselors. MYSA also facilitates participation in forums that address other issues such as environmental conservation. Some members, for instance, have attended courses organized by an organization established by the Nobel Peace Prize recipient Wangari Mathaai. This organization focuses on building leaders in environmental conservation. The above initiatives have contributed to MYSA members' knowledge of health issues as well as their self-esteem and confidence.

MYSA's professional team Mathare United has also gained popularity over the years as one of the formidable soccer teams in the country. A significant number of MYSA's male professional team members also play for the National team, *Harambee* Stars. These players who are sometimes awarded celebrity status by young people are required to fulfill their community service hours. In so doing, they are regarded as role models for many aspiring youths in Mathare. The players' work, for instance, in clean-up activity or HIV/AIDS awareness impacts positively on younger youth in the community.

Lastly, the organization's success is hinged on its efforts to work in collaboration with various stakeholders including parents, teachers, and local government officials. Many of MYSA's members are under 18 years of age and MYSA often engages with their parents when dealing with them, and logistics often require parental consent. MYSA's peer educators also work in close collaboration with various schools and are usually allocated time to share information on various health issues that affect the community. MYSA also interacts with the local chief in planning their meetings and events.

As discussed above MYSA's success is influenced by its appropriate positioning in sports which translates to community activities. The ultimate goal of MYSA is to create behavior change especially with regard to HIV/AIDS, teenage pregnancy, and substance abuse, and to ensure that the youth are able to critically engage with the environmental hazards generated by their living conditions. The next section focuses on the implementation aspects of MYSA by focusing on community outreaches.

Project Implementation

Tackling Environmental Challenges: Clean-Ups

MYSA addresses environmental challenges in the slums by engaging youth in clean-up activities on weekends and school holidays. These activities include garbage collection, clearing of bushes and removal of stagnant water in their neighborhoods. Indeed, these efforts have earned the organization international recognition. MYSA was a recipient of the United Nations Environmental Program award for environmental innovation and achievement in the 1992 Earth Summit in Rio de Janiero. As discussed previously, the enormity of waste disposal in the slums is challenging. MYSA youths understand this and many acknowledge that their clean-up activities probably did not make much impact as the streets end up being littered by the following day. The youth were realistic about the situation as evidenced by their suggestion that the magnitude of the social problems was too great for the organization to change without assistance from other development institutions. Nonetheless, communication played a major factor in motivating youth to continue with their work. The youth were united by a common slogan that *haba na haba hujaza kibaba* (step-by-step we reach the goal) which emphasizes that even the smallest step counts. In this manner, organizational discourse contributed to the idea behavior change on environmental hygiene had to start somewhere, even if that translates to a single step.

A number of youths pointed out that change had already begun by noting that as a result of their initiatives, a number of community members offered to join them and participated in the clean-ups even on days when the youth were not able to show up. Furthermore, MYSA youth efforts have the potential of making a difference in the future because when children who were a part of organization matured, they were likely to continue the community service behavior which was an asset for the community.

One of the limitations of this study is that it does not provide statistical evidence on behavioral change on practices associated with diseases such HIV/AIDs or substance abuse. However, narratives from MYSA members indicated that their participation in the organization and the information gathered had helped in shaping their life trajectories. The time spent engaging in sports, for example, kept them away from drugs, drunkenness, and violent crime. The information provided on HIV/AIDS enabled many to draw from prevention messages provided by peer counselors such as ABC (Abstain, Be faithful, Condoms). This information provided them with options and direction in making decisions in their sexual encounters.

Peer Education

Community service in MYSA's context also entailed peer education and participation in the arts and culture program. MYSA's youth actively engaged in creating awareness about HIV/AIDS, and 300 of its youth had received training as peer counselors by 2006. The trained peer counselors were then responsible for disseminating the information to non-MYSA members in their communities. Peer counselors also shared their knowledge on HIV/AIDS during matches, in schools, and at the organizational setting. Moreover, yearly training workshops on HIV/AIDS were organized, bringing together many children from the slums. The peer approach is especially significant in health promotion because peer-led interventions are based on the assumption that behavior is socially influenced and that behavioral norms are developed through interaction (Visser 2007). Peer interventions also recognize that young people are more likely to be open with their peers and that knowledge can be shared in a language that is comprehensible for young people. More recently, MYSA has introduced voluntary counseling and testing (VCT) programs for HIV/AIDS. These developments provide opportunities for young people to undergo HIV/AIDS testing.

In MYSA's context, school outreach programs in particular are instructive. MYSA youths engaged with their peers on various health issues including reproductive health, drugs and HIV/AIDS. In many cases, youths in these schools actively participated in the conversations. MYSA youths relied on the act of narration; and by using stories, they utilized creativity and appealed to the audience members' imaginations in ways that enhanced their understanding of health issues. Such stories addressed various types of relationships, sexually transmitted diseases, "sugar daddies" (and mummies) and also provided opportunities for both females and males (16–18-year olds) in the class to give their perspectives on the issues. In some cases, narrators did not complete their stories, which generated suspense and interest in MYSA's youth subsequent sessions at the school. By engaging the youths at their level and through the use of personal experience, narrators made knowledge very accessible and credible.

Performance: Music, Dance, and Drama

The arts and culture group utilized music, dance, and drama to engage community members on health issues. Plays were commonly referred to "mirrors of society" because most people in the audience were able to see reflections of their individual lives or of people they knew, enacted in the plays. The group provided entertainment during matches, performed in local public spaces such as shopping centers, and on environmental clean-up days.

MYSA also builds on the orality of African culture in shaping its messages. In their drama performances for instance, youths not only set the stage but also actively engaged with spectators in the development of plots. Plays often presented conflicts that could be resolved in more than one way. Such conflicts provided playwrights and community members with a space to engage with the scripts which enhanced learning. These emergent dialogic spaces also facilitated integrated thinking because in many cases a number of people were involved in coming up with solutions to problems such as drug addiction that affected individual MYSA members and the community as a whole.

Movement Games

The promotion of dialogue was a key characteristic of MYSA. This aspect was facilitated by a number of factors. First, the organization ensured that its programs were tailored to the needs of its target audience—the youth. MYSA understood that even the youth are not a homogenous group. The organization, for instance, used movement games or popular games that were not generally considered professional sports to target younger youths (9–13 years). Movement games enhanced the learning process because certain ideas or concepts, for example, HIV/AIDS that are sometimes too abstract for children to understand were associated with constructs that emerged in the game. This made learning interesting and facilitated significant contributions from children. Facilitators used such forums to talk about HIV/AIDS prevention, transmission, and the associated stigma by drawing analogies between the disease and the game.

Key Lessons and Policy Implications

Holistic Approach to Health

MYSA adopts a holistic or ecological approach to health. Although many of its activities are geared toward creating awareness on various diseases and health hazards, other factors that affect the well-being of youth were prioritized. For instance, through the realization that many children drop out of school because of lack of school fees, MYSA provides scholarships for its members. Two hundred boys and girls had benefited from the scholarship program by 2001 (Wambuii 2003). MYSA also provides employment for a number of youths. One requirement for hiring employees in the organization is that prospective candidates have to be MYSA members. In these ways, MYSA contributed to economic empowerment which is crucial for healthy communities.

Emphasis on Collective Effort

MYSA emphasizes a collective approach to health issues. By encouraging cooperation, MYSA collapses the boundary controls that often limit and bifurcate organizations. Its emphasis on cooperation was also evident in the interpersonal relationships that emerged within the organization. MYSA provided youths with social networks that assisted them in dealing with loss of family to illness, or with sick family members.

Conclusion

MYSA effectiveness is enhanced by the organization's utilization of interpersonal communication strategies that enhance participation and which are embedded in local culture such as drama, storytelling, music, and dance. MYSA uses communication strategies that are accessible and affordable for marginalized populations. These strategies are sustainable and have the potential not only to foster systemic change that improves the quality of life but also to contribute to policies that could be maintained with limited resources.

MYSA provides significant contributions to health approaches that could be utilized in poor urban neighborhoods. MYSA presents a novel way of thinking that promotes the use of sports as a pedagogical tool, or a space where people can acquire skills and generate knowledge on topical issues pertaining to health. These efforts should be strengthened and extended to other social settings. An important step is for the Government to support such initiatives through budgetary allocations that would enable sports programs to expand their activities to include other community service activities. Such developments would ensure that more youth and communities benefited from the programs in both poor urban and rural areas.

The ministry of health could also integrate similar initiatives in its strategic plans to ensure a wider reach. The ministry could adopt an ecological perspective to health as illustrated by MYSA. Health promotions should be characterized by multifaceted approaches that focus not only on the physical well-being but also on other areas such as education and economic empowerment and community building.

The ministry of education could also draw from MYSA's experience, in particular its illustration that effective learning is facilitated through a combination of play and work activities. The use of soccer, movement games, drama and music are effective ways of generating knowledge. Schools could draw from MYSA's model by integrating health information in creative ways in their curricula.

Finally, and importantly, more research needs to be carried out in the sports, youth and development areas, with a goal of developing measurement tools that could be used to evaluate program effectiveness.

References

African Population and Health Research Center (APHRC). (2002). *Population and health dynamics in Nairobi's informal settlements*. Nairobi: African Population and Health Research Center

Airhihenbuwa, C. O., & Obregon, R. (2000). A critical assessment of theories/models used in health communication for HIV/AIDS. *Journal of Health Communication, 5*, 5–15.

Brady, M., & Khan, A. (2002). *Letting girls play. The Mathare Youth Sport Association's soccer program for girls*. New York: The Population Council.

Dodoo, F, N., Sloan, M., & Zulu, E. M. (2002). Space, context, and hardship: Socializing children into social activity in Kenyan Slums. In S. Agyei-Mensah & J. Casterline (Eds.), *Reproduction and social context in Sub-Saharan Africa. A collection micro-demographic studies* (pp. 147–160). Westport: Greenwood.

Government of Kenya. (2003). *Economic recovery strategy for wealth and employment creation 2003–2007*. Nairobi: Government Printer

Hognestad, H., & Tollisen, A. (2004). Playing against deprivation: Soccer and development in Kenya. In G. Armstrong & R. Giulianotti (Eds.), *Soccer in Africa* (pp. 210–226). New York: Palgrave Macmillian.

Kassing, J., Billings, A., Brown, R., Halone, K., Harrison, K., et al (2004). Communication in the community of sport: The process of enacting (re) producing, consuming, and organizing sport.

In P. J. Kabfleisch (Ed.), *Communication Yearbook 28* (pp. 373–409). Mahwah: Lawrence Erlbaum.

MacClancey, J. (Ed.). (1996). *Sport, identity and ethnicity*. Herndon: Berg.

Melkote, S. (2000). Reinventing development support communication to account for power and control in development. In K. G. Wilkins (Ed.), *Redeveloping communication for social change: Theory, practice, and power* (pp. 39–54). Lanham: Rowman and Littlefield.

MYSA. (2013). Our history. http://www.mysakenya.org/Who-we-are/our-history.html. Accessed 12 June 2013

Piotrow, P. T., & Kincaid, D. L. (2001). Strategic Communication for International Health Programs. In R. E. Rice and C. K. Atkin (Ed.), *Public Communication Campaigns* (3rd ed., pp. 251). Sage

Singhal, A., & Rogers, E. (1999). *Entertainment-education: A communication strategy for social change*. Mahwah: Lawrence Erlbaum.

United Nations. (2005). A year of sports. http://www.un.org/sport2005/a_year/ayear_for.html. Accessed 5 Mar 2007

UN-Habitat. (2004). *Global campaign for secure tenure: A tool for advocating the provision of adequate shelter for the urban poor*. Nairobi: United Nations Human Settlements Program

UN-Habitat. (2006). *State of the world's cities 2006/7. The millennium development goals and urban sustainability. 30 years of shaping the habitat agenda*. Nairobi: United Nations Human Settlements Program

UN-Habitat. (2012). State of the world's cities 2012/2013. *Prosperity of cities*. Nairobi: United Nations Human Settlements Program

Visser, M. (2007). HIV/AIDS prevention through peer education and support in South Africa. *Journal of Social Aspects of Health, 4*(2), 678–694.

Wambuii, K. (2003). For the sake of the children. Community-based youth projects in Kenya. In A. Singhal & S. Howard (Eds.), *The children of Africa confront AIDS. From vulnerability to possibility* (pp. 131–148). Athens: Ohio University Press

WHO. (2004). *Joint press release WHO/UNICEF/Rotary International/CDC. West Africa mobilizes for final assault against polio*. http://www.who.int/mediacentre/news/releases/2004/pr13/en/. Accessed 3 Apr 2004

Wilkins, K. G. (2000). Accounting for power in development communication. In K. G. Wilkins (Ed.), *Redeveloping communication for social change: Theory, practice, and power* (pp. 197–210). Lanham: Rowman and Littlefield.

Chapter 16
The Internet as a Sex Education Tool: A Case Study of an Online Thai Discussion Board

Thanomwong Poorisat and Arul Chib

Introduction

The focus on abstinence-only sex education in conservative countries (Chamra-trithirong and Richter 2009; Lou et al. 2006) has made it difficult for youth to obtain information about reproductive health issues from scholastic and traditional mass media sources. This problem is compounded in developing countries with limited health personnel and resources, even in urban areas. Evolving sociocultural norms and media influence have led to youth in Asian countries engaging in premarital sexual activity and a low incidence of safe contraceptive practices (UNICEF 2005). Thailand, in particular among Southeast Asian countries, suffers from a high in-cidence of people having unprotected sex with prostitutes (Gubhaju 2002). Faced with a lack of access to correct information, urban youth harbor misconceptions about sex, and remain ill equipped to deal with unwanted pregnancies or sexually transmitted diseases (STDs).

Sexual education is required to create healthy perceptions about sexuality and knowledge of prevention and mitigation of STDs and unwanted pregnancies. Evidence suggests that the Internet could serve as an alternative source of strategic health education (Borzekowski et al. 2006; Nwagwu 2007). Anonymity provided by the Internet makes it a unique and preferred medium for seeking guidance about sensitive issues, such as those involved in sexual and reproductive health. The convenience and low cost incurred provide secondary motivations to urban youth possessing limited time and resources. The problem of reaching an at-risk population of youth can thus be overcome via targeted Internet resources. Indeed, with increasing urban Internet penetration, young adults have increasingly flocked online to seek sexual guidance (Barak and Fisher 2003).

We note that the use of the Internet to disseminate health information remains a largely urban phenomenon, particularly in developing nations. The global digital divide, while shrinking slightly, still constitutes a significant barrier to the use of

T. Poorisat (✉) · A. Chib
Nanyang Technological University, Nanyang, Singapore
e-mail: than0039@e.ntu.edu.sg

C. C. Okigbo (ed.), *Strategic Urban Health Communication*,
DOI 10.1007/978-1-4614-9335-8_16, © Springer Science+Business Media New York 2014

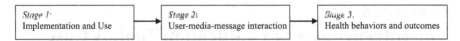

Fig. 16.1 A three-stage model of health promotion using interactive media. (Street 2003)

the Internet by developing countries (ITU 2010). However, urban areas within these developing countries have seen major strides in the deployment of fixed and mobile broadband. We focused this study on the use of new information technologies, particularly the Internet, to improve methods to inform urban youth about sexual health.

From a strategic health communication perspective, the Internet can be an effective dissemination medium in a conservative environment with limited social and institutional support. Social morality stands in stark defiance of actual practice. Almost three-quarters of Thais believed premarital sex of daughters was unacceptable to parents, yet 70 % of young Thai women report sexual relations prior to betrothal (Chamratrithirong et al. 2006). Evidently ostracized by prevailing mores, violators of social rules turn to the Internet instead of approaching medical experts. A similar trend was also observed in urban China (Parish et al. 2007).

In a society with constraining attitudes towards reproductive health, government support services tends to focus mainly on married couples and advocate abstinence-only sex education, ignoring adolescents for all intents and purposes. Government agencies have been criticized for lack of political will and vision, and preference of the status quo. As a result, the majority of existing online sexual health resources has been established largely by the private sector, both profit and nonprofit organizations.

The most common health sites in Thailand present information about sexuality reaching out to a potentially vast online populace (Prachusilpa et al. 2004). The relatively modest 23.9 % Internet penetration in Thailand still translates into a sizeable number of almost 16.1 million users ("ITU" 2009). This chapter contributes to the field by examining how the Internet, specifically health discussion boards, can be used in strategic health communication for a predominantly urban audience in developing countries.

We used the three-stage model of health promotion (Street 2003), to examine an online discussion board for sexual health education. Each stage considers different factors that determine the success and effectiveness of particular health promotion programs (Fig. 16.1). We limited our investigation to the two key factors of user motivation and media characteristics.

To examine user motivation, an important element determining the outcome of technological diffusion, we turned to the first and third stages of health promotion. The first stage of *implementation and use* advocates an emphasis on user needs. Before deciding what type of information to publish online, it is crucial for providers to understand their target audience. Despite monetary and institutional resources invested, online resources may be of little value without addressing specific needs. Further, user perceptions of credibility and usefulness can affect the effectiveness of the strategic health communication.

People are likely to pay more attention to experts and be more prone to the influence of their messages (Bohner et al. 2008). Anonymous members of a discussion board may be motivated to post replies and provide guidance, but if information seekers do not perceive these contributors as credible, then the information could be deemed inadequate. Conversely, and especially for sensitive health issues, the credibility provided by the health specialist could be a key determinant of beliefs about the accuracy of the content (Wathen and Burkell 2002).

According to stage 3 of the model, the impact on positive *health behaviors and outcomes* is the ultimate test of the success of health communication interventions. However, given the level of anonymity and sensitive nature of the topic of sexual health, identification of the direct impact of an online discussion board was problematic. Therefore, we used an indirect measure of the perceived usefulness of a medium to assess the discussion board's contribution to its users' health outcomes. We note that most work conducted in this respect pertains to developed nations (e.g., Kanuga and Rosenfeld 2004; Wynn et al. 2009). We aimed to fill this research gap by examining user factors in a developing nation's urban context.

What are the keys to motivations of users to actively search for sexual health information on an online discussion board, particularly regarding suitability, credibility, and usefulness of the content?

Media characteristics originating from the second stage of User-media-message interaction play a vital role in determining its function (Media Richness theory, Draft and Lengel 1984). In the context of strategic health communication, certain media may possess features more suitable for treatment and problem solving, while others may be better for preventing health problems. The feedback loop provided by an online discussion board distinguishes it from general health websites. While general information seekers may be attracted to the latter, users seeking advice for a particular reproductive health problem are more likely to desire a response from a medium that provides ease-of-use and privacy. We found four characteristics of online discussion boards that would influence people to use them for problem solving in reproductive health, namely, interactivity, modality, asynchronicity, and privacy.

Interactivity is commonly cited as one of the distinctive characteristics of the Internet in relation to other mass media (Barak and Fisher 2003; Dickinson et al. 2003; Gerster and Zimmermann 2005). Instead of passively receiving information from providers, receivers can establish personal agendas and clarify their doubts. Alternatively, providers can tailor responses accordingly, instead of having to publish extensive information which may or may not be relevant to readers. The Health Belief Model (Janz et al. 2002), suggests that perceived susceptibility is an important factor that drives people to take necessary steps. Thus, one would expect that those users with a higher degree of susceptibility, i.e., risk of adverse outcomes, would elicit a higher degree of responsiveness from a doctor, both in terms of content and speed. Using an interactive medium, repliers should provide more educational cues and guidance and do so relatively sooner.

The *modality* of online discussion boards is textual in nature. Users need to type queries and answers into a system to communicate, distinguishing this form of health communication both from face-to-face doctor visits and from website medical information-seeking. The amount of information exchanged is thus limited when compared to these alternative modes. While this characteristic may be a disadvantage for a problem-solving tool because of a perceived lack of completeness of information, this may potentially be compensated by the anonymity provided to the users. Further, in comparison with lengthy medical articles published online, the content written on a discussion board is likely to be more reader friendly as it is more conversational and relevant to issues faced by information seekers. A discussion board can also be used as a preventive tool if users actively post questions online to seek knowledge.

Asynchronous communication is a characteristic of online discussion boards that allows both information seekers as well as repliers, especially nonexperts, to reflect on queries and answer at their own pace. Conversely, for those who need the information urgently, this could be described as a weakness. One criticism of the three-stage model of health promotion is that it neglects to include the role of the service provider in determining program effectiveness. To highlight this point, from a strategic health communication perspective, the function of asynchronicity is an important one, as online communication interventions tend to be subsidiary strategies. Thus, consultant physicians first have to complete their face-to-face routine activities before attending to their online duties, reducing the speed of their response.

The *privacy* afforded by online discussion boards generally allows anyone to access and read all of the information posted, potentially compromising patients' confidentiality. Nevertheless, the popularity of discussion boards addressing sexual health concerns in many countries suggests that users do not mind revealing sensitive information as long as anonymity is maintained. In fact, the anonymity provided might even encourage them to be more open to discussing normally sensitive problems. Considering all these key attributes, this study examined what function a discussion board provides for the improvement of sexual health and investigated the key characteristics of an online discussion board that contribute to effectiveness as a source of strategic health communication, particularly regarding interactivity, modality, asynchrony, and privacy.

Specifically the study considered

- Do online discussion boards favor problem-solving or general health information-seeking behaviors?
- What is the level of responsiveness of the doctors/users replies, both in terms of content and speed?
- Is there a relationship between user susceptibility and quality of response?

Case Study

Among the popular Thai websites providing sexual health-related contents are Sanook.com and Pantip.com. Like many other websites, both are managed by nongovernmental parties. Since both consist of discussion boards addressing a variety of issues (e.g., health, computers, and politics) and focus on the social networking aspect, they ranked in the top 10 most visited Thai websites. Other websites such as TeenPATH.net and Clinicrak.com, on the contrary, are tailored to educate their audiences specifically about sex. TeenPATH.net is managed by an international non-profit organization and has become one of the most sophisticated and content-rich sex education websites targeting youth. However, its average daily visitor count is only 393 ("Monthly Stat" 2009), whereas Clinicrak.com, a simpler website managed mainly by one person, gets 2,104 visits daily ("eTREMe Tracking" 2009).

The Clinicrak website was selected for this study for reasons of historical significance, potential impact, and professionalism. First, the decade-old website includes one of the most organized and established Thai discussion boards providing sexual health information. Second, the wide membership and reach; it had 2,986 registered members (1,009 males; 1,977 females) and 1,346,513 users since October 2006. These attributes serve as an index indicating a certain level of success and qualify Clinicrak.com for a case study assessing the potential role of the Internet for disseminating information related to reproductive health.

In 1999, Dr. Roongroj Treeniti (M.D.) created the Clinicrak website. His professional experiences prompted the realization that Thais had limited knowledge about an array of sexual issues. Thus, he decided to use the Internet to advise and continually educate people. Of the 17 Thai discussion boards he created, a dozen are concerned with different topics related to sexology and family pathology. We selected one of the top two discussion boards, with the most questions posted, "Contraception, Pregnancy and Miscarriage/Abortion," for this study.

To post a question, one is required to register as a member online and submit a copy of their national ID card. Their information is not uploaded but kept as a record offline in case there are any violations of the laws relating to information and communication technologies (ICTs). As suggested by the literature, it was found that when posting a question or reply, users generally opt for pseudonyms (Donath 1999).

A multimethodological approach was used for triangulation of results. Four distinct methods were employed in this study, namely email interviews, content analysis, an online survey, and web-statistics. To learn about the history, implementation and ongoing usage of the discussion board, we engaged in an email-based conversation with Dr. Treeniti.

Content analysis was employed to classify the type of questions and replies posted. Of the 1,800 questions posted between March 2008 and September 2009, 600 were randomly selected to form the sample. To examine the users' motivation, after preliminary analysis, six categories were formed (Table 16.1). The questions posted were also coded into 12 categories based on the topic: "Chance of getting pregnant—do not wish to be pregnant/wish to be pregnant/unable to identify whether the person wishes to be pregnant," "Contraception for female," "Emergency pill," "Condom use," "Miscarriage," "Abortion," "Pregnancy test," "Maternal health," "Pregnancy signs," "Menstruation," "Disease," and "Others." For a posting that contains more than one question (e.g., Is this a sign of pregnancy? What should I do?), each question was analyzed and coded separately.

Table 16.1 Coding scheme based on users' motivation

Motivation	Descriptions	Examples
1. Just for knowledge's sake	Explicitly mention that the question is posted just for knowledge's sake	This is just out of my curiosity, I wonder if…
2. Will this cause pregnancy?	Ask whether – this will/would cause pregnancy. – one can still get pregnant with this contraceptive method. – symptoms they have are pregnancy signs.	I had unprotected sex a day after my period. Will I get pregnant?
3. Instruction-related	Ask for advice regarding what they should do next or how certain things should be done.	When should I take the next emergency pill?
4. Diagnosis	Ask if this symptom is normal, whether he/she has a disease or whether the symptoms are caused by the pills/stress/etc.	My period is delayed for almost a month. Is this normal?
5. Monitor health	Focus on the effect or consequences of a health behavior.	I have been taking contraceptive pills for over 2 years. Will there be any side effects?
6. Others	None of the above	When will my egg be ready? Where can I buy this pill?

In addition, to identify the role of the discussion board, each question was coded into two groups: "problem-solving-oriented" and "prevention-oriented." Seventy-five questions that could not be coded into either of the categories were excluded from the analysis. To assess the susceptibility of a person, questions were also categorized into two groups based on the presence of a symptom(s). As a measure of response quality, the level of responsiveness and interactivity, number of responses, time taken for the first response, length and type of responses (i.e., short answers such as yes/no, answers with some explanation or information in which the reply given is based on, answers with advice of what to do next, answers with explanation and advice for what to do next, and responses with no answer but which ask for clarification) were recorded.

An online survey was conducted among 120 users of the discussion board from 18 February to 22 September 2009. The link to the questionnaire was posted at the discussion board's homepage and sent to users' email address. The sample was predominantly female (65.5%), mainly youth aged between 15 and 29 (90%), university-educated (89.9%), and with a monthly income below 15,000 Thai baht (~US$ 450) per month (79.6%). Participants rated on a 4-point scale (1—"Not much at all," 2—"Not much," 3—"Much," 4—"Very much") the accuracy, credibility, and degree of information filtering provided by various repliers (i.e., in general/by doctors/by other users). In addition, participants rated the usefulness of the discussion board and reported what they used it for.

All of the research communications were in Thai, and coding and analysis were conducted by the Thai-speaking lead author. Web-statistics were used to measure viewership and timing of specific posts on the discussion board. SPSS 14 was used

Table 16.2 Users' perceptions of the Clinicrak discussion board

Topics	Mean (SD)
Doctor credibility	3.30[a] (0.50)
User credibility	2.59 (0.54)
Useful for me or the people I know	3.62[a] (0.55)
Accuracy check by other users	2.60 (0.77)
Accuracy check by the doctor	2.92[a] (0.74)
Provide me better sex education than school	3.46[a] (0.67)
I am confident I can differentiate between facts and false information	3.25[a] (0.68)

[a]Mean is significantly different from the neutral point, 2.5 at $p<0.01$, $N=120$

to conduct statistical analyses. Statistical significance below 0.01 was used for the analyses.

The first research question addresses users' motivations, focusing on the suitability, credibility, and usefulness of the content. We found that the online discussion board was suitable, in terms of usage, when focused on the topics of pregnancy and contraception. Questions were relevant not just to the inquirer, the respondent (primarily the attending physician), but also to the online audience (measured by number of views). Fifty-nine percent of the questions sampled asked whether the person would get pregnant. Many were concerned whether unprotected sex would lead to pregnancy. Others were concerned because they noticed some potential pregnancy signs. One user posted:

> I had sex on January 22 and took emergency pills on January 23. He did not ejaculate inside me. Then I had some blood coming out on February 4 and my period was on April 1st. Now I have constipation and it seems like my tummy is getting bigger. I also feel a bit of pain on the left side of my abdomen. Is it possible that I am 4 months pregnant? How big should the tummy be during the fourth month of pregnancy? Everyone keeps telling me I'm growing fat. Please answer me. Thank you. (*Translated from sample ID 235*)

Nineteen percent of the questions asked for instructions, for example, when they could start taking contraceptive pills after abortion. Twenty percent aimed to gain a better understanding of reproductive health in order to monitor health status, for example, whether there are any side effects of taking contraceptive pills. Less than 1 % of the questions were purely for the sake of knowledge; almost all were seeking information to apply to the users themselves. Sixteen percent asked for help to diagnose their condition, for example, what could have caused painful urination.

Data from the online survey about the Clinicrak discussion board was used to illuminate the issues of user perceptions of credibility and usefulness (Table 16.2). Respondents rated the discussion board as highly credible, especially if it was the doctor replying to questions (vs. users), $t(119) = 14.87$, $p < .00$. They believed that the doctor and other users helped check and filter out erroneous information. This, coupled with data collected from the interview with Dr. Treeniti, suggests that perceived credibility was higher than actual credibility. Therefore, if the information provided contains mistakes, the outcome could be detrimental.

Regarding utility, over 90 % of the respondents indicated that the Clinicrak.com was very useful ($M = 3.62$; $SD = 0.55$). There was a strong correlation between the perceived usefulness of the discussion board and the perceived credibility of the doctor's replies ($r = .45, p < .00$), but not with other users' replies ($r = .16, p = .08$). This implies that in order to use the discussion board to advise people on their sexual health issues, it is important to involve doctors or qualified personnel. Experimental findings from another study on an online health discussion board showed that a doctor's qualification could help to boost credibility by establishing expectations about its validity. However, if a source is a nonexpert, inclusion of explanations or reasons in the answer could help to complement the lack of source qualification, leading to appropriate actions and positive health outcomes (Poorisat and Detenber 2010).

The content analysis was used in combination with the online survey to investigate the second research area concerning the media characteristics of interactivity, modality, asynchronicity, and privacy. Results showed that 70% of the questions posted were oriented towards problem solving; for example, "I touched her with my hand that I just used for masturbation... Does my girlfriend need to take an emergency pill?" Only 13% were prevention-oriented; for example, one user asked when she could have unprotected sex after ingesting contraceptive pills. The survey results revealed overwhelming use of the Clinicrak discussion board (97%) to make decisions and solve problems. A minority (15.2%) indicated use to acquire knowledge, while a mere 3% indicated that they read it just for fun. These findings suggest that people are likely to use this discussion board as an alternative channel to anonymously disclose personal problems and seek guidance. Although most people could have gone through articles published on Clinicrak.com or other health-oriented websites, they chose to type out their questions in order to get a response specific to their problems. Being an asynchronous technology allowed people to post questions anytime and the busy doctor to respond at his convenience. All these findings demonstrated that given the key features (i.e., asynchronicity and anonymity), a discussion board could potentially serve as a channel for people to bring up sensitive questions and get information to help them make informed decisions about specific problems.

The interactivity of the discussion board was measured via an examination of responsiveness, in terms of timing of the posts, the role of the replier, and the presumed susceptibility of the inquirer. Based on the mean difference of the response time, registered users ($M = 1.2$ hrs; $SD = 8.7$) seemed to be more responsive than the doctor ($M = 22.99$ hrs; $SD = 26.17$). However, a closer examination revealed that only 4% of the questions received replies from registered users, while 99.3% were answered by the doctor. About 11% of the users posted another question after the first reply; 72% of them received another reply from the doctor. The analysis indicates high responsiveness on the part of the doctor. Given the small number of other users involved in giving guidance, it can be concluded that the interactivity of a discussion board does not necessary lead to a collaborative online network. This might arise from the users having low confidence in the accuracy and believability of posts by other users, coupled with the general public lacking the specific knowledge and/or confidence to provide medical advice.

Since the discussion board only allowed for asynchronous communication and required people to type out their questions and responses, it might seem to discourage people from clarifying and discussing issues in detail. However, a segment of the discussion board audience did attempt to clarify their doubts (doctor=2%; users=11%), thus lending some credence to this characteristic. Nevertheless, the relatively small numbers suggested that this modality was still incomparable to face-to-face communication with a physician.

It was found that posts which indicated presence of a symptom(s) (i.e., higher susceptibility), in contrast with posts which did not indicate that the user noticed/ had any symptoms, received a longer reply from the doctor $F(2, 593) = 9.07, p < .00$. Further analyses using chi-square showed that users who reported a symptom(s) were likely to receive a reply containing some explanation about their conditions and advice on what they should do next, while those without symptoms were likely to get a short yes/no answer, $\chi^2(8, N = 596) = 42.95, p < 0.00$ with Cramer's V = .27. This distinguishes the Clinicrak discussion board from much of traditional mass media and makes it a suitable tool for problem solving.

Like Thailand, policy makers in many Asian countries have made a concerted effort to promote basic sexual education in schools. However, criticisms remain about the bland, scientific nature of information dissemination and the lack of viable alternatives for young adults (Malikaew 2005). Given the steady rate of urbanization and commensurate rise in Internet connectivity, the role of online sources as effective dissemination alternatives are certainly worth an examination. The current study suggests that, for those seeking particular health information, discussion boards can prove to be cost-efficient and sustainable for strategic health communication.

There is limited access to comprehensive Thai sexual health resources for youth, outside of schools, that can maintain their need for confidentiality, possibly due to a combination of existing social norms and government policies. We used the three intersects of the Technology-Community-Management model (Chib and Zhao 2009; Lee and Chib 2008) to discuss the viability and sustainability of online strategic health communication. The analysis of the Clinicrak discussion board revealed that, even in a limited resources context, it is possible to use the Internet for sex education, given a good understanding of user needs.

From a technological perspective, we note that the Internet cannot be seen as a homogeneous medium. While discussion boards can address problem-solving health behaviors, information seeking related to prevention advice may be better addressed through health-oriented websites. Policy makers need to develop a strategic online approach that addresses the entire gamut of behaviors, particularly as there is the risk of the gap being filled by uninformed users gravitating to peer-to-peer social networking sites. Thus, it is important to design different media formats to cater to different health information needs.

Moreover, there is a need to evaluate the development and the quality of the existing infrastructures, education and regulations in relation to ICTs. Despite the effort and time invested, a website would be useless if the public is not equipped with computer skills or does not have Internet access, as is the case with 80% of Thais. When the Internet is affordable but the regulations for online content or licensing are too strict, nonprofit providers will not be motivated to offer such services. Other media such as mobile phones may also be considered as alternative channels since they are easier to use and have already been widely adopted in developing countries (Chatterjee et al. 2009; Chib et al. 2008).

From a management perspective, key partnerships and financial sustainability are important considerations. Information providers can consider building a co-alition to source volunteers to assist with answering questions. On a macro level, government bodies can play a supporting role by providing intelligence, essential funding and more importantly, technical infrastructure such as servers, storage, and hosting subsidies. A policy-making rationale similar to that used in allocating re-sources for public broadcasting services can be applied to the Internet. Without such support, it will be almost impossible to expect growth and development of high-quality nonprofit websites.

From a user perspective, the Internet possesses various communication capabili-ties, but how it is used depends largely on the community's needs. A huge amount of money may be wasted if one tries to advocate abstinence in the face of changing sexual behavior patterns of adolescents. Instead, information providers might focus on resolving contemporary health issues such as, when building online resources placing an emphasis on different pregnancy signs, the use of contraceptive pills, or unhealthy abortion. It is important to note that there are several advantages as well as disadvantages associated with the use of a discussion board in strategic health-care communication. Findings from this study suggest that some users may have placed too much trust on an online channel and used it as a replacement of an actual visit to a doctor. A small misunderstanding or misinterpretation due to a lack of in-formation can potentially lead to adverse consequences. Therefore, we propose that retrievers should be taught media ecology approaches as part of their formal school sex education to learn to selectively harness information across different media for-mats. This is necessary given that online forums such as discussion groups or social networks are increasingly being used to provide answers that are difficult to acquire offline due to sociocultural constraints.

From a policy perspective, the findings from this study are applicable to a glob-al audience. We found that the Internet is a promising resource for critical health information. However, general content on health websites caters to a mass audi-ence, thus proving inadequate for educating adolescents. It is here that online dis-cussion boards bv can be designed to answer specific queries about topics that are perceived as embarrassing in socially conservative countries. The specific features of online discussion boards, including the benefits of privacy while obtaining pre-cise advice from a health professional in an asynchronous manner, suggests the potential for communicating health messages that may not be as well suited for mass dissemination.

To gain more insight into how the Internet can be used in healthcare devel-opment, future studies can explore comparisons between successful online plat-forms, as well as offline platforms. Examining users' motivations and how the medium is currently being used will help service providers to plan and improve current health communication systems. With a clear understanding of User-media-message interaction, one will be able to use advanced technologies to their full potential. In conclusion, having begun the process of understanding complexities of online communication, a holistic policy-making approach to regulate a hitherto unregulated, though rapidly growing, source of strategic health communication is an immediate next step.

Acknowledgements We would like to express our gratitude to Dr. Indrajit Banerjee, Assistant Director-General, UNESCO who inspired this study. We also want to thank Dr. Roongroj Treeniti for his time and valuable insights. This project would not have been possible without their support. Lastly, we would like to express our sincere thanks to all the website users who took the time to do the survey.

References

Barak, A., & Fisher, W. A. (2003). Experience with an Internet-based, theoretically grounded educational resource for the promotion of sexual and reproductive health. *Sexual & Relationship Therapy, 18*(3), 293.

Bohner, G., Erb, H.-P., & Siebler, F. (2008). Information processing approaches to persuasion integrating assumptions from the dual- and single- processing perspectives. In W. D. Crano & R. Prislin (Eds.), *Attitudes and attitude change*. New York: Psychology Press.

Borzekowski, D. L. G., Fobil, J. N., & Asante, K. O. (2006). Online access by Adolescents in Accra: Ghanaian Teens' Use of the internet for health information. *Developmental Psychology, 42*(3), 450–458.

Chamratrithirong, A., Kittisuksathit, S., Podhisita, C., Isarabhakdi, P., & Sabaiying, M. (2006). *National sexual behavior survey of Thailand 2006*. Bangkok: Institute for Population and Social Research, Mahidol University.

Chamratrithirong, A., & Richter, K. (2009). *Choosing abstinence, being faithful or condoms: Recent trends in sexual behavior in Thailand*. Paper presented at the 2009 Annual Meeting Population Association of America.

Chatterjee, S., Chakraborty, S., Sarker, S., Sarker, S., & Lau, F. Y. (2009). Examining the success factors for mobile work in healthcare: A deductive study. *Decision Support Systems, 45*, 620–633.

Chib, A., Lwin, M. O., Santoso, F., Lin, H., & Ang, J. (2008). Improving healthcare communications via mobile phones in Aceh Besar, Indonesia. *Asian Journal of Communication, 18*(4), 348–364.

Chib, A., & Zhao, J. (2009). Sustainability of ICT interventions: Lessons from rural projects in China and India. In L. Harter & M. J. Dutta (Eds.), *Communicating for social impact: Engaging communication theory, research, and pedagogy. ICA 2008 Conference Theme Book*: Hampton Press.

Dickinson, P., Chataway, J., Quintas, P., Wiel, D., Gault, F., Visano, B. S., et al. (2003). The framework and the model. In G. Sciadas (Ed.), *Monitoring the digital divide*. Montreal: Claude-Yves Charron.

Donath, J. S. (1999). Identity and deception in the virtual community. In M. A. Smith & P. Kollock (Eds.), *Communities in cyberspace*. London: Routledge.

Draft, R. L., & Lengel, R. H. (1984). Information richness: A new approach to managerial behavior and organizational design. In L. L. Cummings & B. M. Staw (Eds.), *Research in organizational behavior 6* (pp. 191–233). Homewood: JAI Press.

eTREMe, T. (2009). http://extremetracking.com/open;sum?login=clinic39. Accessed 31 Oct 2009

Gerster, R., & Zimmermann, S. (2005). Information and communication technologies (ICTs) for poverty reduction? http://www.deza.admin.ch/ressources/resource_en_24102.pdf. Accessed 15 Sep 2009.

Gubhaju, B. B. (2002). *Adolescent reproductive health in Asia.* Paper presented at the Interna tional Union for the Scientific Study of Population Regional Population Conference, Bangkok, Thailand.

"International Telecommunication Union". (2009). *Information society statistical profiles.* http:// www.itu.int/publ/D-IND-RPM.AP2009/en. Accessed 12 Sep 2009.

International Telecommunication Union (2010). *Measuring the information society 2010.* www. itu.int. Accessed 30 Mar 2010.

Janz, N. K., Champion, V. L., & Strecher, V. J. (2002). The health belief model. In K. Glanz, B. K. Rimer & F. M. Lewis (Eds.), *Health behavior and health education: Theory, research, and practice* (pp. 45–66). San Francisco: Jossey-Bass.

Kanuga, M., & Rosenfeld, W. D. (2004). Adolescent sexuality and the internet: The good, the bad, and the URL. *Journal of Pediatric and Adolescent Gynecology, 17*(2), 117–124.

Lee, S., & Chib, A. (2008). Wireless initiatives for connecting rural areas: Developing a frame- work. In N. Carpentier & B. D. Cleen (Eds.), *Participation and media production. Critical reflections on content creation. ICA 2007 Conference Theme Book.* Newcastle: Cambridge Scholars Publishing.

Lou, C. H., Zhao, Q., Gao, E. S., & Shah, I. H. (2006). Can the internet be used effectively to pro- vide sex education to young people in China? *Journal of Adolescent Health, 39*(5), 720–728.

Malikaew, S. (2005, 20 November). Sex education can be creative, say experts. Inter Press Ser- vice. http://ipsnews.net/interna.asp?idnews=31105.

Monthly Stat (2009). http://truehits.net/. Accessed 31 Oct 2009.

Nwagwu, W. E. (2007). The Internet as a source of reproductive health information among adoles- cent girls in an urban city in Nigeria. *British Medical Journal, 7.*

Parish, W. L., Laumann, E. O., & Mojola, S. A. (2007). Sexual behavior in China: Trends and comparisons. *Population and Development Review, 33*(4), 729–756.

Poorisat, T., & Detenber, B. H. (2010). *The roles of source expertise and message completeness in the evaluation of an online health discussion board.* Paper to be presented at the 60th Annual Conference of the International Communication Association: Matters of Communication.

Prachusilpa, S., Oumtanee, A., & Satiman, A. (2004). *A study of dissemination of health information via Internet.* http://library.hsri.or.th/th/download.php?fn=/fullt/res/hs1151.zip&case=2&lang=tha. Accessed 2 Mar 2009.

Street, R. L. (2003). Mediated computer-provider communication in cancer care: The empowering potential of new technologies. *Patient Education and Counseling, 50,* 99–104.

Wathen, C. N., & Burkell, J. (2002). Believe it or not: Factors influencing credibility on the Web. *Journal of the American Society for Information Science and Technology, 53*(2), 134–144.

Wynn, L. L., Foster, A. M., & Trussell, J. (2009). Can I get pregnant from oral sex? Sexual health misconceptions in e-mails to a reproductive health website. *Contraception, 79*(2), 91–97.

United Nations International Children's Emergency Fund. (2005). *Situation review on Adolescents and HIV/AIDS in East Asia and the Pacific.* http://www.unicef.org/eapro/activities_3680.html. Accessed Aug 18 2008.

Chapter 17
Advertising and Childhood Obesity in China

Angela Chang

Obesity

The words "obese" and "overweight" are commonly used in our daily life. To accurately portray obesity or overweight, the Body Mass Index (BMI) is widely adopted. Excess weight and its association with body fatness are measured by the ratio of weight to height (in kg/m^2), according to the Centers for disease Control and Prevention(CDC) (Tuan and Nicklas 2009). For the World Health Organization (WHO), BMI is categorized into three groups: normal (BMI < 25), overweight ($25 \leqq BMI < 30$) and obese (BMI $\geqq 30$) (Zhang et al. 2008). International Obesity Task Force (IOTF) proposes other BMI definitions for children and adolescents on an age- and gender-specific basis (O'Neil et al. 2007) in order to accommodate growth patterns.

Childhood Obesity

Previous studies have not reached consensus and there are no clear clinical standards for defining obesity in children (Chu 2005). To measure obese/overweight children, BMI is used in conjunction with other international reference data. The CDC classifies children as "overweight" if they are above the 95th percentile, and "at risk of being overweight" between the 85th and 95th percentile for their age and sex. Other studies from specific countries have set the criteria for childhood obesity and overweight. Researchers attempt to establish BMIs 18.5 kg/m^2 for children 8-years-old in Asia. The Department of Health in Taiwan defined overweight at BMI $\geqq 24$ and obese at BMI $\geqq 27$, which are different from WHO—Asian's criteria (i.e., overweight at BMI $\geqq 23$, and obese at BMI $\geqq 25$)(Chu 2005). These various criteria of obesity and overweight indicate that the problem and management of

A. Chang (✉)
Communication Department, University of Macau, Taipa,
Macau, China
e-mail: wychang@umac.mo

C. C. Okigbo (ed.), *Strategic Urban Health Communication*,
DOI 10.1007/978-1-4614-9335-8_17, © Springer Science+Business Media New York 2014

obesity are still controversial, and more obesity-related studies that take into consideration the ethnic, geographic, and cultural variables are needed.

Irrespective of the obesity criteria, children's excessive body fat has medical consequences. When these youths mature into obese adults, obesity is linked to various problems such as cancers, diabetes, hypertension, kidney failure, cardiovascular diseases, stroke, respiratory problems, asthma, musculoskeletal diseases, colon, breast and prostate cancer, and mental illnesses (Harker et al. 2007). The implications of childhood obesity on the nation's health care costs are to be huge.

Worldwide Childhood Obesity and Overweight Situation

Childhood obesity is becoming an epidemic worldwide according to the World Health Organization. Increasing levels of children obesity in the Western world in recent years have been issues of concern by academicians, researchers, food and drink advertising industries (Harker et al. 2007; Hastings et al. 2003; Young 2003), as well as policy makers in organizations like UK Standards Agency (Ambler 2006). In the United States, it is one of the passions of the First Lady, Michelle Obama.

Numerous reports have documented trends in childhood obesity over extended periods of time in various countries. The prevalence of obesity in Irish children is high, two- to fourfold increase in obesity in children aged 8–12 years between year 1990 to 2005 (O'Neill et al. 2007). It is estimated that there are more than nine million obese and overweight children in the United States. Childhood obesity is a worldwide phenomenon in high-income countries (e.g., Australia and United Kingdom) and middle-income country like Brazil, which are found to have increases in overweight children (Laver 2006; Palmer and Carpenter 2006).

Obesity Situation in Urban China

Mainland China is the country with the largest population of children in the world (267 million; age < 15), and has one-third of all the world's obese and overweight children (Population Reference Bureau 2010), more than its share of the world's population (1/5). Increased levels of child obesity in Chinese societies are both real and important. In 2003, it was reported that 9.4 % of children aged 6 to 11 in Mainland China were classified as overweight (Waller et al. 2003). In year 2009, 12 million children were found to be overweight and obese in Mainland China, whereas 85,000 Hong Kong children with proportion of 19 % and 10,000 (15 %) overweight and obese children in Macau, the special administrative regions of China (China Education newspaper 2009, May 20).

Waller et al. (2003) surveyed children ages 6 to 11 living in nine geographically diverse provinces of China in 1997 and found that children living in urban areas are showing a high percentage of overweight than rural children, by a ratio of 14.5

to 8.3%. The female overweight children comprised 10.9%, with comparison to 7.4% of male children. The income of the households of the overweight children was significantly lower than that of the households of the nonoverweight children.

In Taiwan, the sovereignty apart from Mainland China since 1949, the prevalence and problem of obesity has shown a persistent increase. From 1990 to 1995, the prevalence of obesity among elementary school boys and girls was 17.8–21.5% and 16.7–20.5%, respectively in urban areas (Chu 2005). In 2001, increasing obesity and overweight rate in boys was 29.5%, and 22.0% in girls (Chen et al. 2006). The 2009 data show 27% (450,000) overweight and obese children in Taiwan (China Education newspaper 2009, May 20). Among boys, the prevalence of overweight was highest around 34% at the age of 10 and dropped to 15.4% at age 14; whereas in girls, the prevalence of overweight was highest around 23.4% at age 6 and down to 12% at age 14 (Chu 2005). It does not take a long time to change the picture: Chinese children used to be less overweight, more active, and less likely to ingest calories as snacks than children in the United States (Waller et al. 2003).

Potential Causes of Childhood Obesity in Urban China

The increasing problem of childhood obesity is a complex issue. Experts have pointed to a range of important potential contributors to the rise in childhood obesity. From Western experience, a number of socioeconomic or demographic factors affect obesity rate. At the early stages of economic development, overweight and obesity tend to be associated with high socioeconomic status (SES) and urban populations. As local economic condition improved, this association shifts toward those with lower SES, occurring earlier in women than it does in men. In England the situation has been termed as "food deserts" where people simply cannot get access to a healthy diet. Similar trends are evident in the United States: in poor neighborhoods in New Orleans there is easy access to corner stores selling doughnuts, potato chips, or fried chicken, while genuine grocery stores are lacking.

Profound social and economic developments in China over the last 20 years have resulted in shifts in nutrition and physical activity causing obesity problems, predominately in urban areas. The prevalence of overweight was 18.6% (15.1% in men and 22.1% in women) and obesity was 1.2% in men and 2.2% in women (Zhang et al. 2008). Although the prevalence of obesity was low, overweight was relatively high in the Chinese rural women. Like the global epidemic of obesity, it is the result mainly of sedentary lifestyles and the consumption of high-fat, energy dense diets. Zhang and his coresearchers further indicated that Westernized diet and drinking increased the risk of obesity and obese and overweight participants were more frequently sedentary, consumed quantities of alcoholic beverages, and were devoted to an unhealthy diet. Increasing urbanization and ongoing economic growth mean that health risks attributable to overweight and obesity are likely to rise, especially for children.

Urbanization

According to the per capita annual living expenditure report in 2005, urban households in China spend a significantly greater share of income on food items and housing, and a lesser share on clothing and services, compared with the rural households. In China, the urban population increased from 31 to 41 % in 10 years from 1995 to 2005 (Chen 2008). Rapid urbanization provides the background for children's development in consumer socialization. Urban residents now represented about 42 % of the population in China, but contributed two-thirds of the total retail sales.

According to the urban–rural theories (Chen 2008), first, rural families are more likely to be larger and have senior members. Children as consumers are able to use their growing financial resources from parents and four grandparents from both the mother and father's sides to express themselves through hedonic consumption from an early age. Second, urban families are likely to see children as economic assets. Mainland China has implemented a Single-Child policy in urban area since 1979. These only children have a substantial amount of their own money to spend and exert a great influence on their family members. Children are not only seen as consumers on their own, they are also gaining more control over their own eating habits and the family food choices. It somehow explains why there is increasing advertising and marketing communication targeted at children. Third, urban consumers in China are inclined to shop at well-known, large-scale stores and stores with quality customer services due to better shopping and consumption environment, compared with poor retailing and insufficient after-sale services in rural area.

The gap between children living in urban and rural areas can be examined from children's attitude and behavior. Due to the exposure to different media environment for urban and rural children, urban children were more skeptical toward advertising than rural children (Chen 2008). As anticipated, modern urban children simply watch more TV, or are more likely to play video games and spend quality time on the Internet than rural children. The sedentary lifestyle may increase snacking and consumption of high-fat, high sugar, or salt foods.

Take Taiwan's urbanization for example, more and more cities are packed with highly dense convenience stores. With over 8,500 convenience stores in this small island, 7-Eleven is undoubtedly children's favorite one for making purchases. With 52 % of market share in Taiwan and over 3.3 billion US dollars net income in 2010, it is proved to be a sales triumph.

Children's Choices and Food Advertising

With the globalization of markets, there is an excessive supply of food with increased portion sizes of calorie-dense products readily available in the supermarket, convenience store, and street shopping environment. Waller et al. (2003) analyze the snacking behavior of children in China and found that 11 % of the 6–11-year-old participants report consuming snacks. Snacking behavior related to obesity is influenced by products availability and accessibility. Convenience, expediency, and immediate gratification for children are evident toward food and drinks purchase.

Children's preferences are not yet well-developed and can be influenced by marketing efforts. Food advertising and promotion on television is influencing children's diet in a number of ways. First, the more food advertisements the children saw, the more snacks and calories they consume (Hastings et al. 2003). Second, food commercials aimed at children often promise a free toy, and some promotions involve other gifts in the food packages or in conjunction with food meals. Taiwanese children express strong preferences for making purchases in convenience stores which can be easily found, close to home, schools, and always on the way to and from school. In addition, children's favorability varies according to purchase situations across product specifics. It is found that those overweight/obese children eat fast food once to twice a week but purchase snacks and drink products at convenience stores on a day-to-day basis. Ready-to-eat breakfast, snacks, and ready-to-go drinks are the items usually sought by obese and overweight children.

Biological differences among age groups may cause differences in the response to the same business environment. Older children in China were less likely to perceive television commercials more truthful than younger children. Younger children liked television commercials more than older children (Chen 2008). On the issue of obesity and eating habits, food decisions have greater personal importance and relevance to girls than to boys. In addition, Children's age is widely agreed to be a key factor in the effect of advertising, especially in regard to children's food choices (Livingstone and Helsper 2006; Palmer and Carpenter 2006). For example, younger elementary school children (grade 1–2) are less immune-competent than older children (grade 5–6), and therefore more vulnerable to an advertising world. Although children of all ages are affected by advertising, those who are 7 to 11 years old are more likely to be targeted and persuaded by advertising in the development of their consumer knowledge and skills (Harker et al. 2007).

Advertising and Childhood Obesity

Advertising is being accused of damaging the health of the nation by pushing "inappropriate" food and drink onto consumers, promoting harmful dietary choices, and misleading children with messages that undermine parental authority and governments' positive eating messages (Harker et al. 2007; Lvovich 2003). The role of advertising seems to be the catalysts to make children overweight.

In the last 10 years, advertising for fast food outlets has rapidly increased. Studies provide evidence that food promotion influences children's food preferences and their purchase behavior (Bridges and Briesch 2006; Hastings et al. 2003; Harker et al. 2007). A study of primary school children shows that labeling and signage on a vending machine had an effect on what was bought by secondary school pupils. Another research also shows that food advertising can influence what children eat such as daily snacks at playtime (Hastings et al 2003; Palmer and Carpenter 2006). Most research on advertising-obesity has been done in the West, and it finds that the socio-economic or demographic factors influence advertising-obesity.

Modern American style television programming and advertising entered the Taiwan market in the 1980s and started to enter Mainland China after 1997. The extensive changes in television viewing patterns are expected to emerge for Chinese audiences. A "melting pot" can describe the mix of Western and Eastern cultural values in Chinese television programs and commercials. Similar to previous studies in the West, half of all ads observed in this study for Chinese children are for foods, dominated by sugared candies/sweets, snacks, and cold drinks for convenience stores, and kids' meal with free gift sold at fast food restaurants. Television food and beverage commercials targeting children may look similar in style, appeal, and content to those aired in America. Dancing, singing, excitement, fast action, and enjoyment are the tone and the mood. The predominant appeal for food and drink ads is fun and cool feelings. The techniques include the use of close-ups, low-angle shots, action, musical jingles, and fast-framing. Some ads for McDonald's and 7-Eleven even provide references to new launching of products with discounted prices. Pre-sugared breakfast cereals, candy, soft-drinks, confectionary and savory snacks are promoted to children in America while iced drinks and ready-to-go food (i.e., rice ball, hot bun, hot dog, and Japanese oden (Guandongjhu) and snacks are for children in Taiwan.

In 2003, Hastings, et al. among others emphasized that there is no evidence showing a direct causal relationship between food or drink advertising and the development of weight problems or obesity. Other studies note that advertising appears to have a very weak positive influence on consumption, and banning ads does not in general reduce consumption. Advertising effects were inconsistent and were not found in all the studies of advertising-obesity. However, there are sufficient studies that suggest that food advertising can, in some context, influence some children's food consumption (Ambler 2006; Harker et al. 2007).

Prevention and Cure Strategies

Ambler (2006) and Lvovich (2003) consider the role of the family—its structure, food patterns and habits, and its socioeconomic status as the most important factors in the development of obesity and overweight. However, the causal relationship could run in the opposite direction for Chinese overweight and obese children by regulating them from engaging in frequent sedentary activities. In 2007, Lau et al. (2007) indicated that Chinese parental influence, especially father's role modeling, was significantly related to attraction to physical activity in overweight Chinese children in Hong Kong. For Chinese boys, both father's and mother's influence were very strong. Parenting style (e.g., role modeling, encouragement, and enjoyment) can universally and positively influence an overweight child's physical activity involvement. In addition, self-report physical competence was also an important correlate of an overweight child's attraction to physical activity. Traditional Chinese society, which emphasizes paternal familial control, may offer a possible solution for this issue.

It would be inefficacy to expect an individual child or family to change its behaviors within the context of a community milieu that is inhospitable to the healthier lifestyle or maintain a normal weight. In urban areas, vending machines and mini-groceries shops for selling sweetened beverages and high-fat or sugar snack foods on campus need to be removed. Instead, nutritious and appetizing foods can become more widely available for children's choice at school. It is expected that school environment should help in reducing exposure to cues that encourage overeating and underactivity, and provide access to health-supporting food and activity.

For Chinese culture, children are more amenable to preventive activities provided by school. Healthy eating has been promoted in some cities of China, Taiwan, Hong Kong, and Macau since 2009 in order to improve children's knowledge of food groups and basic nutrition. School-based programs on healthy weight provide students with knowledge, attitude, and skills and may help establish active lifestyles among young people. This in turn may influence their family, and they themselves will continue to eat healthily throughout their adult lives. The survey from Chu (2005) suggests that school nurses can play an active role and undertake a variety of health-related responsibilities besides measuring growth record, circulating health-related information, and providing emergency services for injury or sudden sickness on campuses.

It is unlikely for the government to restrict the advertising of food and drinks to children in all forms. Children's understanding of advertising is part of their natural development. Removing advertising may hurt child welfare since it would take away an important source of consumer socialization. However, various levels of governments should play an active and aggressive role in not tolerating misleading advertisements to consumers who are trying to eat healthier and watch their weight. In addition, for consumers to obtain healthier choices, the government and the food and drink industry must make sure that companies promote their products honestly and in a proper and balanced way. Messages used to correct dietary imbalance should be found more frequently at retailers reminding and instructing consumers to eat healthier.

Conclusion

Prevention and cure strategies based solely on individual or family will not be maximally effective and must be supported by broader-based environmental programs that provide a counterbalance to the societal trends for the prevalence of childhood obesity. Public policy affecting the food choices and activity for obese children can be formulated at many levels in China. On the community level, schools are prime areas for local policy implementation for the prevention of childhood obesity. Increasing physical program, promoting the nutritional food, and restricting unhealthy food and drinks sold on campus have been the main goals of local policy initiatives.

In Chinese society, it is suggested that advertising affects some overweight/obese children's consumption patterns and brand choices. Chinese children's preferences regarding food and beverages are influenced by TV advertising and promotional efforts of nontraditional ad media. Today's supermarkets, groceries, and convenient stores are filled with scores of products using children's favorite characters to sell them food/drinks. Fast food outlets also make frequent use of cross-promotions with children's media characters from Hollywood or Disney movies in the Chinese community. Due to unhealthy diets on neighborhood shopping, which is easily accessible by children, there are approximately 12 million overweight and obese children in primary schools in Mainland China and 450,000 in Taiwan. In addition, place-based ads and TV ads may play an important role in driving children's requests for brands in these categories. Because advertising messages cannot be completely prevented from reaching children, if one goal of public policy is to promote healthy eating and reduce child obesity, it may be more effective to improve education in media literacy and in children's food categories by using advertising to correct any dietary imbalance.

The increased television viewing time offers increased exposure to food and soft drink product advertisements. Previous studies support the claim that television viewing time correlates positively with obesity in the USA, with children who reduced viewing time significantly decreasing in weight. While previous studies shed some light on how children are affected differently by the same social risk factors, more research into the causes and factors of gender differences for obese and overweigh children in Chinese societies is needed.

References

Ambler, T. (2006). Does the UK promotion of food and drink to children contribute to their obesity? *International Journal of Advertising, 25*(2), 137–156.

Bridges, E., & Briesch, R. A. (2006). The 'nag factor' and children's product categories. *International Journal of Advertising, 25*(2), 157–187.

Chen, K. (2008). Chinese children's perceptions of advertising and brands: An urban rural comparison. *Journal of Consumer Marketing, 25*(2), 74–84.

Chen, L. J., Fox, K. R., Haase, A., & Wang, J. M. (2006). Obesity, fitness and health in Taiwanese children and adolescents. *European Journal of Clinical Nutrition, 60*, 1367–1375.

China Education Newspaper (2009, May 20). http://gov.hnedu.cn/web/0/200905/20081637109.html. Accessed Mar. 26, 2010.

Chu, N. F. (2005). Prevalence of obesity in Taiwan. *Obesity Review, 6*, 271–274.

Harker, D., Harker, M., & Burns, R. (2007). Tackling obesity: Developing a research agenda for advertising researchers. *Journal of Current Issues and Research in Advertising, 29*(2), 39–51.

Hastings, G., Stead, M., & McDermott, L. (2003). *A review of research on the effects of food promotion to children.* Report prepared for the food standards agency by the centre for social marketing, Strathclyde University http://www.ism.stir.ac.uk/pdf_doc/final_report_19_9.pdf. Accessed 30 Apr 2009.

Lau, P. W. C., Lee, A., & Ransdell, L. (2007). Parenting style and cultural influences on overweight children's attraction to physical activity. *Obesity, 15*(9), 2293–2302.

Laver, M. (2006). Childhood obesity--Are food advertisers really to blame? Admap Magazine, 476. www.warc.com. Accessed Feb. 18, 2009.

Livingstone, S. & Helsper, E. J. (2006). Does advertising literacy mediate the effects of advertising on children? A critical examination of two linked research literatures in relation to obesity and food choice. *Journal of Communication, 56*(3), 560–584.

Lvovich, S. (2003). Advertising and obesity: The research evidence. *Young Consumers: Insight and Ideas for Responsible, 4*(2), 35–40.

O'Neill, J. L., McCarhy, S. N., Burke, S. J., Hannon, E. M., Kiely, M., Flynn, A., Flynn, M. A. T., & Gibney, M. J. (2007). Prevalence of overweight and obesity in Irish school children, using four different definitions. *European Journal of Clinical Nutrition, 61,* 743–751.

Palmer, E., & Carpenter, C. F. (2006). Food and beverage marketing to children and youth: Trends and issues. *Media psychology, 8,* 165–190.

Population Reference Bureau (2010). 2009 world population data sheet. http://prb.org. Accessed Mar. 26, 2010.

Tuan, N. T., & Nicklas, T. A. (2009). Age, sex and ethnic differences in the prevalence of underweight and overweight, defined by using the CDC and IOTF cut points in Asian children. *European Journal of Clinical Nutrition, 63,* 1305–1312.

Waller, C. E., Du, S. F., & Popkin, VB. M. (2003). Patterns of overweight, inactivity, and snacking in Chinese children. *Obesity Research, 11*(8), 957–961.

Young, B. (2003). Advertising and food choice in children: A review of the literature. Report prepared for the food advertising unit, August. http://www.fau.org.uk. Accessed Feb. 28, 2009.

Zhang, X. G., Sun, Z. Q., Zhang, X. Z., Zheng, L. Q., Liu, S. S., Xu, C. L., Li, J. J., Zhao, F. F., Li. J., Hu, D. Y., & Sun, Y. Z. (2008). Prevalence and associated factors of overweight and obesity in a Chinese rural population. Obesity, 16(3), 168–171.

Index

Printed in the United States
By Bookmasters